Secret Dublin

Secret Dublin

PAT LIDDY

TWENTY-FIVE ORIGINAL WALKS
EXPLORING THE HIDDEN CITY

PASSPORT BOOKS
NTC/Contemporary Publishing Group

This edition first published in 2001
by Passport Books, a division of
NTC/Contemporary Publishing Group, Inc.
4255 West Touhy Avenue
Lincolnwood (Chicago), Illinois 60712-1975
U.S.A.

Copyright © 2001 in text: Pat Liddy
Copyright © 2001 in photographs: Individual photographers and agencies as credited
Copyright © 2001 New Holland Publishers (UK) Ltd

ISBN 0-658-01381-5

Library of Congress Catalog Card Number: on file
Published in conjunction with New Holland Publishers (UK) Ltd.

Publishing Manager: Jo Hemmings
Design and editing: D & N Publishing, Marlborough, Wiltshire
Cartography: Carte Blanche, Paignton, Devon
Production Controller: Joan Woodroffe

Reproduction by Pica Colour Separation Overseas (Pte) Ltd, Singapore
Printed and bound in Singapore by Kyodo Printing Co (Singapore) Pte Ltd

Photographic Acknowledgements
All photographs by the author with the exception of the following:
Chester Beatty Library plate 29; Mary Evans Picture Library plate 20; Caroline
Jones plates 1, 3, 8, 13, 19, 23, 24; The Irish Picture Library plates 6, 22; Perry
Ogden plate 7 (reproduced by permission of the Estate of Francis Bacon); Peter
Ryan plate 9; Nigel Shuttleworth plate 27; Travel Ink/David Toase plates 4, 18;
Travel Ink/Pauline Thornton plate 21.

Front cover: St Anne's Park, Raheny, Dublin (Ivan O'Driscoll).
Back cover: Oscar Wilde (Caroline Jones).
Spine: Archbishop's Palace, Swords Castle (Pat Liddy).

Contents

Preface

When I wrote *Walking Dublin* in 1998, I knew that I would not have the space to even begin telling the full story of Dublin within its pages. Even now I know that *Secret Dublin*, while taking up some of the slack, still falls far short of doing justice to a fascinating, ancient yet rapidly changing city. The boom economy of the late 1990s and the early 2000s is having a major effect on Dublin. There is unprecedented growth in its population, in the size of the city and in the amount of city-centre building and restoration. The transport infrastructure is about to be fundamentally reorganized and enhanced, which should make walking around Dublin all the more pleasant and the sights more accessible. More importantly, Dubliners have begun to realize for themselves that they are the guardians of a special treasure and that it must be protected and cherished. It is, therefore, with a sense of pride that they have started to enjoy and become more expansive about their own city, and are delighted to welcome more and more visitors to share in that experience.

In putting this volume together there are many to whom I would like to show my warm appreciation. Firstly, let me thank New Holland, who recognized that this city had the capacity to support a second volume in a series that began with *Walking Dublin* in 1998. My special thanks to Jo Hemmings, Publishing Manager and Michaella Standen, Assistant Editor, for their unfailing patience and courtesy. I would also like to express my grateful thanks to the staff of Dublin Corporation's Parks Department, to the owners of properties, to the managers of visitor centres, to the management of Irish Distillers, and to everyone who helped, in big ways and small, with my enquiries as I researched each walk.

Finally, as always, writing books to a deadline always brings a degree of pressure into my household but despite this, everyone not only tolerated my demanding and more than usually eccentric behaviour but actually pitched in and helped with comments and practical contributions, both in putting the ideas and the text together. So let me name names: my wife Josephine (who additionally typed the manuscript), daughter Anne Marie and sons Pádraig and Brendan.

Pat Liddy
Dublin

Introduction

The increased reliance of the motor car and the pressure of modern living has, in a sense, divorced people from the streets and lanes, from the nooks and crannies, from the beautiful architecture of the high street and from the humble backwaters of their own cities. To get out and walk is to rediscover a 'lost' city; so walkers, if they are in sufficient numbers, can help to bring a renewed interest and revitalization to forgotten or bypassed places for the benefit of all.

In the year since first starting to write this book many changes have taken place in the city. I have tried to keep abreast of these changes and to include them in the rewrites. However, in a city where rebuilding and renewal are continuing at a frenetic pace, it is quite possible that some items may not be completely up to date. For any omissions or inaccuracies that may have occurred as a result of this, I beg your forgiveness, and I would hope to make any necessary amendments in the next edition.

The idea behind *Secret Dublin* is to explore those parts of the city that tend to be less frequented by visitors than the main tourist centres. Some of the more popular destinations are, of course, not ignored if they are encountered along the way. With variety in mind, walks by canals, along sea walls, around learned institutions, up byroads, through inner suburbs, in forgotten graveyards, across secluded parks and along countryside lanes are all included. To enliven routine journeys there are even two 'walks' on the DART suburban rail system, which travel over a historic railway system and whisk past interesting backyards and outstanding scenery.

The walks are laid out in a sequence that often allows you to commence the next one, after an appropriate adjournment, without having to travel very far to the starting point. If you have a preference for a particular type of walk, you may find the section Categories of Walks useful. Each walk is preceded by a Summary, which gives a brief overview; this is followed by information under headings such as Start, Finish, Length (of the walk) and Time (how long it will take you excluding visits). These give all the details that you will need for your preparations. For details on public transport see page 14. Opening times and other useful information relating to places open to the public are given in 'Further Information', starting on page 157.

Easy-to-follow maps accompany each walk, with the route clearly marked in blue. Places of interest are individually labelled. A full explanation of the symbols and abbreviations used on the maps appears on page 15.

Historical Background

It is generally understood that Dublin is around a 1,200 years old, and in one respect this is correct. It was the Vikings and not the native Irish who established the first towns in Ireland. For 50 years, from about AD 795, single-boat raiding parties of Norsemen carried out hit-and-run raids on the famous and wealthy monasteries that were scattered all over the country. From the 830s more concentrated attacks were launched from fleets of 50 or more ships. The Vikings decided that to exploit these rich pickings fully they would require more permanent settlements, and so they built fortified harbours around the coast and major waterways of Ireland. They arrived in strength at the estuary of the River Liffey in 841 and soon began to erect a recognizable urban centre. They erected a stockade around the little lake formed by the Poddle, a tributary of the Liffey, and this became their *longphort* or fortified harbour. Beside it they built houses closely packed together and surrounded them with a raised ditch and a wooden stockade. This was the genesis of Dublin, but there were significant settlements in the vicinity long before the Vikings.

As far back as 5,000 years ago there were farming communities of great sophistication along the east coast counties. They built the great monuments of Dowth, Knowth and Newgrange in County Meath. Still standing today, these structures are seven centuries older than the Pyramids of Egypt. At one level they were burial chambers constructed from giant pieces of rock transported from places such as Wicklow, more than 48 kilometres (30 miles) away. But Newgrange, for example, was something more awesome than a mere tomb. In the middle of the last century, it was rediscovered that the building was precisely aligned so that on the mid-winter solstice, the sun would stream through an opening in the roof to light up the inner chamber. The astronomical knowledge of these people was amazing. Sadly, this race seems to have died out or to have become absorbed into later waves of invaders, and their earlier achievements were not followed up. The Celts arrived in Ireland between 500–400 BC and by AD 200 they had built five main roads across the country to connect their main centres. These roads converged in present-day Dublin, at a place called Ath Cliath, the Ford of Hurdles, a crossing point on the River Liffey. The ford was located where today's Father Mathew Bridge (Church Street) crosses the river. A settlement of sorts grew up at this crossing and was active when the Vikings arrived. Another settlement, a Christian monastic community called Dubh Linn (the Black Pool) thrived just south of Dublin Castle and it was in this area that the Vikings built their little town. They moored their boats in the Black Pool, a lake formed by the widening of the River Poddle before it joined the River Liffey. Even though the Vikings routinely pillaged monasteries (as did the native Irish, it must be said), some coexistence developed between the monastery at Dubh Linn and the Norsemen.

Irish techniques and undoubtedly Irish craftsmen were employed to build the houses in Dyflin (as the Viking town became to be known), the excavated remains of which have been uncovered by archaeologists.

In time the Vikings became Christian, and although their fleets held command of the seas their tenure in towns like Dublin was never secure; they only held on by forming alliances with the constantly warring Irish kingdoms. In 1170, the arrival of the Anglo-Normans at the gates of Dublin changed everything. The Vikings were banished to the far side of the river to make their own new town called Ostmantown (literally the Town of the Men from the East) and the Irish were chased off to their own settlements. The Anglo-Normans were followed by English settlers within a couple of years, and from that point onwards, for the best part of 750 years, Dublin and ultimately the whole of Ireland would be ruled by the throne or parliament of England. Naturally, the Irish chieftains challenged the rulers of Dublin, but never very effectively and almost never as a united force. The unsettled political climate caused Dublin to grow very slowly and all the institutions and most of the population stayed within the safety of the encompassing defensive walls until well into the 16th century. By 1592, the Elizabethan Conquests had secured much of the country and it was considered safe enough to erect the new Trinity College a good 800 metres (half a mile) from the city walls. This marked the beginning of Dublin's expansion. A temporary hiatus occurred following the invasion of Oliver Cromwell in 1649, but this was only an intermission before the real flowering of the city.

In the 1660s, after the Restoration of King Charles ii, the shaping of Dublin as we know it today began. The quay walls along the river were constructed and the modern street layouts were commenced. This activity accelerated during the Georgian period (1720–1820). The city became celebrated for its great boulevards and squares lined with terraces of grand houses and lordly mansions. In the latter half of the 18th century, the Irish Parliament even achieved a *de facto* independence, but this was brought to an end by the shamefully arranged Act of Union with Great Britain in 1800. Not that this erstwhile independence was of any great benefit to the Roman Catholic majority. The ruling Protestants had ensured that their Irish tenants and workers would enjoy few privileges. By 1829 an act was passed ensuring Catholic Emancipation, but the English landlord system still kept the native Irish rural population in subservience and poverty. The lot of the working classes in the cities was not much better either. A great famine in the 1840s devastated the countryside; over a million died and as many emigrated. Millions more would emigrate over the next century.

Meanwhile Dublin, after a period of post-Act of Union doldrums, started to prosper again. By the 1880s magnificent new buildings were springing up everywhere, and the emerging middle classes were moving out to occupy the expanding suburbs. But all was not as well as it seemed. The terraces of the once-proud Georgian houses were being let out as tenements to the working classes, many of whom had no work at all or were impoverished by low wages. Vast areas of the city centre became slums, with few examples in the whole of Europe to equal their misery. Revolution was thick in the air, in fact it was hardly ever off the agenda, but all previous attempts at rebellion had ended in miserable failure. In 1916, a rising broke out which took the authorities completely by surprise. Around 800 men and women dared to take on 20,000 British troops. The result was an inevitable failure and the fighting left parts of the city centre in rubble, but the fervour of the people was ignited. The War of Independence broke out in 1919 and by 1921 a truce was called which resulted in the British withdrawal from the 26 southern counties. Tragically, a civil war followed the establishment of the Irish Free State. The result of this was not only the destruction of more of the city centre, but the impoverishment of the country and the alienation of people across the civil war lines that was to last for a couple of generations.

Dublin suffered, and even though there had been a rapid response to repair the damage from all the battles the work soon ran out of steam and the city entered another period of decline. In the 1970s and 80s, many of the shabbier parts of the city were demolished instead of being restored. There was a feeling of shame about the 'old-fashioned' appearance of the city and there was a popular move to modernize it. Unfortunately, while some buildings were indisputably beyond redemption, many were not, and their replacements were ugly, to say the least. By the 1990s there was a general reassessment of the value of the city's heritage and while terrible mistakes had been made in the past there was a new determination to put things right where possible. With the cooperation of the Government (mainly through tax incentives and its own building programmes), the active encouragement of the City Council, private sector initiatives and a host of supportive legislation, the fortunes of Dublin City were reversed before it was too late. The city is becoming a living city again, restoration is a first-choice decision among most developers and quality new architecture is making its own mark.

Every city has its problems and Dublin is no exception. The vibrant economy has made a difference but there are many people who still live off the social welfare system. Crime and drugs are making their lives more difficult and these problems can and do spill over to the wider community. But even here, unprecedented progress is being made. The old and often soulless housing schemes that encouraged negative social attitudes are being demolished and are being replaced with quality own-door developments. Social difficulties are not new to Dublin but today there is an opportunity as never before to wipe out poverty and inequality. This is truly a unique time to live, visit and explore a city in change, a city that has at last discovered its own identity.

Categories of Walks

Each category is not exclusive, as every walk obviously embraces elements from other categories.

Walks of Historical Interest
Ashtown to a Chimney Tall
A Place Apart – St Anne's Park
A Basin at Blessington
Pyramids and Cylinders
Ireland's Eye
Swords to Dublin Airport
Dublin Underground
Some Great Interiors

Parks and Demesnes
Talbot Street to the North Docklands
Ashtown to a Chimney Tall
A Place Apart – St Anne's Park
A Basin at Blessington
Pyramids and Cylinders
Swords to Newbridge Demesne
Mount Street Bridge to Merrion Square
Merrion Square to St Stephen's Green
Charlemont Bridge to Rathmines

Walks in areas of Urban Renewal
Talbot Street to the North Docklands
Ashtown to a Chimney Tall
The Liberties
Pearse Street to the Great South Wall

Suburban Walks
Royal Canal Way – Newcomen Bridge
    to Ashtown
Royal Canal Way – Ashtown to Leixlip
Ashtown to a Chimney Tall
A Place Apart – St Anne's Park

Pyramids and Cylinders
DARTing North
Howth
Ireland's Eye
Malahide to Swords
Swords to Newbridge Demesne
Swords to Dublin Airport
Charlemont Bridge to Rathmines
DARTing South
Dry Greens to Wet Sands

Waterway and Coastal Walks
Royal Canal Way – Newcomen Bridge
    to Ashtown
Royal Canal Way – Ashtown to Leixlip
DARTing North
Howth
Ireland's Eye
Malahide to Swords
Swords to Newbridge Demesne
DARTing South
Dry Greens to Wet Sands
Pearse Street to the Great South Wall

Circular Walks
Talbot Street to the North Docklands
A Place Apart – St Anne's Park
A Basin at Blessington
Howth
Ireland's Eye

Exercise (brisk) Walks
Talbot Street to the North Docklands
Royal Canal Way – Newcomen Bridge
    to Ashtown
Royal Canal Way – Ashtown to Leixlip
Ashtown to a Chimney Tall

A Basin at Blessington
Pyramids and Cylinders
Howth
Malahide to Swords
Swords to Newbridge Demesne
Swords to Dublin Airport
The Liberties
Lanes Beside the Tracks
Dry Greens to Wet Sands
Pearse Street to the Great South Wall

Panoramic Views
Ashtown to a Chimney Tall
Howth
Ireland's Eye
DARTing South
Pearse Street to the Great South Wall

Castles
Malahide to Swords
Swords to Dublin Airport

Dublin Underground
Some Great Interiors

Walks directly served at both ends by DART/Suburban Rail
(most of the remaining walks are still within 20–30 minutes' walk of the DART)

Talbot Street to the North Docklands
Royal Canal Way – Newcomen Bridge to Ashtown
Royal Canal Way – Ashtown to Leixlip
DARTing North
Howth
Ireland's Eye
The Southside Pub Crawl
DARTing South
Lanes Beside the Tracks
Dry Greens to Wet Sands
Dublin Underground

Walks in Order of Length

km	miles	
1	⅔	Ireland's Eye
2	1¼	The Southside Pub Crawl
2	1¼	Lanes Beside the Tracks
2.3	1	The Northside Pub Crawl
2.4	1½	Merrion Square to St Stephen's Green
2.4	1½	The Liberties
2.5	1½	Mount Street Bridge to Merrion Square
2.8	1¾	A Place Apart – St Anne's Park
3.2	2	Charlemont Bridge to Rathmines
3.7	2¼	Dry Greens to Wet Sands
4	2½	A Basin at Blessington
4	2½	Howth
4.8	3	Some Great Interiors
5.6	3½	Ashtown to a Chimney Tall
6	3¾	Swords to Newbridge Demesne
6.4	4	Royal Canal Way – Newcomen Bridge to Ashtown
6.5	4	Pyramids and Cylinders
6.5	4	Malahide to Swords
6.8	4¼	Dublin Underground
7.3	4½	Talbot Street to the North Docklands
8.5	5¼	Swords to Dublin Airport
11.2	7	Royal Canal Way – Ashtown to Leixlip
12.5	7¾	Pearse Street to the Great South Wall
12.9	8	DARTing South
14.5	9	DARTing North

Public Transport in Dublin

Dublin is a relatively small and easy city to get around. With the exception of one walk (the finish point on Pearse Street to the Great South Wall is only served by a maximum of two buses a day) there is an excellent rail or bus service to each of the selected walks. A new light rail system (LUAS) is currently being constructed but it won't be ready until the end of 2002 at the earliest. There is also talk of an underground but there is nothing definite about this yet. The current rail system consists of the DART (Dublin Area Rapid Transit), which serves the coastal hinterland. The Arrow Suburban Rail connects the central DART stations with the west of Dublin on a line that follows alongside the Royal Canal. There is another Suburban Rail line linking Heuston and Newbridge and points in between.

Generally buses in Dublin are green-coloured double-deckers, but there are an increasing number of specialized services with their own colour schemes including City Swift (buses that use the priority Quality Bus Corridors) and Imp (small vehicles that offer high frequency). Dublin Bus has a monopoly situation at the time of writing, but legislation is being prepared to allow competition on certain routes. Many routes require exact change only, so you will need to carry enough small coins or buy a rambler ticket which will allow unlimited travel for a number of days. Day tickets, weekly tickets and family tickets (also interchangeable on DART) are other cost-saving options. Services operate between 06.20 and 23.30 and main routes have a Late Nite service. Further information and prepaid tickets can be obtained from Dublin Bus, 59 Upper O'Connell Street, Dublin 1 (Tel: + 353 1 873 4222).

At peak times there is a DART train every 10 minutes, which reduces to an average of every 20 minutes during off-peak hours. Trains commence at 06.30 (09.00 Sun) and finish at 23.45. Tickets, including discount scheme tickets, can be purchased at any DART station. For more information call (+ 353 1) 836 6222.

Key to Route Maps

Each of the walks in this book is accompanied by a detailed map on which the route of the walk is shown in blue. Places of interest along the walks, such as historic buildings, museums and churches, are clearly identified.

The following is a key to the symbols used on the maps.

⇒	route of walk	●	point of interest
▪	major building	▫	body of water
†	church	▬	railway
♦♦	public toilets	⠿	beach
▦	park		

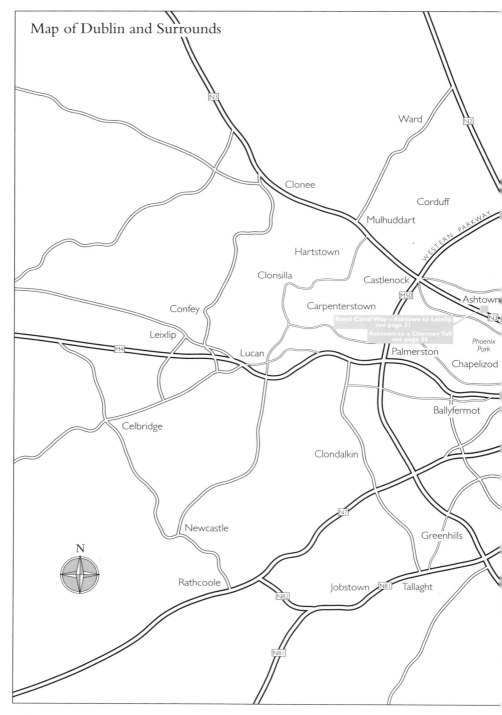

Map of Dublin and Surrounds

N3

Ward

N2

Clonee

Corduff

Mulhuddart

WESTERN PARKWAY

Hartstown

Clonsilla

Castlenock

Carpenterstown

M50

Ashtown

N3

Confey

Royal Canal Way – Ashtown to Leixlip
see page 31

Phoenix Park

Leixlip

M4

Ashtown to a Chimney Tall
see page 36

Lucan

Palmerston

Chapelizod

Ballyfermot

Celbridge

Clondalkin

N7

Greenhills

Newcastle

N

Rathcoole

N82

Jobstown

N81

Tallaght

N81

3,000 m (3,180 yd)

Swords to Newbridge Demesne
see page 78

Swords

Swords to Dublin Airport
see page 82

Malahide

Malahide to Swords
see page 73

N1

Portmarnock

Dublin
Airport
Δ

Ireland's
Eye

Ireland's Eye
see page 68

Kilmore

Baldoyle

Howth
see page 63

Santry

M1

Coolock

Sutton

Finglass

Artane

Howth

Raheny

Whitehall

Killester

Pyramids and Cylinders
see page 54

Dublin Underground
see page 144

R105

A Place Apart – St Anne's Park
see page 41

A Basin at Blessington
see page 47

Clontarf

North Bull
Island

he Northside Pub Crawl
see page 87

N1

Royal Canal Way – Newcomen Bridge to Ashtown
see page 24

Talbot Street to the North Docklands
see page 18

Connolly Sta.

The Southside Pub Crawl
see page 92

Islandbridge

DARTing North and South
see pages 59 and 121

he Great Interiors
see page 151

Pearse Street to the Great South Wall
see page 137

Dublin
Bay

Lanes Beside the Tracks
see page 127

The Liberties
see page 110

Dry Greens to Wet Sands
see page 132

rumlin

R118

Mount Street Bridge
to Merrion Square
see page 97

Merrion

Charlemont Bridge
to Rathmines
see page 116

Rathgar

Booterstown

Merrion Square to
St Stephen's Green
see page 103

Blackrock

Churchtown

N11

Dún Laoghaire

Goatstown

Monkstown

Ballinteer

Dalkey

Edmondstown

M50

Foxrock

Killiney

Ballybrack

M11

Talbot Street to the North Docklands

Summary: Dublin is changing and, we hope, improving, faster than most European capital cities, and nowhere is this more evident than along this walk. The first half of the journey will take you through the heart of the Financial Services Centre, which was built on a redundant 18th-century inner harbour site. Further on, more empty warehousing and railway shunting yards are in the process of giving way to huge office schemes, comprising corporate headquarters, a college campus, apartments, urban squares, light rail junctions, retail and office parks and linear boulevards along both the river and the canals. Then you will come to the outskirts of the modern docklands, which are frenetic with activity and traffic. However, towards the end of the outward section of the walk, the built-up areas yield to sea views, mudflats and parkland. The last part of the journey provides another contrast, as it takes you through an area seemingly left behind by the booming economy; but it, too, is now poised for major redevelopment.

Start & Finish:	Ripley Inn Hotel and Bar, Talbot Street.
Length:	7.3 kilometres (4½ miles).
Time:	1¾ hours.
Refreshments:	There are two hotels, a couple of pubs and a convenience store along the first half of the route. More places are opening all the time.
Pathway Status:	Public pathways everywhere except for a short section of grass and stone path along the seashore.
Best Time to Visit:	During the day is best as towards the evening some of the roads are deserted.
Suitable for Bicycles:	Yes – the homeward stretch of the journey (from Alfie Byrne Road) is mostly along cycle lanes.

From the Ripley Inn, head off down Talbot Street and pass under the Loop Line Railway Bridge. The Loop Line is so called because it connected two separated railway termini in 1890, Connolly and Pearse Stations. Walk over to the opposite side of the street, which should be easy as the street has recently been 'traffic-calmed'. Just before Amiens Street stands a large stone memorial, a grim and poignant reminder of a number of terrorist bombs that ripped through Dublin's rush-hour streets in 1974, killing dozens of people and injuring many more. When you reach Amiens Street, cross over with the aid of the pedestrian lights and turn left towards the impressive Italianate façade of Connolly Station. Originally known simply as Amiens Street Station, it was built in 1844 to the design of William Deane Butler for the Dublin and Drogheda

Connolly Station, Amiens Street.

Railway Company. It was renamed in 1966 in honour of James Connolly, one of the leaders of the 1916 rebellion against British rule. Enter the newly opened station concourse, part of the massive remodelling and upgrading of the interior that was completed in early 2000. The concourse not only leads to the platforms but also directly into one of Dublin's most modern and extensive new developments, the International Financial Services Centre (IFSC).

Something Old, Something New

When you have explored the station, leave by the exit into the IFSC, then stop and take in the view. To the left are some high-tech offices while ahead are the various apartment complexes. To the right are more office blocks, and in between the buildings are gushing fountains and cascading waterfalls. All of Ireland's largest names in the banking and financial services world have a strong presence in the IFSC, but you will also find many leading international institutions as well. Since 1990, these gilt-edged companies have been setting up shop to take advantage of generous tax regimes, Ireland's central role in European affairs and the highly educated home labour market. As you stroll through the centre you will see modern, high specification offices juxtaposed with remnants of the Georgian and Victorian docklands. Known originally as the Custom House Docks, this 18th-century enclave was built around two large inner docks (which now form the core of the IFSC) that were designed to offer shelter from racing tides and gusting winds while the old sailing ships loaded and offloaded their cargos. Head for the lantern-bedecked bridge between Wrights Fisherman's Wharf Restaurant and the Harbourmaster Pub, both an option if you are ready for some refreshment. If not, drop into the pub in any case to experience an atmosphere and memorabilia more associated with sailing days than with blue chips and microchips. Once over the bridge, turn right and walk past an 18th-century warehouse known as Stack A, currently being restored for cultural uses. The stone archway, which stands proudly in solitude, is in fact the old gateway into the Custom House Docks that formerly stood off Amiens Street and was re-erected as a feature in itself. Just beyond the archway is the refurbished Sherzer Bridge, an early-20th-century all-metal lifting bridge. A large concrete dam was deemed necessary to block the Liffey from George's Dock, so the lifting bridge has sadly been retired from its original function.

Turn left onto Custom House Quay. Walk past Jurys Custom House Inn and, on the opposite side, the headquarters of the Dublin Dockland's Development Authority, the state agency in charge of redeveloping the vast tracts of redundant dockland. Its success can be gauged as you continue along North Wall Quay. More impressive office complexes have been and are still being built, each one vying with the next for prominence. Large financial organizations such as Citibank and AIG sit comfortably cheek-by-jowl with a third-level educational establishment (The College of Ireland), a hotel and a block of apartments as part of the strategy to ensure mixed-use developments. Building height is strictly regulated in Dublin, so there are no skyscrapers as such, but developers keep pressing the planners on this issue in this part of the city. For instance, a modestly high-rise scheme was promoted for Spencer Dock, a former railway yard that you come to immediately after crossing another lift bridge, this time over the entrance to the Royal Canal. This is the site of the new National Conference Centre, which should be well under way by the time this book is published. Further impressive development schemes are going ahead or are planned, for this site, for locations further downriver and on the other side of the Liffey. Urban parks, boulevards, quayside promenades and a light railway transit system will add the final flourish to this 21st-century reinvention of the docklands.

Docklands and Wetlands

A typical dockside pub, Vallence and McGrath (established 1908) might prove too tempting to pass by but once past it, keep walking straight on. The monument outside the entrance to shipping agents Dublin Maritime Ltd is entitled *The Mariner* and is by sculptor John Behan. On the opposite riverbank the mouths of the Grand Canal and River Dodder merge to flow into the now widening Liffey. Ahead is the city's easternmost bridge, the East Link Toll Bridge, which can lift to allow ships upriver. Beyond the bridge are the anything but redundant docklands of Dublin Port, now a 24-hour-a-day facility trying to cope with Ireland's booming economy. If you briefly cross to the middle of the toll bridge, you will get excellent views of the port to the east and the city to the west. At the bridge roundabout, you walk past the Point Theatre, a spectacular conversion from an old railway goods depot (built in 1878). You can still see some of the tracks in the car park. There is a scheme called the Point Village planned for around the theatre, which may have started by the time you read this book. The road you are on now, East Wall Road, was once a dockland quay but reclamation has pushed the land limits 2.5 km (1½ miles) further east. In fact, everywhere you have walked and will walk on this tour was, until the last few centuries, covered by the tidal waters of the Liffey estuary. East Wall Road is usually choked with port traffic, much of which will soon be diverted into a new port tunnel that will take trucks directly to the motorway network. When you have crossed the corner of Sheriff Street, railway marshalling yards with a connecting line to the port are spread out on your left.

At the next roundabout, off which is the main entrance to the port and car ferry terminals, turn left and you will quickly arrive at a firm called Rathborne Candles. While employing modern manufacturing methods, this enterprise still makes special hand–made candles using techniques that are centuries old. Rathborne's is Ireland's oldest business and possibly the world's oldest candle-making factory, as it has been in continuous existence since 1488. However, it has only been at this location since 1925. The factory shop is open to visitors. This stretch of East Wall Road is mostly lined with compact dockland housing, small industrial units and business parks. When you reach the next right-hand turn, cross the road and take the right-hand side of the Alfie Byrne Road. This will bring you over the Tolka River, a tidal stream that appears to almost disappear at low tide, and up towards the entrance of East Point Business Campus, a modern business centre comprising many international names, set amid lush landscaping, water features and seafront esplanades. You can take a diversion and visit it if you wish, but remember you still have the best part of 3 kilometres (2 miles) to go to finish this walk. In any event, head a little way up towards East Point and climb to the top of the grassy hill on your left where you will find a pathway along the shoreline. Here the mudflats provide habitats for various wading birds, and the cry of the curlew will be in sharp contrast to the noisy mayhem of the port district through which you have so recently passed. The suburb of Clontarf lies along the north shore of the estuary and in the far distance, beyond a yacht club, is the Bull Island Nature Reserve. Occupying a prominent position at the end of the estuary is a multicoloured sail-like sculpture by Eamonn O'Doherty. Its title is *Wind Sculpture*, and it was erected for the Dublin Millennium in 1988. Beside this sculpture but nearer the road is the memorial to Alfie Byrne himself, a much-loved Lord Mayor of Dublin for most of the 1930s and again in the mid 1950s.

Cross the Alfie Byrne Road to walk left along Clontarf Road, passing under the railway bridge (if you feel too tired to continue at this point, you could take a DART train from the adjacent Clontarf Road DART Station. Alternatively, any bus from here will take you back to Talbot Street). At the junction with the Malahide Road, turn left into the park and take the path lined with rows of dark, brooding maples, oak and beech (if you are on your own and the park looks lonely you might prefer to continue along the roadside footpath). Bearing off to the right is the aforementioned Malahide Road which was a toll road until the mid 19th century (an interesting walk commences from here in *Walking Dublin*). The buildings on the right were custom-built to provide shops, a college and a library as part of an integrated housing development, the first major attempt after the foundation of the Irish Free State in 1922 to begin housing the tens of thousands of unfortunates living in the then appalling slums of Dublin. The park and district are called Fairview because, until the middle of the 19th century, a fair view of the sea was obtainable from here: in fact the sea came right up to the road. Then the railway was built, and its embankment cut off the sea; later, the marshy inlet was reclaimed. Fairview Park is renowned, during the spring and summer, for its array of flowerbeds. After five minutes or so you will reach the statue of Sean Russell, a leader of the Old IRA (as distinct from the modern Irish Republican Army which was activated in Northern Ireland during the riots of the late 1960s). The now defunct Irish script on the plinth of the statue lists his fallen comrades and the provinces and counties of Ireland. The writing on a large boulder further on, at the corner exit of the park, may be difficult to discern if the graffiti is still in place. It commemorates the laying of the final stretch of the water main from Phoulaphuca Reservoir to Fairview in 1994.

Return to the Inner City

Walk across Annesley Bridge passing over the Tolka for the second time. Pass a cement works and a fire station on your left. The residential terraces now begin to give way to a 'mixum gatherum' (as they say in Dublin) of small shops, back-street businesses and offices. There is a general down-at-heel appearance about the place but this is scheduled to change for the better in the near future. Before you reach the overhead railway bridge, turn left into Leinster Avenue. (If you are anxious to reach the end of the walk, keep straight on.) This neighbourhood was developed as a warren of artisan-type houses and in this close-knit community they are generally very well kept. The houses on Leinster Avenue itself are bungalow-style with a basement, commonly referred to as one-up one-downs. Before you reach the railway embankment turn right into Spencer Avenue, then left into James Street North, right along by the embankment and right once more into Northbrook Avenue until you again reach the North Strand. Bear left, passing under the railway bridge, and within a few minutes you will cross over the Royal Canal, the perceived boundary to the central inner city area. The canal was fully opened for business in 1817 but unfortunately closed to commercial traffic in 1961. Engineering works are currently under way along its whole length to make it operational once more for leisure craft. Stop for a minute on the centre of Newcomen Bridge to take in the various aspects. On the left (eastwards) there is a view of the distant docklands. A new lift-bridge system has recently been installed to carry the railway over the canal, which means that the canal can again be opened to waterway traffic. On the other side of the bridge there is a good view of the ultramodern stands of Croke Park, the national stadium for Gaelic football and hurling. Just visible below the bridge level on the Croke Park side is a picturesque lock-keeper's cottage that usually has a profusion of flowers growing outside it in hanging baskets and assorted tubs.

The rather dated public housing flats on both sides of the road, especially those on the left, stand on the site of several streets of terraced houses that were devastated in May 1941 by German bombs, which killed 37 people and injured another 90. A small enclosed park now stands as a memorial to the victims. At the next junction, where five roads converge, there is a decorative lamp column crowned with five lamps, one for each road. Also serving as a drinking fountain, the Five Lamps (as they are rather obviously called) was built as a memorial to a famous Galway man, General Henry Hall, a military campaigner in Britain's Indian army in the late 1800s. Continue on straight along Amiens Street. A number of Victorian edifices, built of brick or stone, are now spread along the street at intervals. These were mostly built to serve the railway, either as offices, a hotel, or, in the case of the elegant triple tower structure, a terminus. Connolly Station is now the terminus for the only international rail connection in Ireland, the Dublin to Belfast service. Another railway bridge, resting on four fluted iron columns, carries the Loop Line over Amiens Street.

At the next junction, turn right and head up Talbot Street to the friendly Ripley Court Hotel and Bar, or continue on up Talbot Street to O'Connell Street.

Royal Canal Way – Newcomen Bridge to Ashtown

Summary: In this walk you get away from the busy city streets and wander alongside the quiet waters of the Royal Canal. This canal was built from 1790 onwards as a rival to the Grand Canal. It stretches from Spencer Dock beside the River Liffey all the way to the River Shannon, which it finally reached in 1817. The canal has been closed to commercial traffic since 1961 and is in the process of being developed for leisure boating. You could walk along the towpath all the way to Mullingar (82 kilometres/51 miles) if you wish, but our little amble involves only a short journey to Ashtown. At the end of the walk, you have three options: you can continue along the canal with the next walk in this book, Ashtown to Leixlip; you can choose another of the walks, Ashtown to a Chimney Tall, or you can return directly to the city by bus or train.

Start:	Newcomen Bridge, North Strand Road. Buses 20A, 20B, 27, 27B, 29A, 31, 31A, 32, 32A, 42, 42A, 42B. DART/ Arrow Station: Connolly Station is only 7 minutes' walk from Newcomen Bridge. Car parking: leave your car in a city centre car park.
Finish:	Halfway House, Ashtown. Buses 22B, 38, 39. Arrow Station: Ashtown.
Length:	6.4 km (4 miles).
Time:	1½ hours.
Refreshments:	The best advice is to bring your own. There are pubs and eating houses within reach of some of the bridges and there is adequate fare at end of the walk.
Pathway Status:	For the first part of the journey, the towpaths are generally laid with tarmac and are in good condition. For the second part, the paths are mostly gravel but are still wide, even and generally dry.
Best Time to Visit:	Any time is suitable, but avoid the dark as there is no lighting along the route.
Route Notes:	The walk is probably best enjoyed in company, as parts of the route can be quite lonely.
Suitable for Bicycles:	Yes, but you will have to negotiate the slightly awkward barriers at each road crossing where there is no towpath

under the bridge. Please show respect to pedestrians on the narrow paths.

Connecting Walks: From Talbot Street to the North Docklands, to Ashtown to a Chimney Tall and to The Royal Canal Way — Ashtown to Leixlip.

The walk starts at Newcomen Bridge in the North Strand area of Dublin, so called because until the 18th century there was a strand, or shore, here, marking the easterly coastline of the Liffey estuary. On the east side of Newcomen Bridge is a new hydraulic lifting mechanism that raises the railway tracks, allowing boats along the canal. The bridges of the Royal Canal (and also the Grand Canal) were named after the directors of the operating company, and so Sir William Newcomen, a director from 1789 to 1810, gave his name to our starting point.

At this point, the canal is quite close to its outlet into the River Liffey, which is only about 0.5 kilometre away at Spencer Dock. This dock was built to transfer goods from ships to the railways, but is now earmarked for a major new development including the building of a large conference centre. The dock and Spencer Bridge, a one-time lifting bridge at Sheriff Street (which you can see in the distance), were named after the 5th Earl of Spencer, Lord Lieutenant 1868–1874.

With your back to the city centre, take the towpath to the left of the bridge and on the left (south) side of the canal, and start heading west. The term towpath comes from the days when horses towed the barges along at a nice leisurely pace. The path is a bit rough and ready at this point, although it may by now have been resurfaced. The road that runs alongside the path is called Charleville Mall. It hardly lives up to the pretensions of its name, although it is graced by a fine old branch library building which is rather spoiled by its vandal-proof roof. You will probably encounter your first ducks on this stretch of the waterway. You may also come across a fair amount of litter, especially on the inner city part of the journey. We may have a beautiful city and incomparable countryside, but unfortunately the citizens of Dublin still drop litter or dispose of the occasional disused fridge or supermarket trolley in rivers and canals. The Dublin Chamber of Commerce has even put up road signs saying 'Welcome to Dublin but excuse the litter'. However, awareness of the problem is beginning to dawn and campaigns to eradicate it are gathering momentum. When you reach the next bridge, Clarke's Bridge, follow the towpath under it. You only actually need to cross over a bridge rather than under it occasionally, but you may want to climb up to road level anyway to view the area. This is the area of Ballybough, a name, like so many in Ireland, derived from the original Irish language place name, Baile Bocht (the town of the poor). You will notice that the bridge over the canal is an elegant arched structure, but that the section over the railway is a more modern and functional straight span. This is because the railway bridge was built much later. The Midland Great Western Railway Company bought the Royal Canal in 1845, not for the value of the canal itself, which had already gone into decline, but to use the land alongside it for building the railway line that is still in use today. This railway line will accompany you for the remainder of the walk, sometimes on your right side, sometimes on your left, and passing trains may keep you company.

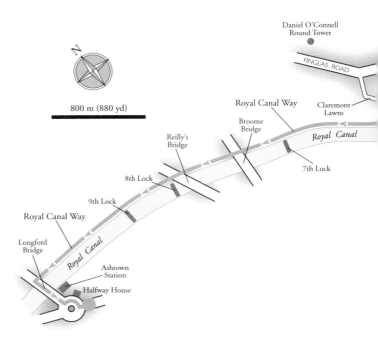

The Auld Triangle

The section of the canal you are now walking along was rebuilt and reopened only in 2000. The reason will be obvious as you approach the mammoth ultramodern Croke Park Stadium. This is the recently reconstructed headquarters of the GAA (the Gaelic Athletic Association) where the national games of Irish football, hurling (an extremely fast field game played with a curved-end stick) and camogie (a ladies' version of hurling) are played with enormous fervour. During the semi-finals and finals, over 80,000 fans, displaying the vibrant colours of their county teams, add great spectacle and pageantry to the proceedings. The railway disappears under the great stand and reappears at the next road crossing, Clonliffe Bridge, commonly called Russell Street Bridge. During the construction of Croke Park, the canal bed was drained and the water was carried through large pipes. Continue along the next section, which was relaid after the new stands were built.

Soon you come to Binns Bridge, named after John Binns, the man mainly responsible for the building of the canal. Binns was a director of the Grand Canal Company, but for some reason he became estranged from his fellow directors. He determined to build a rival canal, from Dublin to the Shannon, although there was very little commercial reason for a second. The Grand Canal Company, when they heard of his proposal, very sensibly suggested sharing the route out of Dublin as far as Kinnegad, where the new canal could branch off to serve the north Shannon region. Binns

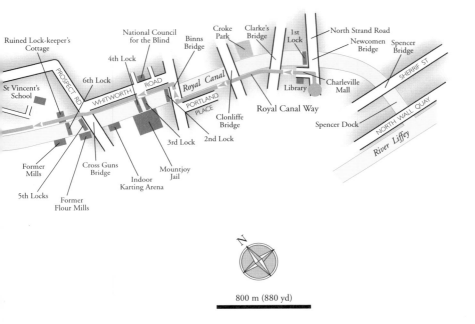

800 m (880 yd)

wouldn't listen, and he persuaded investors to start the Royal Canal at Dublin's North Wall Quay near the mouth of the River Liffey. The final route chosen by Binns and his fellow directors proved to have been poorly surveyed and huge overspending was necessary, especially to cut the canal through the Carpenterstown Quarries (see the next walk Royal Canal Way – Ashtown to Leixlip) and to build the Ryewater Aqueduct at Leixlip. However, the fact that Binns' obstinacy and poor commercial judgement led to a basically unwanted canal is forgivable, given the legacy he has left for future generations.

Cross Drumcondra Road, the main road leading north to Dublin Airport and Belfast, and head up the right bank of the canal. On the other side of the low stone wall is a deep drop to the railway tracks. Ahead is an incline that takes the canal five double locks to ascend between here and Shandon Mills, a short distance away in Phibsborough. The total height gained over this distance is 28.1 metres (92 feet 2 inches). The view along this portion of the canal now becomes more open and pleasant, and you are likely to meet more people walking along the tree-lined towpath. When you come to the next lock gate you can cross it on the wooden platform, if you wish, and recross again at the next lock – but be careful! Running parallel to the railway is Whitworth Road, named after Charles Whitworth, Lord Lieutenant 1813–1817. The Whitworth Fever Hospital, an institution standing about halfway along the road and now the headquarters of the National Council for the Blind, was

27

also named after him. On the left bank of the canal, also about halfway up, are the forbidding walls of Mountjoy Jail which was built between 1847 and 1850. It was laid out in similar fashion to Pentonville Prison in the UK, which was then considered a model prison. The tall chimneys were designed to circulate a complete change of air through the jail every five minutes. Brendan Behan, the famous playwright, was once incarcerated in Mountjoy where he wrote his famous ballad, 'The Auld Triangle', in which he describes life in the jail 'along the banks of the Royal Canal'.

The front end of an indoor karting arena marks the point where a spur once led off from the canal and ended at Broadstone Harbour, the original terminus, which in 1877 was filled in. The spur line was finally emptied and turned into a linear park in 1951. This length of the canal, between the fourth and fifth locks, is popular with ducks and swans.

Still climbing, the path now brings you up to Cross Guns Bridge and, beyond it, to the fifth lock. Prospect Road crosses this bridge and leads to Glasnevin Cemetery and the National Botanic Gardens. The official name of the bridge is Westmoreland Bridge after the Earl of Westmoreland, the Lord Lieutenant who laid the lock's foundation stone in 1790. The name Cross Guns predates that event and has stuck, despite the renaming. Cross the road using the traffic lights and rejoin the canal. The tall stone building rising

Broom Bridge, Royal Canal.

above the fifth lock is now a block of apartments converted from a flour mill. Before 1860 it was Robert Mallet's Iron Works, the company that built the heavy railings of Trinity College, which stretch from College Green to Nassau Street. Just as you approach the next ascent you will notice the remains of a bridge that once carried a railway siding to the mills. At the sixth lock there is another former mill which has also been converted into apartments, and a lock-keeper's cottage that is, alas, in ruins. The canal now levels out, and you can see how far you have climbed by looking over the wall on the right to the railway line below. The distant panorama includes Glasnevin Cemetery (pinpointed by the O'Connell Monument, a large round tower) and the National Botanic Gardens. In the foreground, just behind the railway track, is a large primary school, St Vincent's. The scene becomes quite rural beyond the line of houses on the left. Far below, one set of railway tracks now curves in towards the canal and disappears underneath through a tunnel. This line travels under the Phoenix Park and joins the main routes out of Heuston Station. The other railway line, which has been on your right from the start of the walk, now crosses over the canal and passes by a redundant water tower. At this point the canal takes on a more meandering, river-like appearance.

You are now approaching Broome Bridge and Broombridge Railway Station, both of which are named after William Broome, another director of the Royal Canal Company. The bridge is famous for a reason totally unconnected with canals or railways. Sir William Rowan Hamilton (1805–1865) possessed one of the greatest mathematical minds of the 19th century. At the age of five he was reading Hebrew, Latin and Greek, and by thirteen he had a working knowledge of as many languages, including Persian. By seventeen he was taking the mathematical world by storm, and while still an undergraduate at Trinity College he was appointed its Professor of Astronomy. In 1827 he was appointed Astronomer Royal of Ireland at Dunsink Observatory (not far from Ashtown, your destination on this walk). Walking with his wife into Dublin on 16 October 1843, Hamilton had a flash of inspiration as he passed Broome Bridge. Lest he forget it, he immediately scratched a formula onto the stonework. This formula led to the discovery of quaternions, a breakthrough in algebraic mathematics. A plaque commemorating the event was unveiled exactly a century later by another keen mathematician, President of Ireland Eamon de Valera. For the record, the formula was $12=J2=K2=1jk=-1$. The bridge was renamed Rowan Hamilton Bridge in 1958 but it is still popularly known as Broome Bridge. A second arch was added to the crossing when the railway was built in 1846.

The next section of the walk is through an industrial landscape of factories and warehouse backyards, separated from the canal by hideous security fencing. Once past Reilly's Bridge, however, you leave this behind and a more rural background takes over. Keeping horses is a popular pastime among the young locals, so don't be too surprised if you meet one or two. You will pass the eight and ninth lock before arriving at Longford Bridge. Along the way you may see people fishing for roach, pike or other coarse fish. Longford Bridge is the location of Ashtown Station, where you can get a train back to Dublin. Otherwise you can continue from here on the Ashtown to Leixlip walk, or Ashtown to a Chimney Tall. Whatever you do, you might like to take some refreshment at the Halfway House pub and restaurant, 300 metres (330 yards) away from the station in the direction of the Navan Road.

Royal Canal Way – Ashtown to Leixlip

Summary: If Royal Canal Way – Newcomen Bridge to Ashtown was essentially a waterway walk in an urban setting, then this walk could be described as a waterway walk in a rural environment. It's quite a long journey and should be taken at a leisurely pace unless you are a keen walker and love to burn up the miles. There are many contrasting vistas to enjoy including crossing a motorway interchange complex by a high viaduct, part walking and part scrambling along a densely wooded path skirting a fairly deep gorge, before finally emerging into a wide expanse of level pastureland. The last stage of the walk will take you to the historic village of Leixlip, once a sleepy hamlet of a few hundred souls, but now humming with the activity generated from the nearby huge facilities of some of the world's leading computer and software conglomerates.

Start:	Ashtown Railway Station. Arrow-Suburban Rail: Ashtown. Buses: 22B, 38, 39. Car parking: limited on-street parking.
Finish:	Main Street, Leixlip. Bus 66. Arrow-Suburban Rail: Leixlip Station. Car parking can be difficult to find in the centre of town.
Length:	11.2 km (7 miles).
Time:	2¾ hours.
Refreshments:	Bring a packed lunch or other sustenance, as there will be no opportunities for refreshment until the end of the walk. In an emergency you can leave the canal and make for one of the neighbouring villages.
Pathway Status:	Much of this walk is on hard-packed mud paths or grass, so if it has rained recently there will be muddy stretches and wet grass. If this is the case, wear suitable footwear.
Best Time to Visit:	Any time, but start early enough to avoid finishing in the dark, as there is no artificial lighting along the towpaths.
Route Notes:	Canals can be dangerous places for small children, especially along this walk, as there is up to a 10-metre (33-foot) drop to the Royal Canal in some places.
Suitable for Bicycles:	Partly, but it is not advisable as some of the stretches are very narrow and rutted with stones and tree trunks. Falling off could plunge you headlong into the canal.
Connecting Walk:	From Royal Canal Way – Newcomen Bridge to Ashtown.

Alight from the train at Ashtown Station, a small and newly-built rail halt on the recently improved suburban line linking Dublin with Maynooth. Underinvestment in Dublin's public transport infrastructure bedevilled the city in the 1990s, and an improved economy put more and more cars onto already clogged roads. A rapidly growing population (estimated to double to 2 million by 2011) was pushing the limits of the city further and further into the neighbouring countryside, swallowing up rural villages. Between 1999 and 2001, the single rail line serving Maynooth was augmented by a parallel track, allowing a dramatic increase in the number of scheduled suburban train services. At this point, it's a good idea to climb to the top of the pedestrian bridge connecting the two platforms and view the peaceful scene of the Royal Canal, looking very much like a river as it threads its way from the city and heads off in the direction of Leixlip, your destination, and beyond.

Cross the road from the station and head onto the towpath, keeping the canal on your right and the railway on your left. You are now quite close to the busy Navan Road, and the sound of traffic will be constant until you are beyond the next bridge, but trees and other greenery help to muffle the noise. This stretch of the canal has very few locks, so lock number 11, about 1.5 kilometres (1 mile) from Ashtown, comes as a surprise. At this point the land rises rather steeply and an impressive three-stage lock is required. All the lock gates have been recently restored. After this, you

Ranelagh Bridge, Royal Canal.

approach a complex series of new bridges, flyovers, underpasses and an aqueduct. The first of the modern bridges carries Dunsink Lane (which passes the famous Dunsink Astronomical Observatory) across the canal. This has made the humpbacked road bridge (Ranelagh Bridge) redundant, but the old structure has been preserved as a canal feature. An excellent tarmac path now runs from Dunsink Lane Bridge, and it takes you to a spectacular junction involving interlacing roads, the railway and the canal itself, called the Navan Road Interchange. The M50 motorway passes underneath the canal and the two arms of the roundabout of the Blanchardstown bypass sweep over the railway and the Royal Canal viaducts. This elegant symphony in concrete dates from 1996. When you arrive at Talbot Bridge, a short distance from the interchange, climb up to the road to view some old mills that have been converted into apartments. Regain the towpath and continue though the conurbation of Blanchardstown, one of several former villages on the outskirts of Dublin now being developed as self-contained satellite towns in their own right. One of the advantages of urban growth is the opening of suburban railway stations along what is essentially the railway line to the west of Ireland. So, if you began this walk at Newcomen Bridge (the previous walk in this book) and you feel too weary to continue, you can pick up a train from Castleknock Station, which is just a few strides beyond the next crossing, Granard Bridge.

Even though you are passing through a densely built-up area, a screen of trees and hedging gives a sense of seclusion. This feeling of solitude and stillness intensifies as the channel of the canal drops away from the bank, and the towpath, crisscrossed with exposed roots from the overhanging trees, becomes narrow. Where light penetrates the dark canopy of the woodland, wild flowers grow in abundance, especially limestone-lovers such as cowslip, fragrant orchid and carline thistle. This part of the canal is called the Deep Sinking – its level is as much as 9 metres (30 feet) below the towpath in places. When, in the 1790s, the Royal Canal Company was faced with cutting through the solid limestone of Carpenterstown Quarry, the sheer expense of the operation (which included £10,000 on gunpowder alone) meant that only the narrowest of channels was sliced through the hard rock, with the result that it was not wide enough for two boats to pass. Before a barge entered the Deep Sinking, the boatman would have to blow a horn; if there was no answering signal from another vessel, he could proceed. A constant danger in the days of horse-pulled barges was that a sudden check on the tow rope could, and several times actually did, drag a horse over the edge of the towpath and into the water below. Be mindful of your own safety along this section, and be particularly careful to keep children in check. The Deep Sinking continues past Coolmine Station and the next bridge, which carries the Coolmine Road.

At Kennan Bridge (Porterstown Road), cross over to the right-hand bank. The pathway is still quite high over the canal, but it gradually reaches the same level as the water. The quality and width of the path's surface soon improves, too. Kennan Bridge is named after Thomas Kennan, a director of the New Royal Canal Company, the organization that succeeded the Royal Canal Company when, in 1818, it ran out of funds. An old railway signal box announces Clonsilla Station at Callaghan Bridge (Clonsilla Road). Evidence of the railway spur line from Clonsilla to Navan and

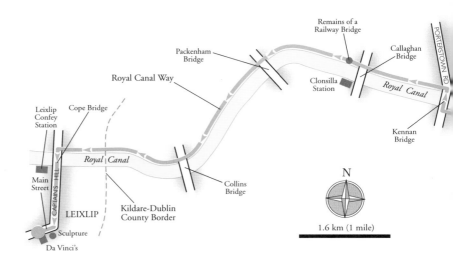

Athboy is provided by the remaining stone abutments of a dismantled bridge, which carries the railway over the canal just west of Clonsilla Station. The Dublin and Meath Railway, a small independent company, started this service in 1862, but the line has long since been abandoned. The present railway track runs very close to the canal bank and you may see the occasional train speeding along it. The canal gently curves to the left, and the surrounding scenery is now of working farms in a rural landscape. A wide grass verge replaces the narrow towpath providing a good place for a picnic, if you wish.

Once over Packenham Bridge (named after Captain Thomas Packenham, a member of the Parliamentary Committee set up to approve the building of the Royal Canal, and later a director of the Royal Canal Company), you are heading towards the penultimate bridge on your itinerary. At regular intervals along this section of the canal, there are numbered markers and concrete ledges jutting out into the water. These are fishing competition stands, which are allocated to competitors randomly; the stand numbers are drawn from a hat. This prevents favouritism, or competitors choosing a spot that they know to be better for fish.

Carry on under Collins Bridge and head towards your last bridge, passing more numbered fishing stands. You might want to ignore the actual numbers, which count down towards the bridge (83, 82, 81 and so forth), to avoid making the journey seem longer. This area is called Confey and it was here that the Royal Canal Amenity Group (RCAG), founded in 1974 to preserve and improve the amenity value of the waterway, built a boat slipway to provide access to the lock-free 12-kilometre (7½-mile) stretch above the twelfth lock at Talbot Bridge. The RCAG was successful in this initial enterprise, and the group now has active branches all along the Royal Canal. These actively lobby for and personally implement initiatives for improving

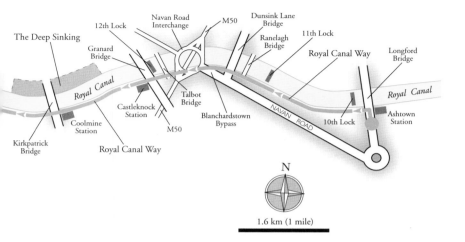

the navigation and condition of the canal. Before you reach the bridge you will have crossed into County Kildare.

The walk now leaves the canal at Cope Bridge and turns left down the nearly 1.2-kilometre (¾-mile) length of Captain's Hill to Main Street, in the picturesque village of Leixlip. Leixlip, once a sleepy backwater on the north bank of the River Liffey, is now a prosperous place with the giant computer corporations, Intel and Hewlett Packard, operating only a short distance away. It was settled by the Anglo-Normans who built a castle (a modernized Leixlip Castle still incorporates much of the original fortification), a stone bridge over the River Liffey (erected in 1308 and rebuilt in the 20th century) and the abbey of St Wolstan, of which little remains. Where Captain's Hill meets Main Street turn right, walk past the sculpture by Jarlath Daly representing the meeting of the Rivers Liffey and Rye, and take a well-earned rest in any of the numerous pubs and restaurants — including the excellent Da Vinci's, an Italian restaurant that serves superb pizzas among its other accomplishments.

Ashtown to a Chimney Tall

Summary: From an almost rural starting point, this walk will take you past modern suburbia, through one of the world's largest urban parks and into a poignant military cemetery, then to an outstanding example of 19th-century barracks architecture. As you enter the city proper you will experience the vibrancy of long-established inner-city neighbourhoods. Finally, after walking along the site of an ancient highway (over which Celtic chariots once thundered), you will arrive at Smithfield, an area transformed beyond all recognition as part of the current programme of upgrading run-down sections of the city. The journey is for the most part gently downhill but at the end it is decidedly uphill, in fact perpendicular – in a glass cabin that swishes its way up to the top of a 38-metre (125-foot) industrial chimney.

Start:	Halfway House, Ashtown. Arrow-Suburban Rail: Ashtown Station. Buses: 22B, 38, 39. Car parking: limited on-street parking.
Finish:	Chief O'Neill's, Smithfield. DART: Tara Street Station (25 minutes' walk). Buses: 37, 39, 51, 51B, 70. Car parking: multi-storey car park on Usher's Quay and some metered spaces along the quays.
Length:	5.6 km (3½ miles).
Time:	1¾ hours
Refreshments:	There are adequate opportunities along the route, but you might like to have a picnic in the Phoenix Park.
Pathway Status:	City and parkland paths. In the cemetery you will have to walk on the grass to view the gravestones.
Best Time to Visit:	The Phoenix Park is at its best in the morning, but any time during the day is good.
Suitable for Bicycles:	Yes.
Connecting Walk:	From Royal Canal Way – Newcomen Bridge to Ashtown, and to The Northside Pub Crawl.

If you have just arrived by train at Ashtown Station (as opposed to having walked here from Royal Canal Way – Newcomen Bridge to Ashtown), take a brief wander to its right to enjoy the peaceful surroundings of the Royal Canal. When you are ready to start the walk, head left towards the Halfway House, passing riding stables on the way. With the Phoenix Park so close by, there are an increasing number of these in the area. From the Halfway House and the roundabout cross the road towards Castleknock. This soon brings you to the Ashtown Gates of the Phoenix Park, one of the world's largest urban parks. It was originally laid out and walled in the 1660s by the Viceroy, the Duke of Ormonde, as a royal hunting park. To this end he stocked it with fallow deer, which still thrive in its great open spaces, and partridge. This walk only takes you along the northern edge, so for a more comprehensive tour, consult *Walking Dublin*, this book's companion guide.

The Futility of War

Turn left at the sign for the Civil Defence School. Note that the antique lamps, which are spaced along most of the roads around the park, are still lit by gas. In a programme of constant renewal, the lines of mature trees are supplemented by saplings. The Phoenix Park School on the left was built in 1848 by the Commissioners of Woods and Forests to cater for the children of their workers, who lived in the various lodges scattered throughout the park. Now a special school, it is also used as a voting centre for local residents, which include the Presidential household. At the next junction, if you have time, you can take the road to the wonderful Ashtown Castle Visitor Centre where you will find full information on everything to do with the Phoenix Park. It also has a coffee shop and rest room facilities. Allow at least another hour and a half if you want to do this. Assuming you are staying on the main route (return to this point if you have visited Ashtown Castle), continue straight on. To the left, behind a pedestrian gate, is the mock Tudor-style Hole in the Wall pub. On the right is a collection of buildings that house the Civil Defence School and headquarters. The

Grangegorman Military Hospital, Blackhorse Avenue.

central building, Ratra House, was formerly the residence of the Private Secretary to the Lord Lieutenant. The first President of Ireland, Dr Douglas Hyde, lived here after his retirement until his death in 1949.

Enjoy the seclusion of the park until you reach the Cabra Gate, where you exit onto Blackhorse Avenue. In front of some flat-roofed apartment blocks is a curious single-storey house with a large mansard roof. Until a few years ago, this was a thatched cottage called Primrose Cottage. The 17th-century wall of the Phoenix Park now runs alongside the road again and you soon arrive at the gates of Grangegorman Military Cemetery. This was opened in 1878 as a family burial ground for members of the British forces serving in Dublin, and is laid out in well-ordered plots. The graves belong to scores of men who were shot in the Easter Rising of 1916 and over 600 servicemen who died during the First World War. The youth of many of the victims gives a sense of the futility of war. The sinking of the RMS *Leinster* by a German U-boat, when it was an hour's distance from Kingstown (Dun Laoghaire) on 10 October 1918, accounts for the largest single group of burials. Only 279 of the 771 passengers (of whom almost 500 were soldiers returning from leave) survived. To add to the tragedy, the Armistice was barely a month away.

Back on the road, continue along Blackhorse Avenue and, on the right, you will shortly see an impressive array of red brick buildings sprouting towers, spires and cupolas. This

600 m (660 yd)

extravaganza (and you are seeing only the rear view) announces the McKee Military Barracks. The complex was built between 1888 and 1892 and was originally called Marlborough Cavalry Barracks. In the British days, over 800 horses were stabled here. During the First World War it was said that departing troops never touched soil from the moment they mounted their steeds in Marlborough Barracks to their final arrival at the battlefields of France, even riding them directly onto connecting ships and trains. The barracks was renamed after Brigadier Richard McKee, who was killed by the British Auxiliaries on Bloody Sunday, 1920.

A Road of Stones

Railway tracks cross under the road, then reappear for a short distance before plunging into the Phoenix Park tunnel. Cross the North Circular Road into Aughrim Street. By its name this street commemorates the bloody Battle of Aughrim in 1691, when the forces of William of Orange decisively crushed the army of James II, thus assuring William the throne of England. A shrine depicting the *Apparition of Our Lady to St Bernadette at Lourdes* stands before the Church of the Holy Family. The interior has been tastefully modernized yet it retains a traditional character. The surrounding streets, with their dense rows of terraced houses, suggest a close-knit community; and if you go into Kavanagh's Pub at the end of Aughrim Street, a turreted Victorian establishment dating from 1901, you may well find some of its members. Don't be tempted to linger too long, though, as you still have a way to go.

You have now arrived at the western edge of the inner city. Turn right into Manor Street and into a road called Stoneybatter, a corruption of Stony Bóthar or Stony Road. The original Irish name for the road was Bóthar na gCloch, or the Road of Stones. This is a reference to the ancient Celtic highway, Slighe Chualann (Cualann's Way), which dates back to the 2nd century AD and ran from Tara in County Meath to Glendalough in County Wicklow. It crossed the River Liffey at the Hurdle Ford (Áth Cliath – the place that has given Dublin its Irish name, Baile Átha Cliath, the Town of the Hurdle Ford). Kirwan Street, to the left, is another attractive street of tightly-packed terraced houses. Also on the left is Stanhope Street School, an old and respected inner-city girls' school run by the Sisters of Charity. Turn left into North Brunswick Street, which, like many in the neighbourhood, is lined with new apartment blocks. Set into the cobbles of Stanley Street (on your immediate left) are the preserved tracks of the old Dublin Tram System. The yard belonging to the mechanical division of Dublin Corporation was once a tram depot. Bear right into Red Cow Lane, which was probably named after a tavern in the locality.

Your destination now spreads before you. Smithfield was laid out by the late 1600s as a marketplace. Some fashionable 18th-century houses were built around it, but fashion soon abandoned it and it became once more a location for horse fairs, cattle sales and food markets. Between Smithfield and Bow Street, John Jameson & Son set up a major whiskey distillery (*see* The Northside Pub Crawl). By the 1970s and 80s, Smithfield had become quite derelict and was best known for a rather shabby horse fair. The horse fair (now upgraded) is still here, but little else remains that even a visitor of five years ago would recognize. Financial incentives encouraged developers to come in, and by 2000, three sides of the open area were rebuilt with apartments and the spectacular Smithfield Village. The fourth side is where you now head for. Here you will find the redundant distillery, which had been empty since the 1970s but was incorporated into a dramatic development involving apartments, a hotel, shops (Duck Lane), an Irish music interpretative centre (Ceol), a whiskey museum (the Old Jameson Distillery) and a theme bar and restaurant (Chief O'Neill's). The old chimney of the distillery was capped with two viewing platforms, offering an unrivalled panorama of the city. You can be whisked up in a lift or you may climb up via the internal staircase. Smithfield Square is now the city's official civil space. It was here, in early 2000, that the rock band U2 received the Freedom of Dublin. The piazza itself was laid out in setts, and 12 huge lighting columns (the sail-like objects are the lights) feature stunning gas braziers with leaping flames that can be seen from many parts of the city.

Feel free to wander around this great space and take in the sights. Take a ride up the chimney to see Dublin spread out before you, and trace the walk you have just completed. Then reward yourself in Chief O'Neill's and/or the Old Jameson Distillery.

Plate 1: *Flanked by the sentinel-like bulk of Liberty Hall, the Georgian splendour of the Custom House (built 1781–92) graces the north quays of the River Liffey (see page 20).*

Plate 2: *The semi-rural setting of the Lockkeeper's Cottage on the Royal Canal at Newcomen Bridge, North Strand, is only around a half a mile (1 km) from the city centre (see page 23).*

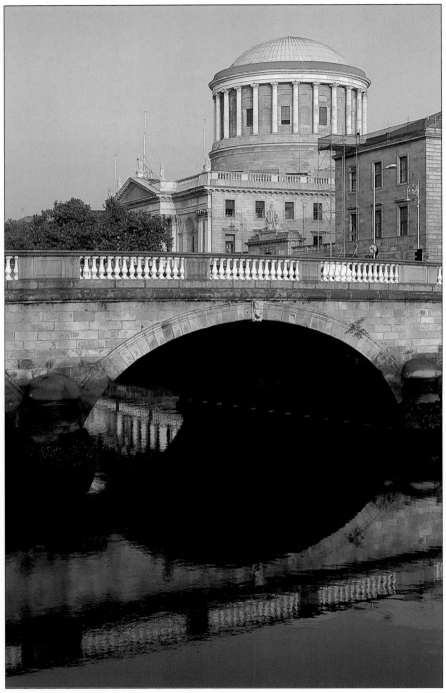

Plate 3: *The Four Courts (built by James Gandon 1786–1802) across the Liffey (see page 89).*

Plate 4: The marina (above) occupies a quiet corner of the busy cross-channel harbour of Dun Laoghaire (see page 123).

Plate 5: Chestnut Walk is one of the romantic hideaways in St Anne's park, a demesne that once belonged to the Guinness family (see page 42).

Plate 6: *A section of the Rotunda Chapel ceiling. The stuccadore, Barthelemi Cramillion, gave the chapel, completed around 1758, the finest rococo ornamentation in Dublin (see page 53).*

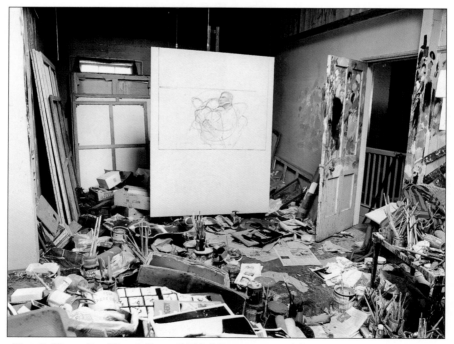

Plate 7: *The studio of Francis Bacon (1909–92) was transported from Reece Mews in London and re-erected in Dublin's Hugh Lane Municipal Gallery of Modern Art in 2000 (see page 52).*

A Place Apart –
St Anne's Park

Summary: Dubliners can consider themselves fortunate to possess abundant fine parklands, several of which are very large. The Phoenix Park is the largest enclosed city-centre park in Europe. Many of Dublin's parks once belonged, at least in part, to exclusive private estates, which were subsequently bequeathed to the state or purchased for public use. St Anne's Park, on the northern coastal fringe of the city, once belonged to that most famous of brewing families, the Guinnesses. Unfortunately the mansion itself is gone, but several generations of Guinness left a wealth of surprises to delight today's visitors. In 1936 the last private owner, Bishop Plunkett, a nephew of the childless Sir Arthur Guinness, sold all but 12 hectares (30 acres) of the 202-hectare (500-acre) estate to Dublin Corporation. Just over 81 hectares (200 acres) were developed for public housing, while the central more attractive section was retained as parkland. Natural planting, a winding stream and a collection of curios make this former demesne one of the most pleasurable and intriguing parks in the city.

Start and Finish:	Mount Prospect Avenue. Bus: 130. DART: Killester Station is 25 minutes' walk via Vernon Avenue. Car parking: on-street.
Length:	2.8 km (1¾ miles).
Time:	1 hour.
Refreshments:	It's advisable to bring your own, but there are a couple of good pubs a few hundred metres along the Clontarf Road in the direction of Dollymount. The proposed Arts Centre (*see* text) may be finished by the time this book is printed, in which case there will be a coffee shop in St Anne's.
Pathway Status:	A mixed bag of gravel paths, stone steps, tarmac and grass swards. Some rough ground might be a little muddy if it has been raining.
Best Time to Visit:	Every season brings its own delight in St Anne's Park, but late spring and summer are the best times to see the Rose Gardens.
Suitable for Bicycles:	The Park is wonderful for bicycles but they are only permitted on the main roads, not along the river or in the various gardens.

Alight from the bus at the stop nearest the lower (coastal) end of Mount Prospect Avenue and cross to the low wall enclosing a sunken garden and a large pond.

Upon entering the park, look across to the seaward side for a panoramic view of the inner Dublin Bay area, Bull Island and (if the tide is out) the mudflats. Bull Island is only about 200 years old and is still growing. This is due to the North Bull Wall, one of the enclosing arms of Dublin Port, which causes a gradual build-up of sand. Bull Island is now a wading bird sanctuary of international importance and is also home to several species of rare plants. It has been designated a United Nations Biosphere, reputedly the only one in the world within a city's limits. You are now in the Sunken Garden, which, from a directional point of view, is at the extreme southeastern top of St Anne's Park. Walk around the pond and head towards the woodland. Pass an old stone archway and tower on the left, one of many follies built around this lower end of the park – but more about them later. Turn right onto a path bordered by a perfectly straight line of trees. This is called Chestnut Walk. Continue straight on until you reach a small lake. Here you will find two more follies, a boathouse (its design based on a Pompeian temple) and an ornamental tower on a hillock overlooking the lake.

Italian and French Modes
At this stage, it is worth knowing something about the origins of St Anne's Park. In 1832 the brothers Arthur and Benjamin Lee Guinness, of the famous brewing family, purchased 13 hectares (32 acres) of land at Heronstown, Clontarf. Two years later they bought Thornhill, an 18th-century house, along with a further 21 hectares (52 acres), from John Venables Vernon, the owner of nearby Clontarf Castle. When in 1837 Benjamin Lee married his cousin, Elizabeth Guinness, he amicably bought out his brother so that he and his new wife could have the place to themselves. They called the estate St Ann's after a holy well, which is close to where you are now. (The 'e' was only added onto 'Ann' when Dublin Corporation acquired the estate.) Benjamin Lee Guinness went on to landscape the estate in typical Italian style, and brought back marble statues from Italy for his walled garden. When he died in 1868 his son Arthur (later Lord Ardilaun) inherited the property and it is to him that we owe the park as it looks today.

Arthur sold his share of the brewery business to his brother Edward and lavished the proceeds on St Anne's (we will add the 'e' from now on). He purchased over 162 hectares (400 acres) of land between 1870 and 1876 and doubled the size of the house. He planted out the vast estate, this time along French lines. The main drive was extended to 2.4 km (1½ miles) in length. The fame of the gardens soon spread far and wide.

Arthur built a large conservatory onto the house but it leaked persistently, something he could never fully cure. The ingress of damp even closed down the central heating system at times, and on such occasions his wife, Olive, Lady Ardilaun, took herself to the Shelbourne Hotel or to stay with her relatives in Iveagh House on St Stephen's Green.

Lord and Lady Ardilaun had no children and in 1925 the property passed to Benjamin Plunkett, Church of Ireland Bishop of Meath. The good Bishop found that he simply did not have the means to maintain the house and lands and so, with the exception of 12 hectares (30 acres) that he kept for himself at Sybil Hill (now

St Paul's College), he sold off the remaining 190 hectares (470 acres). Dublin Corporation was the eventual purchaser in 1936 although the City Manager, John B. Keane, had to pay the required deposit of £50 out of his own pocket while waiting for the City Councillors to debate and agree the acquisition. Shortly after the Corporation bought the land, it was mostly ploughed up to provide allotments to grow crops during the Second World War. During the 1950s some 81 hectares (200 acres) were developed for much-needed housing. What was left was turned into a public park, which today includes 35 playing pitches, 18 hard-surfaced tennis courts, a par-3 golf course and many other pleasures that will be revealed as you resume the walk.

Circle around the lake. On the top of the far embankment, you will see a tower between the trees. This was first erected by Benjamin Lee Guinness on the roof of the mansion, but was removed by Lord Ardilaun to its present position to be used as a summerhouse. It is a replica of the Tomb of Julii built during the Roman occupation of Provence around 40 BC. As you come back around the lake you will find the stone-covered holy well of St Anne, which is now dry. The spring is contained underground until it spills into the lake. Next, at the little Naniken River, take the right-hand bank and walk along the tree-sheltered stream until you reach a tiny bridge. On the opposite bank, you can see a tree growing on the roof of a small grotto made from tufa rock. You may cross the Naniken to view the grotto, but if you do you must return again to the right-hand bank and proceed until you come to a plain concrete bridge. Cross this to continue along the left-hand bank, and you will soon come to a curious rocky outcrop over which is built a Herculanean-styled house, another of Benjamin Lee Guinness's little follies. Herculaneum, like its sister

The Herculanean House, St Anne's Park.

city Pompeii, was submerged by the ash from the eruption of Mount Vesuvius in AD 79. When 18th-century and 19th-century excavations revealed the almost intact details of these cities it became popular around Europe to copy the architectural styles uncovered by the archaeologists. Abutting onto the rock face are the beginnings of an arched bridge, which for some reason was never finished. Next, you come to a three-arched bridge, which you walk under. Overhead, the evergreen trees form a verdant canopy and the stream, moving faster at this point, runs through a gorge. The path now moves away from the Naniken onto more open ground. When it meets a garden wall, turn left. From here, you soon reach the clock tower, which was built in 1854. The tower and the clock itself, the latter designed by James Booth of Dublin, was visible from the great house.

Continue on towards the main avenue and around by the railings that take over from the wall. Go through the gates at the far end of the railings (the railings, gates and piers were recycled from the old mansion) into a charming hidden garden that dates from only 1987, and is planted exclusively with miniature roses. Two fountains splash into the fish pools but, sadly, the fish have long gone, devoured by the herons that are now resident in the park. The clock tower, at the other end of the garden, lends an air of grandeur to the scene. When you have had your fill, return to the gateway and stroll up the long, wide and very straight avenue. Many of the trees along the avenue and the boundary of the park are evergreen holm oak, planted by Lord Ardilaun. To your immediate right, behind the miniature rose garden, is the park depot, and beyond that the vast nurseries which supply not only St Anne's Park but all the other Dublin Corporation parks in the city. The nurseries include the Green Waste Depot where thousands of tons of material, from discarded Christmas trees to garden prunings, are shredded, composted and ultimately resold as compost, mulch and for soft-fall surfaces such as those in playgrounds. Next, you pass by the 12-hole par-3 golf course.

Stables without Horses

When the avenue reaches the football pitches, the Millennium Arboretum is on your right. To celebrate Dublin's Millennium year in 1988 the Parks Department, in co-operation with the Tree Council of Ireland, set aside 6.5 hectares (16 acres) on which to plant 1,000 different varieties of trees, each tree paid for by individual or group sponsors. Turn around and retrace your steps to a path on your right and head off towards the Rose Garden. This beautifully laid-out garden was opened in 1975, and with its scores of large rose beds has been an important centre for International Rose Trials since 1981. Take the east path out of the Rose Garden and walk to the Red Stables, an impressive group of red brick buildings, commissioned by Lord Ardilaun and designed by George Coppinger Ashlin (1837–1921), one of Ireland's most prolific architects. The Lord Mayor's State Coach, a magnificently ornate carriage dating from 1791, is kept here when not in official use. The Red Stables are being converted into an Arts Centre and work should be completed by 2001. You will then be able to take a rest and some refreshment in the coffee shop before commencing the final leg of the walk.

When you are ready, regain the original path, which will bring you to the main avenue again and to a mound at the very end of the main roadway. This is the site of the old Guinness mansion, which was accidentally burned down in 1943 and subsequently demolished in 1968. The avenue, which is still over 1.2 kilometres (¾ mile) in length, was longer in Lord Ardilaun's day and would have made an impressive sight, sweeping away into the distance from the door of the house. Once the domain of the privileged, this vista can now be enjoyed by all. The formal gardens, long since vanished, were just behind the house, although remnants of them can still be picked out in the shrubbery behind the mound. There are plans to re-create the gardens, at least in part. Gone forever, sadly, are the sculptures, carefully garnered from Europe by the Guinnesses, which used to line the criss-crossing pathways.

Now take the side path through the trees, which will gradually descend via more follies, steps and new plantations of trees to the Sunken Garden, the point where the walk began. If you are tall, be careful going under a couple of low arches on the way. You can catch the bus for home or walk down the Clontarf Road towards Dollymount to find the nearest pub. You might also like to walk over to Bull Island later, and cross the sand dunes to view the open sea. This remarkable island is barely 200 years old and was formed by the accumulation of sand that resulted from the building of the North Bull Wall (one of the enclosing arms of Dublin Harbour) in the early 19th century. Bull Island is an internationally recognized bird sanctuary and nature reserve.

A Basin at Blessington

Summary: Despite being so close to O'Connell Street, the main thoroughfare of Dublin, this district and its labyrinth of streets is not at all well known except to the people who live there. For some reason, places on the north side of Dublin, only a mile or so from the city centre, have tended to be thought of as quite a long way out; whereas places the same distance away on the south side are still considered to be very much part of the city centre. In some ways this has worked to the advantage of the north side, as speculators and developers have, by and large, ignored it until quite recently and, while some areas did become run down, the district as a whole escaped the poor developments of the 1970s and 80s. Now, many changes are beginning to happen – for example, you will visit an old reservoir that has been turned into a beautiful secluded park. There are also bound to be more new changes that I won't have made reference to, so just put it down to progress.

Start & Finish:	Gresham Hotel, O'Connell Street. DART: Connolly Station. Buses: most city centre buses are within a few minutes' walk. Car parking: use the Gresham Hotel multistorey car park or any one of several others in the neighbourhood.
Length:	4 km (2½ miles).
Time:	1¼ hours.
Refreshments:	There are hotels and restaurants at the start and finish, and pubs along the way.
Pathway Status:	Footpaths and hard surface all the way.
Best Time to Visit:	Daytime, when the parks are open.
Suitable for Bicycles:	Yes, but dismount in the parks.
Route Notes:	If the route through the King's Inns is locked, an alternative route is marked on the map.
Connecting Walk:	To or from Talbot Street to the North Docklands.

The Gresham Hotel itself has quite a history. The founder, Thomas Gresham, was abandoned as a baby on the steps of the Royal Exchange in London. This inauspicious beginning in no way hindered the young man, however, and after entering domestic service he quickly rose to the rank of butler and determined to run his own business. In 1817 he purchased 21 and 22 Sackville (now O'Connell) Street and three years later he leased No. 20. Using his experience as a butler, he ran his establishment like an extended townhouse, giving a fine and exclusive service to the visiting gentry. The reputation of Gresham's hotel grew and it even attracted royal and noble patrons from abroad. Gresham sold the business in 1865 to a group of Cork businessmen and over the next 50 years or so various alterations and improvements were made. Two hundred guests were trapped in the hotel during the 1916 Rising, but while much of O'Connell Street lay in ruins the Gresham escaped intact. It was not so lucky during the Civil War. In July 1922 Cathal Brugha (1874–1922) occupied the building on behalf of the Anti-Treaty (Republican) forces and during the ensuing clash, Government troops reduced the whole block to rubble. Brugha died of a wound he received as the battle in O'Connell Street drew to a close. Of the five hotels in the block, only the Gresham was ever rebuilt.

Encountering James Joyce

Start walking up O'Connell Street towards the Parnell Monument and swing right into Cathal Brugha Street. This street was created only in 1931 and was named in honour of Cathal Brugha when the Fianna Fail party came to power in 1932. Fianna Fail had been founded in 1926 by Eamon de Valera and represented the defeated Republican side in the Civil War of 1922–1923. Tucked into the corner niche on the Dublin Institute of Technology building on the right is a trio of statues, a reminder that the institute started life as the College of Domestic Science. The figures are of one girl scrubbing and cleaning, another embroidering and the third holding a book to illustrate that success depends on education. On the opposite side, the dark red brick Church of St George and St Thomas is made even darker and more atmospheric by the overhanging foliage of nearby trees. The original church of St Thomas, destroyed in the bombardments of 1922, stood not here but right across the centre of the road. To allow Sean MacDermott Street (then Gloucester Street) to open onto Cathal Brugha Street, the church was rebuilt on an available space beside the new street. It started life dedicated only to St Thomas, but the closure of St George's on Temple Street resulted in the merging of both parishes. Swing left into Marlborough Street, and then turn right into Parnell Street, formerly Great Britain Street, which was renamed in 1911 in honour of Charles Stewart Parnell (more about him later). In recent years, Parnell might not have felt particularly honoured, as along with much of this part of Dublin the street fell into decay over the course of the 20th century. It is only now that reinvestment and redevelopment are beginning to make a positive impact.

Take a left almost immediately into North Great George's Street to find an almost intact Georgian streetscape. For years, the residents of this street have fought to prevent its commercialization and exploitation, and have sought to restore it to its former glory. They have been relatively successful, and at the time of writing there were plans to erect decorative gates at the Parnell Street end. On the right, at No. 35, is the James Joyce Centre, a museum and study centre dedicated to the life and work of the author of *Ulysses*. Crowning the end of the vista is Belvedere House, a mansion designed by Michael Stapleton and completed in 1786 for George Augustus Rochfort, 2nd Earl of Belvedere. It was sold in 1841 to the Society of Jesus (the Jesuits) who have used it as a primary and second-level college ever since. James Joyce attended this renowned school from 1893 to 1898.

Bear right at Belvedere House, and walk along Great Denmark Street and Gardiner Place until you come to Mountjoy Square. This square was built between 1792 and 1818 and was named after Luke Gardiner, Viscount Mountjoy, but it fairly quickly fell upon bad times. Many of the houses became tenements, and by the 1980s nearly half of them had either fallen into complete disrepair or disappeared, leaving unsightly gaps. To all appearances, it has now been completely restored in the Georgian manner. Turn left into Gardiner Street (the Viscount again) and walk up to the classical frontage of St Francis Xavier Church on the right. The Jesuit order had been ministering in Ireland since 1598 when in 1773 it was suppressed by the Pope of the day and ordered out. The order returned in 1811 and laid the foundation stone of St Francis Xavier's in 1829, the year of Catholic Emancipation. In 1898, to combat widespread alcohol abuse, Fr James Cullen formed the Pioneer Total Abstinence Association in the next-door presbytery.

Turn left into Dorset Street, the former Drumcondra Lane, an ancient highway that led to the north of the country. In a sense it still does – it leads to the M1, Dublin Airport and Belfast. At the corner with Temple Street is one of the finest Georgian Churches in Dublin with easily the most elegant steeple. Unfortunately it is no longer a church (the parish was combined with that of St Thomas, whose church you saw earlier) and the steeple has been encased in scaffolding for years. It may have been restored by the time you read this. Cross Dorset Street and turn into Eccles Street (named after John Eccles, a property owner here in the 1770s). On the right-hand

Monument to the Four Masters (erected 1876), Berkeley Road Park.

side, at the entrance to the Mater Private Hospital, is a wall plaque with James Joyce's visage on it. It marks the site of former No. 7 Eccles Street, the home of Leopold Bloom in *Ulysses*. This house, along with whole stretches of the street, was demolished somewhat insensitively to make way for the various extensions to the Mater Hospital. In recent years the hospital authorities have shown more restraint and have begun to restore the remaining Georgian houses in their possession. The old hospital, with its classical frontage, stands at the top of the street and is still in use. It was begun in 1852 and was opened in 1861 by the Sisters of Mercy.

Flames and Fountains

Directly opposite the old hospital, in the pristine little park, stand two interesting monuments. One is in the shape of a Celtic cross and commemorates the Four Masters, four Franciscan friars who, between 1627 and 1637, chronicled the ancient history of Ireland. The second sculpture, a bronze sphere standing on a tree-like pedestal, includes a continuously burning gas flame and is meant to represent the everlasting love of God, as reflected by the Mater Hospital's healing ministry. Turn left into Berkeley Street. St Joseph's Church, opened in 1880, has been in the care of the Discalced Carmelites since 1983. The interior has some wonderful stone and marble work. A sharp right turn will bring you to Blessington Street and into Blessington Street Basin, another delightful park that is relatively unfrequented considering how close it is to the city centre.

In 1803, it was proposed to Dublin Corporation that the new Royal Canal could provide the city with a guaranteed water supply. This was agreed, and to serve and distribute the water, Blessington Street Basin was commissioned in 1810. Water is piped directly from the eighth lock of the Royal Canal. When Vartry Reservoir

System was introduced in 1868, the water from Blessington was used exclusively to service Jameson's Distillery at Bow Street and Power's Distillery at John's Lane. This arrangement continued until the 1970s, when both distilleries transferred to Midleton in County Cork.

As well as being a practical utility, the Basin was laid out as a public park. In 1993 major refurbishment of the water and the walkway areas commenced. Around 6,000 tonnes of silt and debris were removed from the basin; gates, new railings, seating and antique lamp standards were installed, new pavement setts were laid and small sculptures were commissioned. The lake was restocked with fish and the central island was enlarged to provide an improved habitat for wildlife. One of the most beautiful features of the park is the five-jet fountain, a practical part of the water aeration system. For reasons of economy, it spumes only at intervals, but they are regular and frequent. The refurbished park was reopened in 1994.

Leave Blessington Street Basin by the far gateway into a linear park that is actually a filled-in spur of the Royal Canal. This spur once led to a harbour at Broadstone, your next port-of-call. Exit onto the adjoining road, Royal Canal Bank, and turn left, which leads to Western Way. At the corner with Constitution Hill you can see the Egyptianesque form of the former Broadstone Railway Station, designed by John Skipton Mulvany and opened in 1851. The station was closed in 1931 (it is now the headquarters of Bus Éireann, the national provincial bus service) and is due to hum once more with the sound of rolling stock when it becomes a stop for the new LUAS light rail system.

The park on your left belongs to the grounds of the King's Inns. The gates are usually open to the public during business hours, so take a shortcut through the park via the central archway of the King's Inns to Henrietta Street (if the gates are shut, follow the map via King Street North to Henrietta Street). The King's Inns was the last great public building designed by James Gandon in Dublin (he also designed the Four Courts and the Custom House). It is now shared by the Honourable Society of the

Broadstone Railway Station, Phibsborough Road.

51

Benchers of the Inns (the barristers' central organization), and the Registry of Deeds. The King's Inns gets its title from the days when barristers lived as well as studied here. The age-old custom is still for barristers-to-be to eat a certain number of dinners at the Inns before they can qualify. Proceed under the central archway to Henrietta Street. Commenced in the 1720s, Henrietta Street (named after the Duchess of Grafton, wife of the then Viceroy) possesses the finest Georgian mansions in Dublin, but most have become dilapidated. Individual owners have been painstakingly restoring their interiors over the last number of years and there are hopes of refurbishing the exteriors and the street surfaces in the near future. Walk via Bolton Street to Dominick Street, which was originally laid down in 1743 as a fine Georgian thoroughfare of which precious little remains. Enter the grounds of St Saviour's, a Dominican friary, and visit the church if you wish. It was designed in 1852 by J. J. McCarthy, and replaced an earlier chapel in Little Denmark Street. The medieval foundations of the friary were on the site now occupied by the Four Courts. Go around the right-hand side of the church to come out on Granby Lane. Here, in 1925, Matt Talbot, a man whose ascetic and prayerful life had made him a candidate for canonization, collapsed and died. Turn right into Granby Row and left into Parnell Square. One of the grandest 18th-century mansions in the city was Charlemont House, now the Hugh Lane Gallery of Modern Art. The gallery opened in 1933, but its origins go back to the bequest of Sir Hugh Lane (1875–1915), a successful art dealer who collected a large number of important European art works. It is now owned by Dublin Corporation. Its latest acquisition is the complete studio of Francis Bacon, just as it was left at the time of the artist's unexpected death. Next to the gallery is the Dublin Writer's Museum, a Georgian townhouse devoted to the works and memorabilia of famous Dublin writers.

Spears of Peace

Across the road is the peaceful Garden of Remembrance, dedicated to the memory of all who died for Irish freedom. It is built on part of the site of the once fashionable Rotunda Gardens (the entertainments held here were usually fundraising events for the adjoining Rotunda Hospital) and was opened in 1966, the Golden Jubilee of the Easter Rising. The central bronze group sculptured by Oisin Kelly was largely inspired by William Butler Yeat's poem 'Easter 1916'. It embodies the concept that at certain decisive moments of history people and countries are 'transformed utterly'. Kelly decided on the theme of four human figures being transformed into swans, symbolizing rebirth, victory and elegance underscored by pathos. This echoes the Irish legend of the children of King Lir who were bewitched to spend 900 years as swans. The floor of the pool displays a mosaic of weapons from Ireland's heroic age, 300 BC–AD 300. The spears are broken, symbolizing the Celtic custom of throwing weapons into rivers when hostilities were ended. Further down Parnell Square, into the section called Cavandish Row, you will pass the Gate Theatre. Under the direction of Michael MacLiammoir and Hilton Edwards, the Gate Theatre opened in 1928 in the former Great Supper Room of the Rotunda's Assembly Rooms. The Assembly Rooms, like the Rotunda Gardens, were an initiative of Dr Bartholomew Mosse, the founder of Rotunda

Hospital, to raise ongoing financial support for his institution. Passing an elegantly carved drinking fountain, you will come to the junction with O'Connell and Parnell Streets. Ahead, in the centre, is the Parnell Monument. This memorial to Charles Stewart Parnell, a great 19th-century statesman who fought for Irish Home Rule through the parliamentary system, was unveiled in 1911. Cross over to it, and from this vantage point look back towards the Rotunda Maternity Hospital. On the right is the circular Rotunda Room, built in 1764, which gave the popular and now official name to the hospital that was opened in 1757 as the Lying-in Hospital, now possibly the oldest maternity hospital in the world. The Rotunda Room became the Ambassador Cinema and will most likely be a pub by the time you read this. It was designed by Richard Cassels to a plan very similar to Leinster House, the seat of Dáil Eireann (the Irish Parliament), which he also designed. The chapel, which is open to the public, displays the best example of rococo plaster work in Ireland. The stuccadore, Frenchman Barthelmi Cramillion, was commissioned to carry out the work by Bartholomew Mosse. The Gresham Hotel just opposite, or the several other hotels and bars on O'Connell Street or Parnell Street, now beckon and offer solace to your weary mind and feet.

Pyramids and Cylinders

Summary: The title of this walk refers to the various shapes of some of the buildings that you will come across along the way. A subtitle could read 'from Glasnevin to Drumcondra'. These two districts have an ancient history, but as suburbs of Dublin they were only fully developed in the early part of the last century. Some of the places along this route are rarely visited by the general public, but you will find that you are welcome, nonetheless.

Start:	National Botanic Gardens or the Addison Lodge, Glasnevin. Buses: 19, 19A, 134. DART: none. On-street parking, no meters.
Finish:	Cat & Cage Public House, Drumcondra. Buses: 3, 11, 16, 16A, 16B, 33, 41, 41A. DART: none. On-street parking, but watch for clearways.
Length:	6.5 km (4 miles).
Time:	2½ hours.
Refreshments:	Restaurants or pubs are thin on the ground on this walk. You can picnic in a park or take a break in a university restaurant about halfway along the route.
Pathway Status:	Footpaths throughout.
Best Time to Visit:	Any time during the day.
Route Notes:	There may be some access restrictions within the Dublin City University due to the ongoing building programme.
Suitable for Bicycles:	Yes, but you will have to walk the bike in the park and in the centre of the university campus.
Connecting Walk:	None.

This tour starts at the front gates of the National Botanic Gardens (*see Walking Dublin*). Feel free to visit the gardens before undertaking the main walk, but allow one to two hours for this side trip. The Addison Lodge Hotel, which is just across the road, can provide any refreshment you might need before you start the walk. Glasnevin is steeped in history and was just a village until it became absorbed into the city from about 1900. It was the site of an early Christian monastery (there will be more about this later) and eventually evolved into a medieval, and later a Tudor, village. It gained a reputation as a place of ill repute, to judge by a letter written in 1725 by an Archbishop of Dublin: 'Glasnevin was the receptacle for thieves and rogues. The first search when anything is stolen was there, and when any couple had a mind to retire to be wicked it was their harbour.' Uncomplimentary words indeed, and not in any way a reflection on its present good citizens. The National Botanic Gardens occupy the former estate of the poet Thomas Tickell (1686–1740), who was the friend and biographer of Joseph Addison (1672–1719), the English poet, essayist, statesman and secretary to the Lord Lieutenant of Ireland from 1709–1710. The director of the Gardens lives in Tickell's house. Walk northwards towards the pyramid-shaped church. Built in 1972, the Church of Our Lady of Dolours replaced the previous building, which dated from 1881 and was nicknamed the 'Wooden Church'. As you cross the River Tolka you will be able to see, on the left, a corner of the magical Botanic Gardens. Proceed past the Tolka House pub and up the incline of Glasnevin Hill, locally called Washerwoman's Hill. On the right-hand side, where the road bears left, are the entrance gates leading to the Bon Secours Hospital. The hospital and its ground were once the Delville estate. In the 1700s it belonged to the Delaneys, prominent local gentry and friends of Dean Jonathan Swift.

Another Pyramid

Tucked in between Glasnevin Hill and a little road on the right called St David's Terrace is the truncated pyramid of Met Éireann, the headquarters of the Irish Meteorological Service. It was built by John Sisk & Son in 1979 to a design by Liam McCormick. Its limestone-clad walls slope inwards to lessen the effect of the building's bulk on St David's Terrace. The receiving dishes and antennae on the roof are in constant touch with the various weather satellites far out of view overhead.

The convent and schools of the Holy Faith nuns opposite the corner with Ballymun Road occupy the former grounds of Glasnevin House, which was built for Sir John Rogerson, an 18th-century shipping merchant after whom a Dublin city quay is named. Turn up Ballymun Road and take the next right after St David's Terrace into Church Avenue, a secluded road comprising eight cottages on the left and the North Dublin National Schools Project, a nondenominational first-level school, on the right. At the end of the little avenue is a church and graveyard dedicated to St Mobhi. This is usually locked, but it is possible to look at the well-maintained churchyard through the gateway. If you have time to spare you may obtain the key from the ever-obliging residents of No. 3, to the immediate left of the gates. An explanatory booklet (only £1.50) is also available from them. The church dates from 1707, although the tower goes back to the 14th century. Considering the compact appearance of the church from the outside, the dignified interior is surprisingly spacious. The oldest identifiable headstone is dated 1695, but burials undoubtedly took place here for centuries before that. Local legend has it that the leader of the 1803 Rebellion, Robert Emmet, lies here, a claim that is shared by a couple of other cemeteries around the city including St Michan's on Church Street. St Mobhi founded the monastery in the 6th century, picking this site because it overlooked the River Tolka and was directly served by a tributary called the Glas Naíon (the stream of Naíon, the name of the local chieftain). Famous pupils of St Mobhi included St Columcille (otherwise known as Columba of Iona), St Ciaran, founder of Clonmacnoise, St Canice of Kilkenny and St Comhgall of Bangor. St Mobhi died during a widespread plague in AD 544.

When you have finished your tour of St Mobhi's (and you have returned the key), walk along the narrow lane into St Mobhi Boithirin or Mobhi's Little Road. The square white building on the right is the headquarters of the Irish Fisheries Board. Turn left up busy St Mobhi Road, cross the junction with tree-lined Griffith Avenue (at over 3.3 kilometres (2 miles), the longest avenue in the city) and continue up Ballymun Road before turning right into Hampstead Avenue. Near the end of this short road is a gateway, the entrance to Hampstead Private Hospital and Elmhurst Private Convalescent Home. Take a peek through the gates at the expanse of privately-owned land inside, which still contains a working farm. Recently a fair slice of the land was sold for housing development. Explore the rustic lane a little further. At the end of the left-hand-side stone wall, go through the two sets of gates into Hampstead Park, also called Albert College Park. When Albert College was closed in 1978 (*see* next paragraph) Dublin Corporation acquired much of its grounds for a public park. It is designed as a woodland park complemented by floral schemes. You might like to relax here for a while before continuing the walk.

And now the Cylinders

Follow the perimeter path to take you back out onto the Ballymun Road, and turn immediately right to enter Dublin City University (DCU). The driveway will bring you to the campus origins, the former Albert College. For over 130 years Albert College was a centre for agricultural education and research. The potato blight fungus, which led to the deaths of over a million people in Ireland in the 1840s, was first identified here. In 1978 the agricultural faculty at Albert College, by then part of University College Dublin, was transferred to Belfield, on the south side of the city. The college buildings were then occupied by a National Institute for Higher Education (NIHE) dedicated to business, scientific and computer studies. Ultimately the NIHE achieved the status of a university and is now a rapidly expanding institution covering 34.4 hectares (85 acres), with ultramodern facilities for 6,500 students. Feel free to wander around the campus using the map to locate the various points of interest. You can have a cup of coffee in the restaurant, but this is best avoided at lunch time. The brand-new Arts Centre with its concert halls, theatres and exhibition spaces is a must, as you never know what might be on. The RTE (Irish National Radio and Television Service) Concert Orchestra is based here. Follow the map to leave DCU via the exit onto Collins Avenue. This was named after Michael Collins, a key figure in the War of Independence and a minister in the first Free State Government, who was assassinated in an ambush while serving as Commander-in-Chief of the National Army during the Civil War (1922–23). If you have reserves of energy, stride down the avenue (there is little to occupy your attention on this stretch), crossing the Swords Road before turning right into Grace Park Road. This part of Dublin traditionally abounds in convents, seminaries, religious training colleges and other spiritual institutions. Several have since gone, but some have remained and are facing up to the new challenges of a more secular society. A couple of convents on the right-hand side, along the top end of Grace Park Road, provide services such as sheltered housing and a care centre for sufferers from Alzheimer's disease. To fund these developments, their surplus land was sold off for housing. Grace Park Road itself used to be called Goosegreen Lane, after a small village that once stood next to it.

Yet another Church Avenue

Cross Griffith Avenue and enter the lower half of Grace Park Road. On the right up a short lane is another convent, still very much in business. It is the enclosed Carmelite Monastery of the Incarnation, which organizes spiritual programmes in its Hampton Hermitage, a retreat house. Its chapel is open to visitors at the stated times. Opposite St Joseph's School for the Visually Impaired (once the site of a castle built in 1560 by James Bathe), make a sharp right-hand turn into the grounds of All Hallows College. The Vincentian Order, under Father John Hand, founded the Missionary College of All Hallows in 1842. Father Hand had acquired Drumcondra House, a palatial pile designed in 1725 by Sir Edward Lovett Pearce for Sir Marmaduke Coghill, and set up his college to train priests for the English-speaking missions. It still fulfils this role, but on a much smaller scale. Today the college offers diploma, degree and post-graduate courses in humanities, empirical sciences, media studies and information technology. The chapel, next to Drumcondra House, is well worth a visit. Its south-facing rose window is by artist Eve Hone. The college authorities appreciate visitors informing reception before wandering around the grounds.

There is only one more place to visit before the end of the walk. Leave the grounds and take the next right-hand turn into Church Avenue, following

To the Memory
of
Captain Francis Grose
F.R.S
Who whilst in cheerful Conversation
With Friends
Expired in their Arms
Without a Sigh
10th of May
1791
Aged 60
Also his Friend
James Gandon
Architect
Born 1743 died 1823
Captain Grose
was a friend of Robert Burns
And the inspiration of Tam O'Shanter

Gravestone of architect James Gandon, Drumcondra Cemetery.

the perimeter wall of All Hallows. Church Avenue is where Taoiseach (Prime Minister) Bertie Ahern was born and raised – his father was head gardener of All Hallows. Go through the gate of the Church of St John the Baptist, built for the Church of Ireland in 1743. Dublin's famous architect, James Gandon (1742–1824) is buried in a grave shared with his friend, antiquarian Francis Grose (1731–1791). The grave is marked by a horizontal headstone supported by four stones. The inscription reads 'To the memory of Captain Francis Grose, who whilst cheerful in conversation with his friends expired in their arms without a sigh. Also his friend James Gandon'. Patrick Heeney, composer of the Irish National Anthem *The Soldier's Song* (which was written in 1907 to words supplied by Peader Kearney), also lies buried in the graveyard.

A short journey to the end of Church Avenue will bring you to the Cat & Cage where, like Captain Grose, you can engage in cheerful conversation – without, of course, meeting the same untimely demise.

DARTing North

Summary: Like its south city counterpart route, DARTing South, this journey is not a walk as such but simply a convenient means of getting to the start of a couple of the other walks. However, there is plenty to glean about this side of Dublin from just looking out of the carriage windows, and the commentary below should help to enrich the experience enormously.

Start:	Pearse Station, Westland Row. Buses: 1, 3, 5, 7, 8, 45, 46, 84. DART: Pearse Station. Within 10 minutes' walk of Grafton Street/Trinity College. Very limited on-street parking.
Finish:	Howth DART Station. Bus: 31. DART: Howth. Ample public car parking.
Length:	14.5 km (9 miles).
Time:	21 minutes.
Refreshments:	There are many restaurants and taverns at the journey's end.
Best Time to Visit:	Any time, although it is best in daylight – darkness reveals a wonderland of lighting in the city centre and again on the approach to Howth, but the journey in between is then difficult to discern.
Suitable for Bicycles:	Cycles are not allowed on DART trains.
Route Notes:	On the outward journey, sit on the right side facing forward. For convenience, purchase a round trip ticket or a cheaper family ticket if applicable.
Connecting Walk:	Howth, Ireland's Eye and DARTing South.

For this journey you will be using the DART, the acronym for Dublin Area Rapid Transit. For years, Dublin's suburban trains, first steam trains and then diesel engines, were unreliable, uncomfortable and infrequent. All this changed in 1984, when 40 two-carriage train sets were delivered by the German manufacturer Linke-Homann-Busch to Iarnród Eireann (Irish Rail). These were the latest in energy efficiency at the time; for instance, they have a regenerative braking system – the slowing down process actually creates electricity, which is then fed back into the grid. Computers control all the signalling, level crossing barriers and even the speed of the trains. At peak times, trains can run safely at only four-minute intervals. From its inauguration in October 1984, the new DART service proved immensely popular with the public. The suburban service has recently been supplemented by the purchase of extra trains and the extension of existing lines.

Loop Line Section

Begin the journey at Pearse Street Station (*see* DARTing South) and wait on the northbound platform. Make sure you pick a train with Howth as its destination, as there are a number of other commuter lines. When the train departs, it will leave literally through a hole cut in the station's wall. When Westland Row Station, as Pearse Street was then called, was built in the mid-19th century, it served as a terminus for the Dublin to Kingstown (now Dun Laoghaire) Railway. In 1890 a new Loop Line was built to connect Amiens Street (Connolly) Station with Westland Row. As the platforms of both stations were above street level, it was necessary to build a series of bridges and arched embankments to connect them. The portion of the line crossing the street at Westland Row is carried over a cast-iron bridge that possesses some design merits.

The journey time between here and the next station, Tara Street, is less than one minute so you will have to be sharp-eyed to take in the sights. To the left, immediately on exiting the station, is the Church of St Andrew (1832-1837), which has some interesting internal features but is more famous as the place with the 'cold smell of sacred stone' in James Joyce's *Ulysses*. For the next few seconds the DART glides across the northeastern end of Trinity College, passing beside the glass envelope of the O'Reilly Institute and the modern science wings before wheeling away across Pearse Street. Note the knife-edged triangular corner of the EBS building on the left before the train slows down into the purely functional Tara Street Station.

A Brush with Dracula

As you pull out of Tara Street, you can catch a fleeting glimpse of one of the best views of the River Liffey, both upriver and downriver. There is too much to see to attempt to describe it all here, so concentrate your attention on the Custom House to the right. If you wish to appreciate its graceful classical lines the usual view from the riverfront is probably better, but the view from the passing DART gives a marvellous close-up of the complete design and arrangement of the building from three sides. It was built between 1781 and 1791, designed by James Gandon, and is one of the jewels in Dublin's architectural crown.

When the Loop Line was built, several buildings had to be demolished to allow the trains to pass through, and the openings cut between the rows of houses on Gardiner Street and Talbot Street will be obvious if you watch out for them. The DART now eases into the back end of Connolly Station (*see* page 18), Ireland's only international railway terminus (it serves the Dublin to Belfast Enterprise Express). The suburban platforms are beyond the main platform areas, almost as far out as the shunting yards. Towards the end of the platform, on the left side, is an old turntable (for turning around steam engines to face in the opposite direction) and a water tower reminiscent of a bygone era. The greatest concentration of railway networks in Ireland crisscrosses your line as you move out of Connolly Station. Lines branch off to the left, and other lines from the docklands join up or pass underneath. Today, there is less use for all these rails than there was a hundred years ago, but traffic is starting to increase on them again as a result of the gridlock conditions on the roads. Below you are the closely-packed streets of terraced houses built for artisans and dockers of the labour-intensive but poorly-paid industries of the 19th century. The next waterway you will pass over is the Royal Canal with a good view to the left of Croke Park, the main stadium of the Gaelic Athletic Association. The docklands area will come into focus as you trundle over the Tolka river, then you arrive at the maintenance workshops for the DART fleet and the recently opened station of Clontarf Road, set amid the greenery of Fairview Park. On the far right is the ultramodern business park of East Point. From Fairview Park to the far docklands, all the land has been reclaimed from the sea over the last couple of centuries.

As the electric-powered engine gently picks up speed again, you will have only a few seconds to note Marino Crescent, a curving terrace of houses to the left, just beyond the bridge over the Clontarf Road. Here, in No. 15, Bram Stoker, the creator of *Dracula*, was born in 1847. Don't open the carriage window in case a stray bat gets in! The line is still raised on an embankment, but once over the Howth Road it sinks to ground level and passes the Clontarf Golf Club, then below ground before reaching Killester Station.

A Sea View

Now travelling through cuttings, the DART will speed its way through a succession of nondescript stations: Harmonstown, Raheny (a historic area in its own right) and Kilbarrack, until it reaches Howth Junction. Here the line divides for either Howth or the main Belfast route. After Bayside Station and more sprawling suburbia the line approaches Sutton Station, the gateway to the Howth Peninsula. A brief view of the sea is obtained on the left.

St Fintan's Church, Sutton.

Sutton is an ancient place, with archaeological evidence of human habitation going back 5,000 years. The graveyard contains the ruins of the 9th-century church of St Fintan, the patron saint of Howth. Just before you reach the level crossing (yes, the line is back at road level) you might notice some converted red brick sheds to the right. These were the old tramway sheds for the celebrated Hill of Howth trams that ceased operating in 1959. A fully restored tram from this line is on display in the Howth Transport Museum. Once out of Sutton, past the golf links and a row of coastal houses, you will have an unrestricted panorama of the sea, Lambay Island in the distance and Ireland's Eye lying a mere mile or so from Howth Harbour. The train fairly rattles along this stretch of track but it soon begins to decelerate as it approaches the final halt on the line, Howth Station, which looks more or less the same today as it did when first built over 150 years ago.

Walk slowly through and out of the station and take in the scene from the front door. The abutments of an old stone bridge stand on either side of the facing road. This was the bridge that carried the graceful Hill of Howth tramway, now just a memory. If you wish, you could now indulge yourself in the Bloody Stream, an award-winning seafood bar and restaurant attached to the station, before undertaking the next part of your itinerary.

Howth

Summary: Howth has always been a magnet for Dubliners and visitors alike, who are attracted by the scenery, the fishing fleet, the marina and yacht club, bracing walks along the piers and the numerous taverns, some of which offer evenings of traditional Irish music. For all its popularity, Howth still has its nice nooks and crannies that the casual visitor may pass by. This walk is really just an excuse, if you need one, to visit one of the most charming places in Dublin. (A walk taking you around the whole peninsula of Howth and explaining the village itself, the Transport Museum and Howth Castle is featured in the companion volume to this book, *Walking Dublin*.)

Start and Finish:	Howth DART Station. Bus: 31. DART: to Howth Station (the terminus).
Length:	4 km (2½ miles)
Time:	1½ hours.
Refreshments:	Howth is renowned for its restaurants and taverns, some of which are expensive, some very reasonable. There are plenty of suitable spots for a picnic, either on grass or on seats sheltered from easterly sea breezes.
Pathway Status:	Footpaths and piers. Be very careful walking along the pier where working trawlers are tied up. Netting, cables and other pieces of equipment may lie across the path and trip the unwary. Here and there, the surface of the East Pier can be a bit uneven and there can be gaps between the granite slabs, so mind where you place your feet.
Best Time to Visit:	Anytime during daylight hours, although dark evenings have their own charm. At night, keep to the well-lit sections of the walk.
Route Notes:	Avoid the East Pier in stormy weather or when a strong east wind is blowing, particularly the upper level, as it can be washed with great spumes of water.
Suitable for Bicycles:	Yes, but only on the lower piers. Watch out for cables and other fishing paraphernalia strewn across the West Pier.
Connecting Walks:	From DARTing North and to Ireland's Eye.

As this walk leads on directly from DARTing North we shall assume you are already outside the Bloody Stream pub and restaurant. Continue along Harbour Road, bearing left onto the West Pier, which will take you to the commercial end of Howth Harbour. On the outward journey, stay on the left side of the pier. You will pass several shops belonging to the major fishmongers, such as Beshoffs, Wrights, Reids and the aptly-named 'Nicky's Plaice'. If you are so inclined, you can buy the freshest fish in Dublin here – although you would do well to wait until you are ready to return home. The tracks running across the road lead from a slipway to boat repair yards, where trawlers are refurbished or refitted. You will pass a boat supply store, which literally sells anything from a needle to an anchor. Through gaps in the buildings along the pier you will be able to see Claremont Strand, a popular bathing place between Howth and Sutton. Most premises along the pier are constructed from the local reddish-brown Howth stone. Walk past the former Harbourmaster's building, now occupied by a number of fish merchants and the Irish Fisheries Board, a statutory fishing regulatory and development organization.

Meander on to the end of the pier taking in the sights. On the return you will have an opportunity to study the trawlers themselves – providing the fleet is in, of course. Climb the curving steps at the pier's end and scan the horizon in all directions. There is an excellent view of Sutton and Claremont Strand to the west, and Portmarnock, Malahide and Donabate to the northwest. Almost due north is the island of Ireland's Eye (*see* the next walk, Ireland's Eye), and to the east lies the East Pier. Beyond it (although you can't see it from here) is the coast of Wales. Swinging towards the south, you have a panorama of the harbour itself with the headland of Howth rising behind it. Howth village and its hilly hinterland, both well served by public transport, became much sought-after and, inevitably, expensive residential districts. This placed enormous pressure on the remaining but fragile landscapes of the peninsula. Thankfully, the threat was recently removed by legislation which sets out to protect these areas from any future development and to maintain them for all to enjoy.

Trawlers, Howth Harbour.

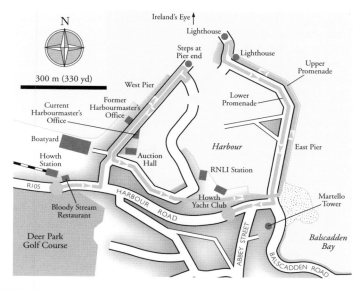

A Bad Mistake Come Good

This is a good point to sit for a while on the steps and watch the world at work and play. There are usually a number of people fishing with rod and line, looking for a bite in the open waters of the sea. Families or couples tend to gather here, pottering around or simply gazing at the scene. You will probably see yachts and pleasure craft skimming in and out through the mouth of the harbour. An occasional trawler, surrounded by wheeling seagulls, may be seen approaching cautiously from the east, making a wide swing around the mouth of the harbour to avoid treacherous sunken rocks. In 1800, it was suggested that Howth Harbour should become the cross-channel mail packet station for Dublin. At this time, the city's own harbour was unsuitable for large ships because of the shallowness and the tidal fluctuations of the River Liffey. So, in 1807, work commenced to create an enclosed port of 21 hectares (52 acres). In 1809 the East Pier was being built when a new engineer, John Rennie, was appointed to oversee the construction. He suggested an additional West Pier, and by 1813 the harbour was completed. Rennie and other prominent locals had foreseen the problem of silting due to the local tidal currents, and this indeed proved to be the case. Low water and a rocky bottom also caused damage to some ships. After barely a couple of years, everyone realized that Howth would never work for large ships, so in 1815 the building of Dun Laoghaire Harbour was authorized instead (*see* this book's companion volume, *Walking Dublin*). When this new harbour was ready in 1821, Howth was abandoned to fishing and pleasure craft. It was a monumental mistake to build a mail packet harbour at Howth in the first place, but this decision has nevertheless given us a treasure that we would not have had otherwise.

Return up the pier on the left-hand side, taking care not to trip over tying-up ropes, hawser lines, nets, fish boxes and all the trappings of a busy fishing port. There are about 40 vessels of all shapes and sizes in the Howth fishing fleet, although the once traditional small wooden trawler is now almost a thing of the past, and the gargantuan ocean-going trawlers-cum-processing-factories are mainly concentrated in Ireland's south and northwest ports. The Howth fleet confines itself almost entirely to the Irish Sea, and the fish landed here are mainly cod, plaice, whiting, haddock, sole, hake, mackerel, herring and prawn. Looking down into the decks of the trawlers, you can easily see how tough and hazardous the profession is. A major rebuilding of the harbour was undertaken and finished in 1986, when additional piers and facilities were built. One such facility is the Auction Hall into which the fish are directly delivered from the trawlers.

After passing the Auction Hall and repair slipway, turn left onto another pier and head away from the working harbour towards the leisure end of things. On your left the Howth lifeboat usually rides at anchor beside the Royal National Lifeboat Institutions (RNLI) small but attractively designed station. The first lifeboat was stationed here in 1816 by the Corporation for Preserving and Improving the Port of Dublin, and the RNLI took over in 1862. Straight ahead you can hardly miss the premises of the Howth Yacht Club with its jaunty architecture and colouring. It is the largest yacht club in Ireland, and was formed in 1968 from the amalgamation of the Howth Sailing Club (1895) and the Howth Motor Yacht Club (1933). The present clubhouse was opened in 1987. The rows of moored yachts, with their forest of masts, range in size from dinghies to ocean racers, and are a magnificent sight.

This part of the north-facing pier is bordered by a grass strip ideal for a picnic. If a blustery east wind is blowing, you can have your alfresco snack on the lee side of the East Pier wall, which you are now approaching.

Surprised by a King and Guns

Until relatively recently, the village of Howth itself was somewhat of a backwater. As you can see for yourself, Harbour Road is now alive with boutiques, shops, restaurants and apartments. When you reach the East Pier you have a choice – you can take the upper parapet walk or the lower pier walk. If it is very windy and waves are crashing over the higher path, steer well clear of it. On the vast majority of days, when there is absolutely no danger, I suggest you walk out on the upper level and return on the main pier level. Before commencing, take in the seaward view to your right towards the cove of Balscadden Bay, which is overlooked by a scattering of houses clinging to the side of the hill. When you are ready begin walking in the direction of the far lighthouse. The pier was begun using stone from the quarry of the Earl of Howth but his prices turned out to be too high, so granite was shipped in from Dalkey on the far side of Dublin Bay instead. The foundations were laid using a red gritstone from Runcorn in Cheshire. Up to 700 men were employed in the pier's construction and a settlement, the forerunner of today's village, was built to accommodate them. The East Pier is 61 metres (200 feet) wide at the base, 11.5 metres (38 feet) high and originally ran 458 metres (1,503 feet) from the shore, heading due north, before turning northwest for another 301 metres (990 feet). A further short extension was added in the 1980s. The hewn granite is slightly uneven in places, so watch your step. The walk you are now on has been a favourite promenade for Dubliners since Victorian days.

There have been two famous landings at Howth. One was by the newly-crowned King George IV of England, who arrived unexpectedly in 1821 on an ordinary steam packet, because his own royal yacht had been becalmed at Holyhead. The other landing was deliberately kept secret, except to those who were anxiously waiting. It was by the yacht *Asgard*, skippered by Erskine Childers, which landed guns and ammunition for the Irish Volunteers in 1914.

At the end of the pier is the lighthouse, and steps going down to the lower level. You can obviously linger here for as long as you wish. When you start on the return leg, you will pass the old premises of the Howth Sailing Club. At the time of writing, this was occupied by the Howth Boating Club (founded 1985), which may now have moved to a new clubhouse. Look out for signs indicating the departure point for Ireland's Eye passenger boats (*see* the next walk, Ireland's Eye). The signs and embarkation point are frequently moved depending on the day's tides.

You are now on the home stretch. Ahead, a hill overlooks the harbour, with a Martello tower perched on its summit (*see* Ireland's Eye). From this vantage point you will be able to study more closely the lines of yachts moored at the extensive marina of the Howth Yacht Club. Ireland's so-called 'Celtic Tiger' economy has certainly enabled some people to indulge their love of sailing, and many large and expensive craft are in evidence. When you reach the end of the pier you can disappear into any of the many pubs, hotels or restaurants in the centre of the village or along Harbour Road before taking the bus, car or DART home.

Ireland's Eye

Summary: Ireland's Eye, a craggy little island lying a short distance north of Howth Harbour, has always held a fascination for visitors to the seaside village, but few venture out to experience it first hand. It is a paradise for bird-watchers, beachcombers or for those who want to explore an unspoilt natural habitat. There are regular boat trips during the summer and there is now an all-weather boat that operates in the winter as well (*see* below). A ruined early Christian church and a Martello tower are evidence of past human habitation. The boat trip itself, especially if it rounds the eastern side of the island, is stunning. If you don't want to disembark, you can stay on the boat and complete the round trip in one go.

Start & Finish:	East Pier Howth. For getting to Howth *see* the Howth walk. Boats leave regularly from 11.00 in the summer. At other times of the year you could chance turning up, or phone 087 267 3211 to check times.
Length:	The sea journey is a little over 1.6 km (1 mile). The island is quite small, so distance is not an issue.
Time:	The sea crossing takes 15 to 35 minutes depending on the direction the boatman takes (*see* main text).
Refreshments:	Bring a picnic if you want to stay for more than an hour or so.
Pathway Status:	There are no paths. Rocks, grass, beach and fern-covered ground make up the terrain.
Best Time to Visit:	Obviously stormy weather is out. Any reasonably calm day is good, but a warm sunny day is heaven.
Route Notes:	The island is perfectly safe and the long beach is suitable for picnicking and bathing. However, the cliffs are extremely hazardous and everyone, especially children, must exercise great care in that area. Watch out for rabbit holes when walking, too.
Suitable for Bicycles:	No.
Connecting Walks:	DARTing North and Howth.

To start this boat trip and exploration you need to get to the East Pier in Howth. If you are continuing on from the Howth walk, you will be on the pier already. In any case, walk along the pier until you find the signs for the Ireland's Eye day trip boats. Their exact location cannot be pinpointed on the map as it is moved around to suit the tides. There is at least one boat company which is Department of Marine

Howth lifeboat against the backdrop of Ireland's Eye.

approved, but if you are in any doubt about the service's credentials ask to see the Department certificate which should be on display. The 15-minute journey across to the island is enchanting. As you cruise slowly out of the harbour, you will get a sailors-eye view of all the yachts bobbing around at their moorings, and the less luxurious fishing trawlers offloading catch or preparing for their next voyage. Direction signs, depth levels marked on quayside walls, warning buoys and all the other paraphernalia of the seafaring world glide past as you curve towards the narrow opening between the east and west piers. Cruising in waters that can sometimes be choppy or heaving with swell requires an intimate knowledge of the undersea sandbanks and buried reefs. The seas around Dublin Bay are littered with the wrecks of sailing ships that, in past centuries, had the misfortune to get caught in bad weather and drifted onto rocks or were swamped, but don't worry – modern aids and experienced seamanship will see you safely back to Howth's embracing piers. The day trip boats usually go straight to the landing point on Ireland's Eye, but you should ask the boatman if he could possibly take you on the scenic route around the 'Stack', a stark headland cut off from the island by erosion. Wave a copy of this book at him and he may be more disposed to oblige. (This was an informal agreement made by the author with the boatman!) The following description assumes that he agrees to take you on this route.

When you are in the open sea approaching Thulla, a low rocky platform off Ireland's Eye, you may be lucky enough to spot grey seals cavorting in the water. There is a plentiful supply of fish available for them here, mainly mackerel. Cormorants may be standing like sentinels on protruding rocks, often with outstretched wings. Looming up in the near distance will be the huge outcrop of rock referred to as the Stack, which, as you get closer, will reveal an astonishing sight. Thousands of guillemots, perched precariously on every available toehold, swarm, swoop and flutter across the sheer face of this inhospitable-looking crag. Above and below them, terns and gannets fight for space, while razorbills and opportunistic great black-backed gulls bob about on the waves. You might see colourful little puffins darting about as well. Admittedly, all this activity is usually only evident during the breeding season (April to July and sometimes into August). As Ireland's Eye is a special reserve for seabirds, it is interesting to list the numbers of birds recorded during a single season (survey compiled in 1997 by Birdwatch Ireland): gannet (110 pairs), cormorant (250 pairs), shag (30 pairs), puffin (10 pairs), razorbill (292 pairs), guillemot (2,268 individuals), herring gull (250 pairs), great black-backed gull (100 pairs), and kittiwake (1,200 pairs).

To the east of the Stack, look out for a cave-like fissure in the rock. This is a spot called 'the long hole', where the infamous Kirwan murder took place in 1852. An artist named Kirwan came to the island with his wife to paint, but when the boatman returned to collect them, she was missing. Her body was later found at the long hole. Kirwan claimed that while he was painting somewhere else, she wandered around the island and must have toppled into the sea and drowned. His story was not believed and he was eventually sentenced to be hanged for her murder. However, he was reprieved from the gallows and served 27 years in prison before joining his erstwhile mistress in America. This extramarital liaison may have been the reason for Mrs Kirwan's untimely death, or it may indeed have been a tragic accident: we will never know.

As you continue to cruise around, you will be confronted by a cavernous opening on the northeast cliffs. It is said that a natural underwater tunnel leads from this cave all the way to the mainland, coming out again inside the grounds of Howth Castle. Believe this story if you wish! The boat will soon round the western headland and then glide to the landing stage, or rather a few shapely rocks that serve as a landing stage. Hop off here to begin your exploration of the island, but not before arranging the time for your return trip with the boatman. Clamber up the gentle slope until you reach a level area with a full view of the Martello Tower. This fortress, along with dozens of replicas around the east coast, was built between 1804–06 to fend off a possible invasion by Napoleon. The invasion never materialized, which probably accounts for the tower's undamaged state today. It is possible to clamber down to have a good look around this elegant bastion.

After exploring the tower, climb higher towards the island's peak. If you wish, you can branch off towards the cliff edge – but not too close to the sheer drop! As well as the birds already mentioned, you may see linnets feeding from grass seeds, rock pipits hopping around the cliffs, and blackbirds, robins and wrens. An occasional rabbit may cross your path darting to and fro. This part of the island is littered with rabbit burrows, so be careful not to catch your foot in one. As you get higher the views become more panoramic. It is hard to believe that you are only a

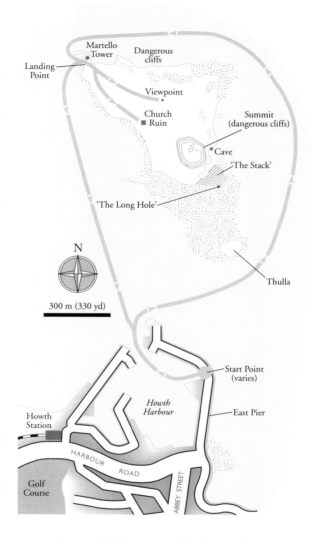

few miles from a teeming capital city as you look around at what is a relatively unspoilt landscape.

From this vantage point, you can decide for yourself which direction to take, but be very wary of going all the way to the high cliff edges. On the southern slope of the island, a short distance up from the beach, you will notice the ruins of an old church. The history of this building goes back to the 8th century when the three saintly sons of Nessan, of the Royal House of Leinster, forsook civilization and founded their own little church. It flourished until the Vikings paid unwelcome visits to Dublin during the 9th and 10th centuries, and by 1235 the small community had transferred itself to the mainland. In 1843, well-meaning antiquarians reconstructed the ruins you see today, and in so doing they altered the shape of the original. St Nessan's or Kilmacnessan (literally, 'the church of the sons of Nessan') stands amid a forest of ferns that are home to the tiny wren.

In Celtic days the island was called Inis Erean – Eria's Island. Eria was a woman's name but it became confused with Erin, the Irish name for Ireland. When the Vikings arrived they swapped the word Inis for Ey (meaning 'island' in Norse) and so it became Erin's Ey and, finally, Ireland's Eye. The sweep of land that you can see from the higher levels takes in, from the south, the Hill of Howth, the village and the harbour, with Baldoyle and Portmarnock to the right and the plains of Fingal beyond. On the island itself there are no trees except for a few stunted elders. Nettles, thistles, heather, ferns and cow parsley all thrive, not least because of the huge volume of bird droppings. You will occasionally come across evidence of the birds' meals in the form of fish bones. Pick a spot for a picnic, either on the rocky slopes where you can listen to the cries of the wheeling birds, or down on the sheltered sandy beach. When you are ready, take a boat back to Howth. There, you can follow the example of the island's birds and what they eat, and enjoy a fish meal in one of the restaurants for which Howth is justly famous.

Plate 8: *The beach at Portmarnock, one of Dublin's principal seaside resorts, provides a fine seaward aspect of Ireland's Eye (left) and the Howth Peninsula (right) (see page 74).*

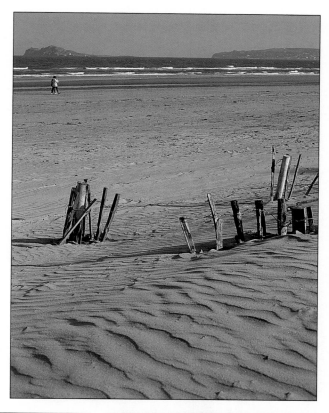

Plate 9: *A fine collection of commercial and public transport vehicles, several dating back to the early 20th century, are on view in the National Transport Museum, Howth Castle (below left; see page 62).*

Plate 10: *Boats moored at the Howth Yacht Club (below right), the largest yacht club in Ireland (see page 66).*

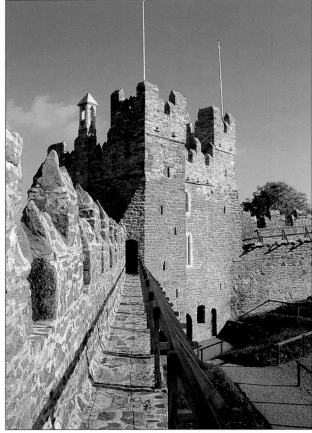

Plate 11: *Every available foothold and niche of Thulla Rock (above), an outcrop off Ireland's Eye, are crowded with seabirds during the breeding season (see page 68).*

Plate 12: *Swords Castle was built for the Archbishop of Dublin at the end of the 12th century (see page 77).*

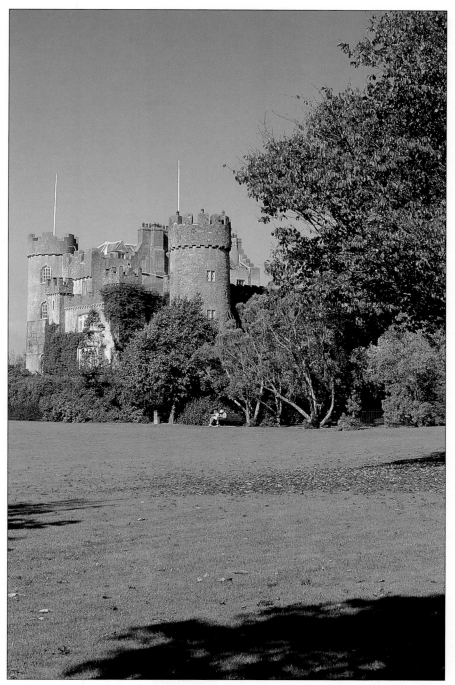

Plate 13: *The town of Malahide owed its medieval existence to the wealth and protection of Malahide Castle, which lies only a short distance from the start of the Malahide to Swords walk (see page 74).*

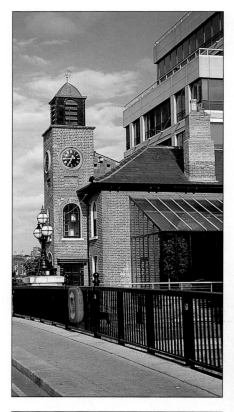

Plate 14: *The former offices of the Master of the Custom House Docks are now a pub and restaurant in the heart of the International Financial Services Centre (see page 91).*

Plate 15: *As its names suggests, The Legal Eagle (below left) is a haunt of barristers, solicitors and their clients fresh from their campaigns in the nearby Four Courts (see page 89).*

Plate 16: *Leinster Market (below), connecting D'Olier Street with Hawkins Street, is a re-creation in the style of Tudor Dublin (see page 93).*

Malahide to Swords

Summary: When the embankment and bridge were laid down for the railway connecting Dublin and Drogheda in the 19th century, they split Malahide Estuary in two and thus created very sheltered waters in the inner half, known as Broadmeadow Estuary. The shallow inner estuary is now ideal for dinghy sailing and sailboarding, especially for learners. Different breeds of water bird congregate in various spots, and farms are still worked along the shore road. This is a gentle walk among, literally, the backwaters of Dublin and ends inside the walls of a real medieval castle.

Start:	Duffy's Pub, Main Street, Malahide. Buses: 32, 32A, 43. DART: Malahide Station. Car parking: in the side streets, but watch for single and double yellow lines where parking is forbidden.
Finish:	Swords Castle, Swords. Buses: 33, 33B, 41, 41B, 41C. DART: None. There are a number of surface car parks, some of which are fee paying. On-street parking is available but you might have to find it on the outskirts of the town.
Length:	6.5 km (4 miles)
Time:	1½ hours.
Refreshments:	Only at the start and finish, where each town has an ample supply of taverns, restaurants and hotels.
Pathway Status:	Footpaths and hard surface all the way.
Best Time to Visit:	Any time in any bearable weather.
Suitable for Bicycles:	Yes.
Connecting Walks:	Swords to Newbridge Demesne, and Swords to Dublin Airport.

If you have arrived by train, walk up the hill from the faithfully preserved period-style railway station and turn left onto the Dublin Road. Bus passengers will join at this point. Pass the graceful simplicity of the church of St Sylvester, which was built in 1846 and has an equally simple and dignified interior. Walk on until you reach the crossroads at the centre of the award-winning village of Malahide. Turn down New Street past the boutiques, coffee shops, restaurants, taverns, antique stores and other speciality shops, all housed in modestly sized buildings more typical of an Irish country town than a suburb of Dublin. But Malahide was not always a suburb: it is only in the last two or three decades that the conurbation has caught up with the village. Its former isolation has probably helped to preserve its old-world charm, which, despite some discordant modern intrusions, the people of Malahide now jealously maintain.

Gracious Seaside Living

It is worth noting at this point that parts of Malahide not covered on this walk, including the eastern part of the village and Malahide Castle and Demesne, are dealt with in this book's sister, *Walking Dublin*. The history of Malahide goes back to pre-historic times. The quiet waters of the Broadmeadow Estuary and the beaches of Portmarnock attracted settlers who farmed the rich hinterland and fished the abundant waters. Later, Vikings, Normans and monks all laid claim to the valuable fishing rights along the coastline. The Anglo-Norman knight Sir Richard Talbot arrived from Shrewsbury in King Henry II's entourage in 1172. Five years later he was granted land at Malahide by the king and he commenced the building of a massive castle. The Talbot family continued to live there with only one break (during the Cromwellian period) until 1976. Today, the castle is without its extensive curtain wall and outer towers, but the huge central keep remains, although it has been radically remodelled over the centuries to make it more habitable. Malahide developed into a fishing port (famed for its oysters), which prospered in the 17th and 18th centuries. The opening of the railway between Dublin and Drogheda in 1844 brought many of the wealthier classes to Malahide to indulge in bathing and golfing. It developed into quite a fashionable resort, as you can see from the number of large seaside terraces that still exist. From the middle of the 20th century it became less important as a resort, as people started taking foreign package holidays or travelling further in Ireland thanks

Broadmeadow Estuary

300 m (330 yd)

Railway/Viaduct

Island Golf Links

Malahide Yacht Club

Marina Village

Malahide Marina

Grand Hotel

SEA ROAD

YELLOW WALLS ROAD

MILLVIEW ROAD

STRAND ST

NEW ST

THE MALL

STRAND ROAD

Malahide Railway Station

R106 DUBLIN ROAD

St Sylvester

to the freedom offered by the family car. Malahide then entered a new phase in its history with the arrival of thousands of new residents from the 1970s onwards. It is now a highly sought-after district that is reinventing its own identity. At the bottom of New Street is the latest sign of this renaissance, Malahide Marina, a nicely designed complex of apartments complete with a large yacht marina. Walk over to the low sea wall and take in the view. Yachts might be sailing between the two shores on their way to or from the open sea. On the opposite shore is a finger of land stretching from Donabate which all but closes off the estuary. The renowned Island Golf Links is located on this peninsula. To your right is the Grand Hotel, now much enlarged but once the elegant country hotel much favoured by the gentry who came to Malahide to 'take the waters'. Stroll along by the wall, passing under the overhanging restaurant and the busy marina. If you can't afford any of the yachts you can always admire them from the shore.

Make your return journey along the main road that leads to the apartments until you reach Strand Street, at which point turn right into Sea Road. When you emerge from under the railway bridge, the expanse of the Broadmeadow Estuary stretches before you. The inlet may well be peppered with the brightly coloured sails of numerous sailboards, many in the hands of learners for whom this stretch is an ideal training ground. The railway line goes straight across the estuary, carried by the viaduct that was designed by Robert McEntire and constructed in 1844. Lining the road on

Railway Bridge, Malahide.

the left are a mixture of houses, some modern, some 19th-century, and there is even a thatched cottage.

When you arrive at the Malahide Yacht Club you will have to turn inland for 700 metres (½ mile), carrying on up Sea Road until you reach the junction with the Yellow Walls Road. This road gets its name from the days when the local dye works hung out their wool to dry on walls. Turn right here, cross over a small stream by way of a stone bridge and continue until you meet another T-junction. At the T-junction, turn right again onto Estuary Road and the next left will bring you to Seatown Road and to the shores of the estuary once more. Apart from some motor traffic this is a very tranquil part of the walk. Farmland lines the left-hand side, but for how much longer in the face of housing pressures no one would like to predict. The estuary itself begins to narrow and becomes more shallow and marshy, and this area of mudflats and salt marshes provides a suitable habitat and rich feeding ground for a wide range of birds. Waders include oystercatchers, black-tailed godwits, redshanks and curlews. Watch out for herons, often seen patiently standing on one leg, waiting to pounce on an unsuspecting fish or eel. Winter guests include the Brent geese that fly all the way from Arctic Canada. Tufted ducks, mallards and great crested grebes seek their share of the food supply but not without competition from the assertive black-headed gulls.

Ramparts and Dungeons

The official end of this walk is in the town of Swords to which you now head by taking a left turn up the continuation of Seatown Road. However, if you want to combine this walk with the next one, 'Swords to Newbridge Demesne', you have a choice: you can continue on to Swords for rest and recuperation, or ignore Swords for now and keep to the estuary road. If you want to do the latter, turn now to page 78. Otherwise follow the next set of directions. Walk along Seatown Road until you reach the busy Belfast Road. Cross over using the footbridge to access the second part of Seatown Road. The modern but tasteful headquarters of Fingal County Council stand at the end of the road, on a site that was previously the town park. Before that, it was the location of Swords House, the home of Francis Taylor, Lord Mayor of Dublin in 1595. He refused to take an oath to Queen Elizabeth's Act of Supremacy on religious grounds, and so he was cast into prison where he died seven years later. He was beatified by Pope John Paul II in 1992. From the Fingal headquarters, cross the road towards a castle partly hidden behind a pub. You have now arrived at Swords Castle, an impressive medieval stronghold that has remained remarkably intact considering its turbulent past.

In 1183, John Comyn, the first Norman Archbishop of Dublin, built a fortified summer palace and surrounded it, as was prudent in those days, with defensive walls and towers. Comyn held jurisdiction over the whole territory and his courts sentenced criminals to hang on nearby Gallows Hill. In 1316 the castle was attacked by the Scottish army of Edward Bruce and was extensively damaged. Repairs were made, but eight years later the Archbishop of the day moved his summer palace to Tallaght on the other side of Dublin and Swords Castle was abandoned. It remained in church ownership until 1869. It was then sold into private hands, where it remained until Dublin County Council (the precursor of Fingal County Council) took it over. Perhaps it was lucky to be ignored for so long, as its walls were never dismantled to provide stone for other buildings, a common practice elsewhere. Since the late 1990s Fingal County Council, in association with FÁS, the state agency that provides trained and apprentice workers to help rehabilitate historic sites, has been painstakingly rebuilding and restoring the castle.

The entry into the courtyard might be through the main gate, but will probably be through a small postern gate on the west wall around to your left. Once inside, you can explore the visitor centre, stroll around the yard, visit a tower or climb up onto the timber-beamed rampart walks to play knight or archer in your imagination. When you have had enough, you can try out the coffee shop, which is due to be opened by the time of this book's publication. If it is not, you will find ample alternatives outside in the village.

Swords to Newbridge Demesne

Summary: Birds, a wildfowl reserve, a road flooded at high tide, a sweeping demesne, a country mansion and a 19th-century traditional working farm are just some of exciting elements that make up this wonderful walk. It will be hard to imagine that you are on the capital's doorstep, and not at least a hundred miles away.

Start:	Swords Castle. Buses: 33, 41, 41B, 41C, 43. DART: none. On- and off-street car parking is available around the town.
Finish:	Newbridge House. Bus: 33. DART: none. Train: to Donabate Station. Car parking is available in the grounds.
Length:	6 km (3¾ miles).
Time:	1¼ hours.
Refreshments:	Only at both ends of the walk (nonalcoholic at Newbridge).
Pathway Status:	Hard surface and pathways. Walking on the beach is an additional option for part of the journey.
Best Time to Visit:	Any time during the opening hours of Newbridge House.
Route Notes:	This is the only walk in the book subject to the ebb and flow of the tides. A 0.4 km (¼ mile) length of road on the north shore of Broadmeadow Estuary becomes submerged at high tide. When this happens you take a rough pathway built on top of a wall, or simply wait a while until the tide recedes.
Suitable for Bicycles:	Yes.
Connecting Walks:	Malahide to Swords and Swords to Dublin Airport.

Depart from Swords Castle (*see* Malahide to Swords) in the direction of the new Fingal County Council offices, cross over onto Seatown Road and continue until you reach the roundabout. Cross the busy Belfast road, using the footbridge, to reach the second half of Seatown Road, and turn left when you reach Broadmeadow Estuary. If you are continuing on from the Malahide to Swords walk, this is where you join the route. A ten-minute hike will bring you to a T-junction, where you swing right. This will bring you to Lissenhall Bridge, a curious structure spanning the twin rivers, the Broadmeadow and the Ward. It is in reality two bridges – a stone section built in 1903, and a metal-railed span erected in 1895. The road curves to the right, skirting the entrance and walls of Lissen Hall Estate, and the river begins to break up into little streams and reed-filled inlets. By the end of the estate walls the estuary comes into view again.

Not So Wild Swans

A short distance further on, an extraordinary sight will greet you. Where the road and the water meet, a group of 50 or more mute swans gather at a spot know as the 'swannery'. The birds will either be floating on the water, or, more probably, sitting or strutting around on the road in the hope of being tossed pieces of bread by passers-by. The estuary now becomes a good deal wider. At low tide it can be reduced to just a series of mud flats with streams dissecting them, whereas it is filled with water at high tide, but rarely to a depth of more than 1 metre (3 feet). The road soon reaches Prospect Point, a piece of land that juts into the estuary and to which a decrepit old jetty is attached. From here the road turns abruptly left. This is the stretch that gets completely submerged during high tide, as evidenced by the sea-weed scattered on the surface. However, if the tide is in when you arrive there is no need to turn back or wait. Simply climb on top of the low sea wall that separates farmland from the water, and walk along the parapet. At Newport House turn right, then almost immediately left again to walk up a country lane. If you want to post-pone leaving the estuary, the sea air and the views, you can temporarily continue along the gravel path and then the beach, but you will have to retrace your steps to this point.

Enjoy the rustic avenue for about 2 kilometres (1¼ miles). When it meets the road to Donabate go straight across and in through the gateway of Newbridge Demesne.

Lord Chancellor's coach (built 1790), Newbridge House.

This 150-hectare (370-acre) estate was bought by Fingal County Council, then known as Dublin County Council, in 1985. As you enter the rolling parkland you will get some sense of the great estates of 18th-century Ireland. Archbishop Charles Cobbe acquired the lands in 1736 and engaged Charles Fritzell, of the famous Wexford family of surveyors, to landscape the grounds. Vast open areas, a walled garden, an arboretum, woodlands, walks and playing pitches all combine to make this an exceptional place. Follow the pathway from the gates and it will eventually lead you to the great house itself, Newbridge House. Cobbe built this fine Georgian mansion when he procured the estate and it remained in the family for almost 250 years. There is still a standing arrangement with the family that allows them to reside in apartments in the house from time to time. A generous concession by the family allows visitors to view the original furniture, pictures and objets d'art. The house contains several fine ceilings, not least that of the Red Drawing Room, which also features an outstanding white marble chimney piece, a carpet that matches the ceiling and 18th-century curtains and wallpaper. There are guided tours for visitors, and a coffee shop and rest rooms that you may wish to use before undertaking the last part of the walk.

When you are ready, head for the rural museum and the traditional 19th-century working farm. Here, in the restored 18th-century cobbled courtyard, in the rehabilitated old buildings surrounding it and in the various outhouses, paddocks and fields, you will see the machinery and techniques used in rural Ireland before the advent of

Lanestown Castle, Newbridge Demesne.

electricity and tractors. You will find all the animals you might expect on a 19th-century farm, along with some rare breeds, and much of their food is grown in the adjacent fields. The trade skills necessary to supply and work the farm are also demonstrated. A prized possession of the rural museum is the resplendent gilded coach of the late-18th-century Lord Chancellor, Lord Fitzgibbon. Built in London in 1790 at a cost of £7,000, its massive size required six horses to adequately pull it. It was restored in 1982. Once you have seen enough, leave Newbridge House via the car park and the main road exit, passing Lanestown Castle, an old tower house, on the way. Fortified tower houses such as this example were very numerous throughout Ireland from the 15th to the 17th century, and were necessary to protect English colonists from the aggrieved Irish from whom the land was taken in the first place. The bus stop to Swords and Dublin is right outside the main gates. Alternatively, you can follow the signs to Donabate train station.

Swords to Dublin Airport

Summary: Swords, once a small village on the northern outskirts of Dublin, is now a huge sprawling suburb of the capital. It is also home to several thousand people who work at nearby Dublin Airport. St Colmcille founded Swords as a monastic settlement in the 6th century, and a holy well and a round tower survive from these early days. Swords Castle, a medieval archbishop's residence, is another direct link with the past while at the other end of the walk, Dublin Airport is a direct link with the present and the future. There is also an excellent vantage spot for enthusiastic aircraft spotters.

Start:	Swords Castle, Swords. Buses: 33, 41, 41B, 41C, 43. DART Station: None. On- and off-street car parking available around the town.
Finish:	Great Southern Hotel, Dublin Airport. Buses: 33, 41, 41A, 41B, 41C, 43 plus frequent express Airlink coaches. DART Station: None. Fee-paying car parks available. Patrons are allowed free car parking at the Great Southern Hotel.
Length:	8.5 km (5¼ miles)
Time:	1¾ hours.
Refreshments:	Only at both ends of the journey. There are two hotels at Dublin Airport plus terminal restaurants and snack bars. Swords has one small hotel, pizza and other restaurants and several good taverns.
Pathway Status:	Footpaths (*see* route notes).
Best Time to Visit:	Any time. Forest Road, which is not yet lit, may be dangerous for pedestrians after dark.
Route Notes:	There are plans to build a path along part of Forest Road, but at the time of going to press it was not yet built, so be very careful of the traffic. For this reason the walk may not be suitable for young children.
Suitable for Bicycles:	Yes.
Connecting Walk:	Swords to Newbridge Demesne, and Malahide to Swords.

Swords Castle (*see* Malahide to Swords) forms an appropriate backdrop to the ancient town of Swords. Prehistoric man certainly settled in the area, but it achieved its earliest fame for its substantial monastery, established by St Colmcille (also known as St Columba) on a hill overlooking the town in around AD 550. Before Colmcille retired to the island of Iona, off the west coast of Scotland, he placed St Finian the Leper in charge of the monastery.

Round Towers and Holy Wells

With the castle behind you, turn right up Bridge Street and go over Mill Bridge (as the name suggests, a corn mill once stood here, worked by the Ward River). Take the next left turn up Church Road, passing some old cottages on the right and some rather nice stone apartments on the left, which were built in the same style as the former vicar's 17th-century house and appropriately called 'The Old Vicarage'. A bit further along on the right is the entrance to the old monastery site, which is open to the public. It is now the grounds of a more recent parish church belonging to the Church of Ireland but there are still remnants of the earlier foundations. The tower at the side of the church is 14th century, and was the belfry tower of the medieval abbey. It is sometimes possible to ascend to the top of the tower and view the surrounding countryside, Swords town and Dublin Bay. Times for this are listed on a nearby board, and you may be able to climb it at other times if it is convenient for the verger. The adjacent round tower, 23 metres (75 feet) high, is the only part of the old monastery to survive, although it was built later, around the 10th century. The erection of round towers, a peculiarly Irish feature found in almost every monastery in Ireland, was in response to the many attacks by Vikings from the 9th century onwards. The tower acted as a belfry, a lookout post, a safe storage area for valuables and a refuge from the Vikings, who were more interested in the quick seizure of spoils than the sustained siege of an embattled tower. The

St Colmcille's Well, Swords.

conical roof and cross surmounting the tower are relatively recent, dating from the 19th century. A solemn occasion took place in the abbey on Good Friday 1014 when, after the Battle of Clontarf, the bodies of the slain High King of Ireland, Brian Boru and of his son, Morrough, were laid to rest here overnight on their long journey to Armagh.

Next, proceed down the hill (it is still Church Road), passing the old Royal Constabulary Barracks on the right before recrossing the Ward River. On the left is the excellent Old Schoolhouse Restaurant, originally built in 1834 as the Junior School to the Old Boro School in Main Street. The building still retains its original ceiling, wood panelling and timber floors, and even some of the former pupils' names etched onto the walls. Bear left into Well Road until you reach an apartment block on your right. Just before this block, there is a tiny temple-like structure that once housed a water pump. This is the actual location of Colmcille's Well, which is the origin of Swords' name, *Sórd Cholaim Chille* or 'the pure (water) of Colmcille'. After a pause (and perhaps a prayer to the saint) continue onto Main Street, turn right and right again at the Lord Mayor's Pub onto Forest Road. Highfield Road (on your right, but don't take it unless you want a diversion) leads into the beautiful Ward River Valley Park, a linear park developed along the river by Fingal County Council. (Fingal is a name derived from Fine Gall, which means the territory of the foreigner.) Forest Road is a fairly long stretch of road, with a footpath along it that peters out after the village of Forest Fields and its roadside water pump. There are plans to continue the footpath but these may not have been carried out at the time of publication, so in its absence walk in single file on the right-hand side of this busy road. As the road curves to the left, passing Forest Little Golf Course, you will get an inkling of what lies ahead in the form of a large revolving radar dish. After another couple of bends you will come onto another road that leads to a spectacular panoramic view of Dublin Airport. Cross the road carefully to the grass verge along the airport perimeter fence. Ahead, in the distance, you will see a range of airport buildings, from massive hangars to radiating terminals. Nearer to you is the complex network of taxiways and runways. These are usually busy with aircraft, but the amount of activity depends on the day's wind direction and which runways are in operation as a result. Although it serves only a relatively small country, Dublin Airport has become a major international airport – the Dublin to London service alone is now the busiest route in Europe.

The 'Eagle' Flies Again

If you are an enthusiastic plane spotter, you can stay here for as long as you like. When you are ready to move on, walk along the grass verge with the airport on your right until you reach the Cloghran Roundabout. Turn right and continue along the Swords Road. Coming up on your right, partially hidden by a wall, is Castlemoate House. Originally built in 1822, in 1877 it was extensively rebuilt and the garden landscaped, both in Italian style. Aer Rianta, the Dublin Airport Authority, has preserved the house and uses it as a training centre. On the opposite side of the road is a lovely old stone bridge, which leads to Kinsealy, and the Coachman's Inn, a much-enlarged former stagecoach stop. Your journey will now bring you to another roundabout, upon which is a soaring monument ending in a sharp point, entitled the *Spirit of the Air*. It was built in 1991, made of rein-forced concrete and clad in Dublin granite, and was designed by Richard Enda King.

After turning right at the roundabout, the path brings you into the airport prop-er and you are soon walking alongside a gigantic hangar. This mammoth but attrac-tive building, owned by FLS Aerospace, dates from 1990. It is big enough to house two jumbo jets and four Boeing 737-sized aircraft simultaneously for overhauling. For a good overall view of this lower end of the airport complex, climb to the top of the pedestrian bridge and take a look around; then regain the path, which soon passes between two lines of shrubbery. Over on the left is the Airport Church (which is open during daytime and where this author was married many moons ago). It was built in the mid 1960s and was very modern for its day. In fact its stained glass Stations of the Cross were considered so avant-garde that the archbishop of the day ordered their removal. They have since, thankfully, been restored. Various technical buildings and hangars are now the main features on one side, while multi-storey and surface car parks dominate the other. Keep to the right side as you circumnavigate the buildings. Turn left at a security hut to head towards the main terminal, but first note the slightly curving white-fronted building directly ahead with a control tower on top of it. Opened in 1941, this was the airport's first permanent terminal. It was designed by Desmond FitzGerald, chief architect with the Office of Public Works, and was modelled on the bridge of a luxury liner, reflecting the close relationship between sea travel and aviation at the time. The history of Dublin Airport started during the First World War when Collinstown (the name of the district) was selected as a base for the Royal Flying Corps. After the establishment of the Free State in 1922, the airfield was abandoned until construction work began on a new civil airport in 1937. The first passenger flight took place on 19 January 1940 when a full Aer Lingus aircraft took off for Liverpool. The management of Dublin Airport is vested in a state company, Aer Rianta (which literally means Air Prepared). Aer Lingus (from Aer Loingeas meaning Air Fleet) was founded as the state airline in April 1936 with a single aircraft, a DeHavilland 84 Dragon named *Iolar* (eagle). Aer Lingus still owns a sister aircraft which has been renamed *Iolar*, but the original was shot down during the Second World War, after it had passed out of Aer Lingus's ownership. The current aircraft is still perfectly airworthy and is often seen at air shows.

Walk up the ramp towards the departures building and go inside to survey the scene. This particular terminal has recently been doubled in size, and several other terminals have been added on over the last few years to try to cope with ever-increasing numbers using the airport. Over 14 million passengers arrive and depart annually – over 3½ times the total population of the Irish Republic. There are limited public observation areas of the busy tarmacs, but you could cross over to the highest multi-storey car park and take in the views from the rooftop. When you are ready to leave the terminal (or the car park), proceed towards the exit road past a somewhat unexpected sight, a Georgian-style country mansion, situated near the bottom of the ramp leading to the departures terminal. Known as Corballis House, it was built as a country house in the early 1700s. One of the earliest occupants was Thomas Wilkinson, Lord Mayor of Dublin. Internally, except for minor alterations, the house remains much as it was over two hundred years ago. It has been used as an airline training centre since 1954.

At this point, decide whether you want to board a bus directly from the airport, in which case return to the arrivals level of the main terminal where you will find the bus stops. Alternatively you could wine and dine at the Great Southern Hotel, the tall yellow building about 600 metres (650 yards) away, or indeed at the Trusthouse Forte Hotel directly opposite.

The Northside Pub Crawl

Summary: This may start as a walk, but if you don't take care to resist most of the temptations along the way it may degenerate into a staggering meander, with all fixed focus on the final destination hopelessly lost. It is not for nothing that visiting a number of pubs in sequence is called a pub *crawl*. I will nevertheless uplift the proceedings by concentrating on the history of the neighbourhoods, which will hopefully woo you away from all the hospitable pub landlords may offer.

Start:	The Old Jameson Distillery, Bow Street, Smithfield village. DART Station: Tara Street is 25 minutes' walk away. Buses: 37, 39, 51, 51B, 70. Car parking: multi-storey car park on Usher's Quay directly across the river. Metered on-street spaces available on the quays.
Finish:	Harbourmaster Pub, International Financial Services Centre. DART Station: Connolly Station. Buses: you are only 7 minutes walk away from all city centre buses. Car Parking: some on-street metered parking available but you would be better off using the multi-storey car park behind Jurys Custom House Inn.
Length:	2.3 km (1½ miles).
Time:	1 hour.
Refreshments:	Need I say anything!
Pathway Status:	City paths throughout.
Best Time to Visit:	This depends on whether you like your pub quiet (before 4.00 pm) or bursting at the seams (after 6.00 pm until late). Pub opening hours have recently been extended. They may now stay open until 12.30 am on Thursdays, Fridays and Saturdays, and until 11.30 pm on other days. There is an additional half-hour drinking-up time.
Suitable for Bicycles:	Yes, but bring a good bicycle lock with you and stay sober.
Connecting Walks:	From Ashtown to a Chimney Tall, and to The Southside Pub Crawl or Talbot Street to the North Docklands.

It seems appropriate that this walk should start at a former distillery, which is now a visitor centre. In 1780, John Jameson bought a small distillery on Bow Street, and from these small beginnings he built up a huge enterprise that became known the world over as John Jameson & Son Ltd. In 1966 Jameson's was united with the John Power & Son and the Cork Distilleries labels to form the Irish Distillers Group.

In 1971 the distillation process was moved from Dublin to Midleton, Co Cork, leaving the premises at Bow Street vacant. For years, its chimney stacks and grey stone warehouses stood lonely against the bleak and desolate area that Smithfield had become. Its one salvation was that in 1980, Irish Distillers converted the old spirit store that faced onto Smithfield into their corporate headquarters, and opened a small visitors' centre in another warehouse opposite the main complex in Bow Street. In the general rejuvenation of Smithfield, which began in the late 1990s, Irish Distillers played their part by investing £7 million to recreate a replica of a working distillery. Here, in an atmosphere redolent of a bygone industrial age, you can follow the steps involved in whiskey-making before being offered your own complimentary glass. However, you don't have to take the tour to wander around the main reception area and view the iron supports and oak beams, cranes, storage cellars and bric-a-brac associated with the business. You can also visit the self-service restaurant without taking the tour. Incidentally, whiskey is an Irish invention that dates back to the days of the early Christian church. It seems that some monks, while visiting the Near East, spotted the locals using a distillation process to make perfume. They decided on a better use for the process – to make what became known as *uisce beatha*, or the water of life. In the cold damp monkish cells of the 8th century, the *uisce beatha* probably helped (along with prayer) to keep body and soul together. In the 12th century, the word *uisce* was corrupted to *fuisce* by the invading knights of King Henry ll, and ultimately became 'whiskey'. The Scots dropped the 'e' to give 'whisky', a drink that is distilled only once, whereas Irish whiskey is distilled three times.

Legal Eagles

You might, of course, be tempted to stay in the distillery and not do the walk at all! However, the panoply of splendid taverns that you will visit, from the traditional to the chic, should encourage you to continue on. When you are ready to tear yourself away, leave the outside courtyard via the pot-still (a large copper vessel used to distil whiskey) and Duck Lane and enter Smithfield (*see* Ashtown to a Chimney Tall for further information about this area). Turn left and left again at the Children's Court and walk down New Church Street. On your right is the headquarters of the Irish Distillers Group, and ahead is the tower of St Michan's Church, the oldest parish church on the north side of the city. Originally founded by the Vikings in 1095, it was the only parish church north of the Liffey for nearly 600 years. The main reason for this historic church's fame is some 17th-century mummified bodies that lie in full view in the underground vaults (*see* Dublin Underground). At the corner with Bow Street is the public house attached to the old Jameson Distillery, the Irish Whiskey Corner Bar. It may be closed until around 5.00pm, depending on the day and time of year. Bear right down cobbled Bow Street, named after John, Baron Bowes, a former resident and one-time Lord Chancellor (1761). The whole of this area was virtually derelict until a few years ago, but it is now crowded with new apartment blocks.

Next, head left into Hammond Lane, once famous for an iron foundry and now home to Maguire & Patterson, well-known match-makers. Hammond is a corruption of Hangman, indicating a somewhat sinister past. Upon arrival in Church

Street turn right towards the River Liffey. This street could just as easily be called Barrister Boulevard, as it swarms with legal eagles flittering between the Four Courts (on your left) and their offices, which are spread along this street. At The Quill, one of the local pubs haunted by the legal profession and their clients, cross Church Street to walk towards the city centre with the river on your right. The impressive bulk of the Four Courts dominates Inns Quay. It was designed by James Gandon and built between 1786 and 1801. The actual Four Courts were the Courts of Exchequer, Common Pleas, King's Bench and Chancery, although a fifth court, the Judicature, also sat here from the beginning. The five statues by Edward Smyth which stand on the lofty perch are of Moses, holding the Tables of the Law, accompanied by Justice, Mercy, Wisdom and Authority. Diagonally across Chancery Place is The Legal Eagle, a hostelry well worth dropping into if it is lunch time. Here, if you pretend not to listen, you may well hear discussions about the morning's legal dramas and the afternoon's likely dénouements.

Continuing on your worthy quest, go back to the riverfront, noting Dublin Corporation's impressive Civic Offices on the far bank. Turn left to walk a very short distance along Upper Ormond Quay, then swing left again at the Chancery Inn, yet another lawyers' drinking hole. This establishment proclaims that it is a Tea, Wine and Spirit Merchant, so it would appear that you could request a nice hot nonalcoholic cuppa. As in many city centre pubs, it offers traditional Irish music at stated times. You are now in Charles Street, named not after King Charles II, as you might expect from his association with the Duke of Ormond (after whom Ormond Quay is named) but after Charles Coote, a contemporary of Ormond and Earl of Mountrath. Cross over and enter Ormond Square, an oasis of tranquillity for the residents who live around the pleasantly designed open space, upgraded from a run-down condition in 1998 by Dublin Corporation. A right turn into Arran Street will take you back once again to the river. If you are a fan of James Joyce you

Madigan's Pub, Lower Abbey Street.

simply must drop into the Ormond Hotel, the setting for the 'Sirens' chapter in *Ulysses*. The hotel has been extensively remodelled since 16 June 1904 (the day covered in the book and now immortalized and annually celebrated as Bloomsday) but the spirit of Leopold Bloom still lives on. On the far side of the river, stretching from here to O'Connell Bridge, is the famed Temple Bar area, but there is more about this district in the next chapter. Moving on, pass by Grattan Bridge House, an office block converted from a Presbyterian Church. Cross Capel Street onto Lower Ormond Quay. At the corner with Jervis Street is one of the chicest hot spots in town, especially with young professionals and the stars of the entertainment business – the Morrison Hotel. Its plush, ultramodern Café Bar, Morrison Bar and Lobo's (where Japanese food is a speciality) attract the jet set from noon until late.

A Gauntlet of Bars

The Millennium Bridge, a new pedestrian bridge (built in 1999), signals your proximity to Zanzibar, one of the newer theme bars. Here you can imbibe in a splendidly exotic atmosphere, although it may be closed when you arrive as it only opens at 4.00 pm (12 noon on Saturday and Sunday). A little down Liffey Street, at the junction with the venerable Ha'penny Bridge (built in 1816), is Pravda, a pub with a Russian Revolutionary theme. It's different, and it's very popular, too. Such bars are becoming increasingly popular in Dublin and are seriously challenging the more traditional pub. There is, however, no danger of the latter becoming extinct. The sculpture on the pavement outside, of two tired shoppers sitting down (*Meeting Place* (1988) by Jakki McKenna), was dubbed by the ubiquitous Dublin wits as the 'Hags with the Bags'. No statue or monument in Dublin is safe from its witty and sometimes acerbic rhymesters. Along Batchelor's Walk you'll find antique shops, apartments, a restful chapel, and oh! a pub, the Knightsbridge Bar, part of the Arlington Hotel.

With the aid of the traffic signals, make your way across O'Connell Street, one of the widest thoroughfares in Europe. This end of the street was nothing but a lane until it was widened by the Wide Streets Commission in 1789 to connect the proposed Carlisle Bridge (now O'Connell Bridge) to Sackville Street (now Upper O'Connell Street). The new street was called Sackville Street Lower. In 1924 it was renamed O'Connell Street in honour of the Liberator, Daniel O'Connell, whose monument, sculpted by John Henry Foley and unveiled in 1882, stands proudly facing the bridge. Enter Abbey Street and prepare to run a gauntlet of pubs. On the right are Wynn's Hotel, The Plough (just around the corner in Marlborough Street) and the bar in the Abbey Theatre (to which you will only gain entrance if you attend the evening's play). On the left is Madigan's, a fine traditional house. On the corner with Marlborough Street is The Flowing Tide – though it's about 350 years since the sea lapped at its door. The Life, another modern, candlelit 'in' place, is at the top of Northumberland Square, which leads into the car park and shops of the Irish Life Centre. This sextet of pubs is joined on the street by a religious bookshop, a Methodist Mission Hall, a Presbyterian church, the Salvation Army and a health insurance organization. Is somebody trying to tell us something? But the offices of the National Lottery are close to The Life – what better incentive to ignore them all and spend, spend, spend!

If by now you are thoroughly exhausted, and well you might be, head once more for the balm of the River Liffey by skirting around the Custom House (*see* Talbot Street to the North Docklands) and find the Harbourmaster Bar in the International Financial Services Centre. In the 19th century this was the dockmaster's office, and many of the office trappings and samples of examined cargoes are stacked on the high shelves. The bar also includes a fine restaurant. Unless you are made of stern stuff you will hardly want to undertake the Southside Pub Crawl today, but then again, it takes all kinds....

The Southside Pub Crawl

Summary: If you have survived The Northside Pub Crawl, or if you haven't yet attempted it, you might be foolhardy enough to undertake this little number. Of course it is all in the cause of historical research – after all, you must want to follow in the footsteps of those Dublin literary characters of great renown who blessed many of the selected establishments with their company. Mind you, many of their footsteps may not have been directed in coherent straight lines and could therefore be difficult to follow… Seriously, though, on this walk you can soak up the various atmospheres of mostly traditional (but some trendy and modern) pubs, and learn a little about their individual stories and the history of their locations. You can, of course, reward yourself with the occasional pint of stout, shot of spirit, cup of coffee or a plain soft drink and naturally, the chat.

Start:	Mulligans Pub, Poolbeg Street. DART: Tara Street Station. Buses: all city centre buses are only a few minutes' distance away. Car parking: some metered on-street parking in neighbouring streets and quays. Fleet Street has the nearest multistorey car park.
Finish:	Davy Byrne's, Duke Street. DART: Tara Street. Buses: it is only a 5-10 minute walk to all buses. Car parking: there are several multistorey car parks in the vicinity.
Length:	2 km (1¼ miles).
Time:	1 hour (or perhaps 21, depending on your thirst!)
Refreshments:	Liquid (and also the more solid variety) is available at each port of call.
Pathway Status:	All city footpaths.
Best Time to Visit:	During pub opening hours!
Suitable for Bicycles:	It wouldn't seem the best idea to bring a bicycle. Besides, the Temple Bar area is a pedestrian zone.
Route Notes:	Several notable pubs are not included here as they appear in some of the other walks.
Connecting Walks:	From The Northside Pub Crawl, or Talbot Street to the North Docklands.

If you are on your way to Poolbeg Street up Tara Street from the DART station or from the last walk, you will notice the elegant Florentine-style tower of the former Tara Street Central Fire Station. The 38-metre (125-feet) high structure was built in 1907 to serve as a lookout tower, in the days before telephones were available to call brigades to the scene of a fire. It was also very useful for hang-drying wet fire hoses. The tower clock and its mechanism were modelled exactly on London's Big Ben. In a new hotel and bar development (not on this itinerary, but well worth a separate visit) the old fire station building has been sensitively preserved. The new Central Fire Station has been relocated a few strides around the corner in Townsend Street, which dates from at least 1674 and at that time literally represented the eastern extent of the built-up city, or the town's end.

Mulligan's Pub, Poolbeg Street.

Temple Bar

The first turn to the right will bring you to Poolbeg Street, and the official start of the walk, Mulligan's Pub. This is a relatively small, unpretentious establishment, with low wooden-beamed ceilings. The owners have resisted modernizing it or extending it in any way, as is the current trend. Its interior is completely genuine and old-world, and the passing of recent legislation means that it and several other pubs cannot now be altered in any way without statutory permission. It dates from 1782. Poolbeg Street, then called Shoe Lane, was originally a late medieval lane leading to the Poll Beag (Small Pool), a small deep-water berthage near Ringsend. Leaving Mulligan's, turn to the right past Greer & Son, a saddlers shop that has been trading here since the early 1900s. The ugly (by today's perceptions) glass and panel office block on your left, Hawkins House, replaced the much-loved Theatre Royal, which was demolished in 1962. A more successful modernization is the Corn Exchange, an apartment block which backs onto the old Corn Exchange Building on Burgh Quay. Crossing Hawkins Street, enter under the mock Tudor archway of an Bord Gais (the Gas Board) into Leinster Market. Now lined by mock but pleasing Tudor façades (built in the 1930s) this lane was indeed a market in the 19th century, selling second-hand clothes, periwinkles (edible sea snails) and sweets. When you come out onto D'Olier Street, turn right towards O'Connell Bridge to cross over to the far side of Westmoreland Street. Many of Dublin's streets are named after former Lord

Lieutenants, the English monarch's representatives in Ireland until 1921, when the Irish Free State was established. Westmoreland Street, laid out in 1801 by the Wide Streets Commission, commemorates John Fane, 10th Earl of Westmorland (without the 'e'), Lord Lieutenant 1790–94. Turn left down Westmoreland until you encounter Bewleys Café, part of the chain founded by Joshua Bewley in the 1840s. It has been in Westmoreland Street since 1896 (*see* Some Great Interiors). More to the purpose of this walk is Bewley's latest venture, The Bridge, a bar with a 1920s look but which only opened in the late 1990s. It has a wonderful collection of curiosities and oriental artefacts, both upstairs and in the several themed rooms downstairs.

Upon exiting, wheel right into Fleet Street and enter the heart of Temple Bar, a cultural centre where noble artistic and educational pursuits are buttressed by the city's greatest concentration of bars, restaurants and hotels. The first of these is one of the most genuine, and definitely calls for a stopover – the Palace Bar, a shrine to authentic Victorianism. The old-fashioned carved mahogany shelving units, counter screens and the counters themselves are finely complemented by a collection of brass vessels, bric-a-brac and framed pictures and cartoons of notable and historic Irish people, especially from the literary world. The back room is entered through a snug-like door. When you leave the bar, have a look at the antique-style lamp outside. It was sponsored by the Palace Bar, and bears an inscription attesting to the fact. Further up the street is Buskers, a bar-cum-disco, laid out on a traditional shop-fronts theme complete with stone floors. It is part of the Temple Bar Hotel. The Oliver St John Gogarty is next on the list. The present building has an attractive 19th-century boarding house appearance, the result of a redevelopment completed in 1994. The genesis of the pub itself goes back to 1850. Irish traditional music is played here every day in the late afternoon and at night-time. Ad hoc musical sessions often start up when musicians drop in for a drink. Oliver St John Gogarty (1878–1957), a one-time friend of James Joyce and the model for the character Buck Mulligan in Ulysses, was a writer, poet, wit, a senator of Dáil Éireann and a medical doctor by profession.

From here on, the going gets tough and gallant pub-crawlers will have to resolutely hack their way through a forest of pubs. Up Anglesea Street you have the Left Bank Bar and a little further away, Blooms Hotel. Across from the Oliver St John Gogarty is another traditional music venue, the Auld Dubliner.

A Cultural Square

Now you move into a street called Temple Bar, which gives the whole district its name. It was ostensibly named after Sir William Temple whose residence and gardens previously stood in the area in the early 17th century. However, as there was already a Temple Bar leading onto a Fleet Street in London, it might follow that these names were imported by Dublin's many administrators and developers who hailed from London, and to honour the well-regarded Temple family almost incidentally. The earliest record of Temple Bar is on a 1673 map of Dublin. A 'bar' or 'barr' is an estuary sand bank or, as is the case in London, a barrier or gate blocking the entrance to the city. A sandbar could easily have existed here before the reclamation of the land in the 16th and 17th centuries. Today, Temple Bar is taken

The Porterhouse
Fitzsimons
Temple Bar Galleries
Clarence Hotel (Octagon Bar)
Black Church Print Studios
Buskers
Bewleys
Leinster Market
Corn Exchange
The Auld Dubliner
Palace Bar
Mulligan's Pub
WELLINGTON QUAY
ASTON QUAY
BURGH QUAY
GEORGE'S QUAY
POOLBEG ST
BUTT BRIDGE
ESSEX ST EAST
TEMPLE BAR
FLEET STREET
Gaiety School of Acting
TEMPLE LA
FLEET STREET
Tara Street Station
DAME
Crown Alley
Left Bank Bar
Oliver St John Gogarty
Tara Street
Irish Film Centre
STREET
TOWNSEND STREET
The Ark
DAME LANE
Gallery of Photography
Eustace Street
Bloom's Hotel
Fire Tower
N
National Photographic Archive
Stag's Head
Eamonn Doran's
The Temple Bar
SOUTH GREAT GEORGES STREET
The Norseman
GRAFTON
DUKE STREET
200 m (220 yd)
Davy Byrne's

to mean the area bordered by Fishamble, Dame and Westmoreland Streets, and Wellington Quay. Crown Alley, apart from being the busy pedestrian route between Dame Street and the Ha'penny Bridge, is also the home to Eamonn Doran's, a New York-style pub and restaurant. The pub is an important venue for rock and pop music as well as the more traditional kind. As you continue along Temple Bar, a more cultural element begins to creep in. Temple Bar Galleries and Studios provide exhibition spaces, while in the overhead studios, 22 resident artists work on their latest creations. Next door, the Black Church Print Studios incorporates a gallery on the ground floor and print studios on the upper three floors. On the opposite side, at the corner with Temple Lane, is The Temple Bar pub, established in 1849 and popular for its daily traditional music. Next, at the intersection with Eustace Street, are two hostelries – one supposedly the oldest in Temple Bar, and the other, one of the newest: the Norseman first traded in 1696 and Fitzsimons opened in 1993. A quick detour into Meeting House Square will place you in the middle of a cultural oasis. There is access from the square to the National Photographic Archives, the Gaiety School of Acting, the Irish Film Centre, the Gallery of Photography and the Ark, a cultural centre for children. On Saturdays, an organic food market takes place in the square itself (which is named after the adjacent Quakers' Meeting House).

As you walk along Essex Street there should be a couple of new drinking emporiums on the left, but at the time of writing work had just begun to redevelop the whole block. On the right-hand side, the penultimate building before Parliament Street is the Clarence Hotel. Standing on the site of the original Custom House (the riverfront around here was the heart of Docklands in the 18th century), the Clarence and its Octagon Bar are both sophisticated and trendy. Is it any wonder? The Clarence is owned by the rock band U2. One of the more unusual pubs of this ramble is The Porterhouse, standing at the corner of Essex Street and Parliament Street. The large copper vats indicate that this pub brews its own stouts and beers, and it is worth a visit to taste both the pub's unique flavours and its ambience: traditional, blues and jazz music feature nightly.

A Gorgonzola Sandwich

So far this tour has been a bit of an obstacle course, and it is now time to speed up a little. A good brisk walk should stir up a genuine thirst, so you will have to ignore all but one pub until you reach your destination. This will take some resolve on your part, as quite a few of Dublin's 700 pubs still lie in wait to ambush you. Turn left into Parliament Street (it was once the main route to the House of Parliament from the northside) with the magnificent City Hall at its head. With the aid of the traffic lights, cross to the opposite side of Dame Street, then onto South Great George's Street and into Dame Lane until you reach Dame Court (all these Dames were named after a medieval dam across the River Poddle near the City Hall). You have now reached the Stag's Head in all its authentic Victorian red brick splendour. It goes back to 1770, but received its Victorian embellishments in 1895. They include the usual carved mahogany, a granite-topped bar, a stained glass ceiling (at the back) and several stained glass windows based on the stag theme. Thus fortified with the offerings of the Stag's Head, make your purposeful way to Duke Street via Dame Court, Exchequer Street, Wicklow Street and Grafton Street. At 21 Duke Street you will find the illustrious Davy Byrne's immortalized in James Joyce's *Ulysses*. In the chapter 'Lestrygonians', Leopold Bloom satisfies his lunch-time hunger by calling in at the 'Moral Pub', his description of Davy Byrne's. Davy Byrne opened his bar in 1873 and personally attended his business for the next 50 years. By all accounts he was not the most charming of men. Here Bloom had a glass of Burgundy and a Gorgonzola cheese sandwich with mustard. You could try the same. Every year on Bloomsday (16 June), Joycean enthusiasts gather at Davy Byrne's, many in 1904 costume, the year in which the great novel is set. Whatever the day of your own visit, just close your eyes and let your imagination take over. You can smugly reflect that your pilgrimage today would certainly have earned the approval of James Joyce.

Mount Street Bridge to Merrion Square

Summary: Starting at a junction that saw some of the heaviest fighting during the Easter Rising of 1916, this is a walk along some streets that are off the beaten track and an encounter with a newly refurbished but forgotten little park. There is also a visit to a major city park that holds many hidden delights.

Start:	The Schoolhouse Hotel/The Inkwell Bar, Northumberland Road. Buses: 5, 7, 8, 45, 46, 84. DART: Pearse Station, Westland Row (10 minutes' walk). On-street disk parking only for a maximum of 3 hours.
Finish:	National Gallery of Ireland, Merrion Square. Buses: 5, 7, 8, 45, 46, 84. DART: Pearse Station, Westland Row (5 minutes' walk). Several nearby multistorey car parks or on-street disk parking.
Length:	2.4 km (1½ miles)
Time:	1¼ hours.
Refreshments:	There is no shortage of hotels and pubs along many parts of the route.
Pathway Status:	Pavements throughout, and grass sections in the parks.
Best Time to Visit:	Any time of the year during the daylight opening hours of the parks.
Suitable for Bicycles:	Yes, but you will have to walk your bicycle through the parks.
Connecting Walk:	Merrion Square to St Stephen's Green.

Depending on whether you arrive by foot, bus or DART, make your way to the Schoolhouse Hotel on Northumberland Road. This attractive red brick building was, until relatively recently, St Stephen's National School. During the rebellion of 1916, a column of Sherwood Foresters passed along Northumberland Road on its way to reinforce the British Army garrison in Dublin in its offensive against the Irish rebels. Without warning, as the soldiers were about to pass the school, they were caught in crossfire directed at them from the corner buildings (now demolished) on the far side of the canal bridge. Dozens of unfortunate British soldiers were killed and wounded in the action.

Start the first leg of the walk by proceeding down the side road past the hotel entrance. This will lead you to Estate Cottages, a neat row of brick and stone terraced cottages built for the workers of the Pembroke Estate, the landlords of much of this part of Dublin. Keep going straight alongside the Grand Canal. This short

Schoolhouse Hotel, Northumberland Road.

stretch of bank was used during the Second World War to store turf, brought here by barge from the midland bogs. When the grassy path reaches the next bridge, turn to the left over the bridge and cross to the far side of the road. This area, once occupied by light industry, town gas manufacturing and warehousing, had been growing ever more derelict until the upsurge in the economy during the late 1990s, when new businesses and apartments were attracted here, giving some of the old stone buildings a fresh lease of life. Ocean, a telecommunications company, used the curve in the canal to create an interesting design feature for its new headquarters. Turn into cobbled Clanwilliam Terrace, which is lined on both sides by offices that look more like houses. Towering over the offices is the Treasury Building, the former Bolands Mills premises that has been marvellously modernized with a stunning interior and a new cladding to the outside walls. This was another well-known rebel strongpoint during 1916. Éamon de Valera, a future President of Ireland, led the insurgents here. Note the intriguing sculpture of a man climbing up the sheer wall of the building. This is appropriately named *Aspiration* and is by Ronan Gillespie (1995).

When you come to the railway bridge, mind your head, as the clearance must be the lowest in Dublin – it just about allows a car to pass under its centre. ESAT, another telecommunications giant, occupies a modern building to the left and a former malt house, now converted to offices, lines the canal side. Grand Canal Quay, the road you are now on, brings you to the Waterways Visitor Centre, which is well worth visiting if you want to know more about Ireland's rivers and canals. Opposite the visitor centre, dominated by a lovely cut-stone tower block, is the Pearse Street Enterprise Centre, currently in the process of being converted into a research and development centre for Trinity College. The large expanse of water here, and the even larger dock across Pearse Street at the next bridge, are part of the Grand Canal Docks, a 19th-century sheltered harbour that was connected to the River Liffey by an arrangement of lock gates. This valuable facility is now attracting the building of apartments and the development of water leisure activities.

A Baby Boom

Walk up Pearse Street and cross over to the far side at the next lights. Until the late 1990s, this whole area had become quite run down. Pearse Square Park (which was known as Queen's Park in honour of Queen Victoria when it was first laid out in 1839), where you will arrive next, was one of the environmental catalysts for improvement when it was restored in 1998. The refurbishment design was based on the formal layout of the park shown on a mid-18th-century Ordnance Survey map. The central sculpture, a bronze entitled *Harmony,* is by Sandra Bell. Directly across Pearse Street is the former St Andrew's National School (1895), now a local community resource centre, an example of decorative yet everyday Victorian architecture. Moving on from here you will pass the Holiday Inn before coming to the junction with Erne Street Lower. Take a peek up Erne Street to view some very contemporary apartments lying opposite more old-fashioned local authority flats. Stroll up Erne Street Upper, a street still possessing a few dainty inner-city Victorian terraces. Walk under another railway bridge, this time without any danger to your head. At the right-hand corner with Hogan Place is a brand new replica of a 1940s car garage (formerly known as Archer's Garage and an architecturally protected building) that was knocked down for development in 1999, but following public outrage was immediately ordered to be rebuilt. Continue on up Holles Street, which goes past the National Maternity Hospital, founded in 1894. The present buildings date from 1934–38, along with the neo-Georgian façade of the Nurses' Home that faces onto Merrion Square. At the peak of the Irish baby boom of the 1980s, this hospital recorded the highest number of annual births in Europe for a hospital of its kind.

Merrion Square is one of the classic Georgian squares of Dublin (geometrically it is not a square at all – the longer sides are almost double the length of the other two). A plaque on the wall of the maternity hospital states that John Robert Godley, the founder of the Province of Canterbury in New Zealand, was born at this site in 1814. Cross over to the far side of the square, to the railings of Merrion Square Park. For safety reasons you should do this in two stages using the traffic lights. At the next entrance gate, turn into one of Dublin's grandest parks. The Roman Catholic Church bought the park in 1930 as a site for a new cathedral, but this project never went ahead. It is officially named Archbishop Ryan Park in memory of the Archbishop of Dublin who handed the 4.75 hectares (11.7 acres) to Dublin Corporation in 1974. As you wander around the park, note the many beautiful antique lampposts located along the pathways. Dublin once had (and still has, to some extent) a vast array of ornamental street lamps, and many of the rare and more endangered ones were re-sited in the park to preserve them for posterity.

Heads and Shoulders

At the next fork take the right branch and cross the grass to examine a couple of the monuments. The first upright stone commemorates the children who died at birth in the National Maternity Hospital between 1894 and 1994. Inscribed on the slab is a moving poem by Eavan Boland. In the far corner is a large bronze of *Eire* (Ireland) leaning on her harp. Originally crafted in 1932 by Jerome Connor (1876–1943), it was presented to the park in 1976 by the Buttercrust Bakery on their centenary and in memory of their founder Sir Joseph Downes, High Sheriff of Dublin (1900–1901). From here, you get a good view of the park in general. When it was taken over by the Corporation, it was decided that the park would provide passive recreation only – no football or sports activities would be catered for. The theme would be ornamental, based on the designs of Victorian horticulture. As a result, there are abundant flowerbeds, and cherry trees mingle with planes and other trees around the perimeter. Ninety per cent of the trees are evergreen, the remaining ten per cent deciduous. Over 150,000 shrubs were planted and every year 150,000 new bulbs are laid (the old bulbs are transplanted to other parks and motorway verges or given as charitable donations to institutions), resulting in carpets of daffodils, tulips, crocuses, snowdrops and hyacinths. These flowers are supplemented in season with wallflowers, pansies and lilies. The hill on the far side, which children love to roll down, is actually a soil-covered Second World War air raid shelter.

Regain the path, which, like all the other paths in the park, is edged with old limestone street setts. To the left, set amid elderberry, cypresses and heather, is a delightful carved granite piece, *Mother and Child* by Patrick Roe (1985), again a reference to the maternity hospital. At the next junction turn sharp right. Tucked away in the far corner is *The Tribute Head* by Elizabeth Frink. It was donated by Artists for Amnesty and was unveiled in June 1983, the 20th year of Nelson Mandela's imprisonment. He served another eight years before his release, and waited another four for his historic election as President of South Africa in 1994. When the path reaches the railings, turn left and visit the exquisitely laid out conifer and heather garden with its natural sculptures in bog oak. Up against the screen of shrubbery is the impressive bust to Bernardo O'Higgins, recognized as the Liberator of Chile, who was born of Irish descent in Chile in 1778 and died in Peru in 1842. The Republic of Chile presented the memorial to Ireland in 1995.

Now head towards the northwest corner of the park, first passing a children's playground on the left and the distant façades of the Georgian terrace on the right. At the corner you will find one of the true gems of Dublin – Danny Osborne's Oscar Wilde Memorial (1997), a relaxed Oscar Wilde reclining on a huge quartz rock. Scrutinizing the great man are a pregnant female figure (representing Constance, Oscar's wife) and a male torso (Dionysius, the god of drama and wine), each surmounting a pillar upon which is written a selection of Wilde's one-liners. The forty-eight quotes were selected by leading figures in Irish society and written in the style of their own handwriting. They include, 'Most people are other people', 'Whenever people agree with me I always feel I must be wrong', and 'The telling of beautiful untrue things is the proper aim of art'. This colourful statue, reflecting the flamboyance of Wilde's life, is composed of jade, thulite, porcelain, glass, black granite and bronze. It faces the last house on the opposite square, which was Oscar's home during his formative years.

Continue along the path to the rear of the Rutland Memorial Fountain, a Georgian masterpiece built simply to supply communal drinking water. It was designed in 1791 by Francis Sandys and commemorates Charles Manners, 4th Duke of Rutland and Lord Lieutenant from 1784–87. Take the path directly in front of the fountain, passing, on the right, the bust of intellectual A.E. (the pseudonym of George William Russell (1867–1935), a prominent figure in the Irish Literary Revival at the end of the 19th century) by Jerome Connor, which was presented to the park in 1985. Turn right at the crossing, passing two more busts. The limestone bust is of 18th-century Irish parliamentarian, Henry Grattan (1746–1820) by Peter Grant (1982). The bronze, by Dick Joynt (1990), is of the supreme military tactician of Ireland's War of Independence, Michael Collins (1890–1922). Collins was one of the primary negotiators of the Treaty with Britain, but was tragically assassinated in an ambush when he was Commander-in-Chief of the pro-Treaty forces in the following Civil

Rutland Fountain, Merrion Square.

War. Turn right again to view the statue group *The Victims* by Andrew O'Connor. O'Connor was born in 1874 in Worcester, Massachusetts, USA and died in Dublin in 1941. The statue, which was sited in 1976, depicts the dead victim (symbolic of any casualty of violence) laid out with one woman kneeling, her hands clasped in prayer, and another standing at his feet.

Return in the direction of the Rutland Fountain and exit the park just before you reach the memorial. You can now see the fountain from the front, and if you are in luck the water may be flowing. Thanks to some well-known contemporary prints of the Rutland Fountain from the Georgian period, it is easy to imagine the clusters of servants from the surrounding houses fetching water from the fountain and at the same time exchanging gossip about their masters and the latest scandals (has anything changed?). If the site gives you a thirst, or even hunger, you could do worse than cross the road and head for the scrumptious coffee shop in the famous National Gallery of Ireland, or try the nearby Mont Clare or Davenport Hotels.

Merrion Square to St Stephen's Green

Summary: This walk will take you along some of Dublin's most elegant Georgian streets, but you will also experience more private areas and back lanes. You will see where modern developments during the 1970s and 80s despoiled some Georgian streetscapes, and discover a wondrously ornamented but secluded park that was only officially opened to the public a few years ago, and is still undergoing development.

Start:	National Gallery of Ireland. Buses: 5, 7, 8, 45, 46, 84. DART: Pearse Station. Several nearby multistorey car parks or on-street disk parking.
Finish:	St Stephen's Green Hotel, St Stephen's Green. Buses: 10, 11, 14. DART: Pearse Station or Tara Street Station (15 minutes' walk). Several nearby multistorey car parks or on-street disk parking.
Length:	2.4 km (1½ miles).
Time:	1 hour.
Refreshments:	There is no shortage of hotels and pubs along many parts of the route.
Pathway Status:	Pavements throughout, as well as grass sections in the parks.
Best Time to Visit:	Any time of year and during the daylight opening hours of the parks.
Suitable for Bicycles:	Yes, but you will have to walk your bicycle through the park.
Connecting Walks:	Mount Street Bridge to Merrion Square, The Liberties, and Charlemont Bridge to Rathmines.

As the starting point for this walk is the National Gallery of Ireland, you might well be tempted to browse inside it first. Most of the greatest Irish artists are represented, along with many of the European Masters and Schools. Enquire at the ever-friendly reception desk for further guidance. The statue on the front lawn of the Gallery is a tribute to William Dargan (1799–1867), a 19th-century railway entrepreneur, whose efforts in assembling works of art for the Great Industrial Exhibition, which was held on this site in 1853, led directly to the opening of the Gallery in 1864. The statue, by Thomas Farrell, was unveiled on the same day. This was a somewhat unusual honour for a living person, and Dargan was still very much alive at the time.

A Street of Celebrities

With the Gallery behind you, turn right and then pause before the railings in front of Leinster House, the seat of the Irish Dáil (Parliament). It was built as a town house for the Duke of Leinster in 1745, then passed to the Royal Dublin Society in 1815. The society surrounded the house with a complex of learned and research institutions, which eventually led to the establishment of the National Library, the Natural History Museum and the National Museum. The government acquired Leinster House for use as the country's legislature in 1922. The obelisk standing in front of the house is in memory of Michael Collins (*see* page 101), Arthur Griffith and Kevin O'Higgins, who were all involved in the struggle for Irish independence. To the left of Leinster House is the Natural History Museum (1857) and to its left stands the massive Government Buildings (1904–1922). This block is dealt with in more detail in the chapter 'Georgian Dublin' in the companion book *Walking Dublin*.

Cross over the road to walk along Merrion Square South. Laid out in the mid 1760s, Merrion Square is, for Dublin, a unique Georgian square in that all its original 18th-century houses remain intact. Many of them have fine stucco ceilings, which can be observed from the pavement if the rooms are lit. Most of the houses are no longer lived in, but a few still are and there is now a slowly growing trend to reconvert Georgian houses from offices back to homes and hotels. It is worth noting who once lived in some of the houses and indeed who occupies them now. A.E. (George Russell), poet and patron of the 19th-century literary circle, worked in No. 84 (*see also* page 101), while poet William Butler Yeats lived at No. 82. Sculptor Andrew O'Connor (*see* Mount Street Bridge to Merrion Square) answered the door at No. 77. The Central Catholic Library occupies No. 74 – it was moved here from Hawkins Street to be close to the proposed new cathedral, which was to have stood where Merrion Square Park is today. The library shares the house with the Irish Georgian Society. Their neighbour in No. 73 is, fittingly, the Irish Architectural Archive. The reclusive horror storywriter, Joseph Sheridan Le Fanu, wrote from midnight to dawn in the eerie candlelit gloom of No. 70, now the headquarters of the Arts Council. Nobel Prize winner, Edwin Schrödinger (1887–1961) spent the Second World War in No. 65 working on theoretical physics. The august institution of The Royal Society of Antiquaries of Ireland is housed at No. 63. Daniel O'Connell, who in 1829 achieved emancipation from the harsh Penal Laws for Roman Catholics and dissenters, lived at No. 58. As you walk along, notice the elegant doorways of each house. While they might all appear the same at first glance, in the little details such as fan lights, side windows, column orders, door panelling and paint colours the variety is endless. If you want to know more about Merrion Square Park, *see* 'Mount Street Bridge to Merrion Square'.

Anyone for Tennis?

When you reach the end of the terrace, turn into Fitzwilliam Street Lower. This was named after the Fitzwilliams who developed this whole area in the latter half of the 18th century. Immediately across the road is Number Twenty Nine, a restored Georgian house converted into a visitor centre. It is run by the Electricity Supply Board (ESB) in association with the National Museum of Ireland, and is furnished to reflect the interior of an upper middle-class home of the late Georgian period. The ESB's involvement in this worthy endeavour is somewhat of a contrast to its actions in 1965, when it demolished a row of 12 Georgian houses and replaced them with an office block. The public outcry then and since has achieved nothing tangible, but the streetscape may perhaps be rehabilitated eventually.

Fitzwilliam Street offers a remarkable Georgian vista, particularly from Leeson Street, where you can look down the unbroken length of the combined streets. Once past the ESB offices turn right and walk under the archway into Fitzwilliam Lane. This was the original entrance lane for the back-door deliveries to the Georgian houses of Merrion Square and Baggot Street. Many of the rear entrances still have the brick archways that allowed the entry of horse-drawn carriages. The back gardens and former stables are now mostly given over to small firms and mews-type houses. At McGrattan's Restaurant, with a good view of the Government Buildings straight ahead, turn left into Baggotrath Place and out onto Baggot Street. These two place names are derived from Robert, Lord Bagod, to whom the Manor of the Rath (the local district) was granted in about 1280. Cross Baggot Street, another Georgian street that has been somewhat scarred by developers, and enter Pembroke Street, named after the 11th Earl of Pembroke who inherited the bulk of the Fitzwilliam estate in 1816. Many of the houses along here, especially those surrounding Fitzwilliam Square (1825), are occupied by medical consultants, but less today than formerly; other professionals such as lawyers, accountants and architects have now moved in alongside them. Fitzwilliam Park, which divides Pembroke Street into two, is still a private park with access only permitted to the residents of the square. It is well cared for, with attractive walks, lawns and planting that includes horse chestnuts and holly trees. During the 1890s the Irish Lawn Tennis Championships were held here. A prominent Dublin club owes its origins and name to the park even though it is now situated elsewhere – the Fitzwilliam Lawn Tennis Club. Walk around the square, noting the various name plaques and houses where the famous once lived. No. 2 was the home of William Dargan (*see* above); the painter Jack Yeats (1871–1957) lived at No. 18 and his poet brother William Butler Yeats (1864–1939) lived nearby at No. 42, but just for one year in 1928, immediately after retiring from the Irish Senate. When your scrutiny is complete, come out onto Fitzwilliam Street Upper (1780) and thence into Fitzwilliam Place (1800).

Cascades and Fountains

The last couple of buildings to the left of Fitzwilliam Place, with their façades facing onto Leeson Street (1765), might look like Georgian buildings but are in fact additions to the streetscape built only during the 1980s. Turn right into Leeson Street, a street renowned for its basement nightclubs. It is named after another 18th-century bigwig, Joseph Leeson, Earl of Milltown, who developed part of his estate near St Stephen's Green. Crossing over the road, enter Hatch Street (1800), where

National Concert Hall, Earlsfort Terrace.

Georgian buildings soon give way to modern office blocks. The most significant building on this street is University Hall, opened by the Jesuits in 1913 to provide hostel accommodation for male students, a function that it still performs. Cross obliquely from Hatch Street into the forecourt of the National Concert Hall on Earlsfort Terrace (1839). The Concert Hall only occupies the central portion of the building; the wings contain part of the Medicine, Architecture and Engineering faculties belonging to University College Dublin. The complete edifice was built in 1865 as part of the Dublin International Exhibition. Walk to the right side of the building towards the rear and you will find a small doorway in the garden wall which leads into Iveagh Park, a public park maintained by Dúchas The Heritage Service (for Ireland).

For now, take the pathway facing you. You will circulate around the park, discovering all its secluded features, in due course. The initial development of the park started in about 1700 when a Michael Gleeson built his house and gardens here. Up to that point, this area was known as Leeson's Fields, and before that was part of the commonage of St Stephen's Green. In the 1770s the first houses along nearby Harcourt Street were built, and by 1777 the Earl of Clonmel, John Scott, had built his mansion, Clonmel House. He took in Gleeson's gardens and they became known as Clonmel's Gardens. After his death they were renamed Coburg Gardens. By 1860 Benjamin Lee Guinness (Lord Iveagh), one of the Guinness brewing family, had built Iveagh House on St Stephen's Green, and he bought Coburg Gardens to have as his backdrop. Three years later he leased most of the land to the Dublin Exhibition Palace and Winter Garden Company, which built the impressive exhibition building surrounded by the lofty glassed-in Winter Gardens for the Dublin International Exhibition of 1865. The grounds were designed by landscape architect Ninian Niven. Initially, the Dublin Exhibition was a success, but within a year or two it ran out of steam and the buildings fell into disrepair. In 1872, the Dublin Exhibition of Arts, Industries and Manufacturers brought about a brief revival – it was held over 154 days and attracted nearly half a million people. This latest endeavour proved not to be sustainable and it too was closed down; all the glass sections of the Winter Palace were demolished and the gardens were given back to Lord Iveagh. The central stone building (today's University and Concert Hall complex) survived by virtue of becoming the examination centre for the Royal University from the 1880s. The Royal University later became part of University College Dublin (UCD). The front façade was redesigned by R.M. Butler in 1918 for UCD, and the building became the UCD main campus until the new facility in Belfield was developed from the 1960s. UCD still occupies most of the building, but the old Great Hall was converted to become the National Concert Hall in 1981. Meanwhile the park itself, bought from Lord Iveagh by the university in 1939, was taken over by the state in 1994 and the 3.4 hectare (8½-acre) site has since been undergoing an intensive programme of improvements.

First, stroll along the north walk, passing the large sunken lawn on the right. This is, in fact, Ireland's only purpose-built archery field. It is believed that an elephant lies buried under its east end. Apparently the animal died in Dublin Zoo during the 1920s and was brought here for research (which was never carried out) by the veterinary students of UCD. Note some nice holly trees along the path. When your reach the end of the path, turn left and walk past the lovely caretaker's house until you reach the Cascade, an immense rockery over which 1,360 litres (300 gallons) of water a second plunge into the pool below. The cascade is built from large rocks garnered from every county in Ireland, including limestone, sandstone and granite. Continue on to the far wall, turning left into the box hedge garden. Here, there is a miniature copy of London's Hampton Court maze. Just beyond the maze, flanked by two high rockeries, is the Rosarium (rose garden) enclosed by the graceful arches and tracery of a circular pergola. The roses form Ireland's largest collection of Portland Roses, a variety that is difficult to keep free from disease. Leave the rose garden by the steps and wander along the east path. On your right is an area left deliberately wild. The glass-enclosed Winter Gardens stood here and you can see evidence of their existence in the large cut stones, plinths and occasional statues lining the pathway. When you reach the steps, guarded on each side by statues, turn left and pause to look down the main avenue towards the cascade. This would also have been the view confronting visitors to the exhibitions as they entered the gardens. You may now promenade down the central parterre to enjoy the lawns and fountains on either side. This section of the park is more formal, its design inspired by the Bois de Boulogne in Paris.

When you are ready to leave the park, return to the caretaker's house where you will find the exit into Clonmel Street. The original buildings of this quiet cul-de-sac have been supplanted by modern counterparts. Only one on the right-hand side, which houses the Equality Agency, complements the sense of place. Turn right down Harcourt Street, named after the 1st Earl of Harcourt, Lord Lieutenant (1772–1776). Facing you at Nos 17–19 is the former Clonmel House, the earl's home. Harcourt Street is another Georgian street that looks relatively intact, but several of the houses have only period façades disguising modern office developments within. As you near your final destination, look over at no. 6. This was the home of John Henry Cardinal Newman, rector of the new Catholic University from 1852 until 1859. No. 4 Harcourt Street was the birthplace of Edward Henry Carson (1854–1935), founder of the Ulster Volunteers in 1912 and Unionist leader of the new Northern Ireland in 1922. Carson's house has now been renovated and absorbed into the new St Stephen's Green Hotel, your final port of call.

The Liberties

Summary: This walk is through an area that has changed substantially in the last few decades. The Liberties were those parts of Dublin granted a certain amount of autonomy by the British monarch in the Middle Ages. For instance, the Liberty of Christ Church was under the jurisdiction of the Dean of Christ Church Cathedral. As well as being responsible for the welfare of his citizens, the dean could pass laws and punish transgressors. Large areas around the centre of the city remained outside the jurisdiction of Dublin Corporation until the mid-19th century. Today, the term 'the Liberties' has come to mean the part of inner Dublin approximately west of Aungier Street and south of the River Liffey. The places that you will visit still have connections with either a turbulent past or a grim one in which political upheaval or dire poverty were the order of the day. In the 17th century, they were wealthy districts, when the crafts of the immigrant Huguenots had a ready market. When, in 1699, the English slapped penal duties on Irish imports, the Liberties were plunged into a despair that lingered until relatively recently. The once terrible slums and dereliction of the past have since been wiped away and you will pass a succession of pleasant and busy streets, a pair of former graveyards now converted into tiny city parks, and the spot where the patriot Robert Emmet was executed, before finally arriving at the extraordinary visitors' centre attached to the world-famous Guinness Brewery.

Start:	Stephen's Green Hotel, St Stephen's Green. DART: Pearse Station (15 minutes). Buses: 10, 11, 11A, 11B, 13, 15A, 46A. Car parking: College of Surgeons and the St Stephen's Green Centre multistorey car parks. There is metered on-street parking around the Green.
Finish:	Visitors' Centre, Guinness Brewery, Market Street. DART: none. Buses: 123, 68A, 78A.
Length:	2.4 km (1½ miles).
Time:	1 hour.
Refreshments:	The route will take you past some taverns, but the walk is hardly demanding – the Start and Finish venues should be adequate to meet your needs.
Pathway Status:	Public footpaths.
Best Time to Visit:	Any time providing the Guinness Visitor Centre is open when you arrive.
Suitable for Bicycles:	Yes, except for parks.
Connecting Walk:	From Merrion Square to St Stephen's Green.

From the Stephen's Green Hotel, saunter up Cuffe Street. This street has utterly changed since it was first laid down in around 1677. It was named after Sir James Cuffe, the son-in-law of Sir Francis Aungier, Master of the Rolls in early 17th-century Dublin, who gave his name to nearby Aungier Street. Today, Dublin Corporation flats have replaced the Georgian streetscape. One of these blocks, Mercer House on the right, has been restored and is now a very fine building indeed. Turn into Wexford Street, an original medieval road on which a gateway stood to guard the entrance into the Liberty of St Sepulchre. The right-hand turn into Camden Row will bring you, on the right, to the arched entrance of St Kevin's Park, a small converted graveyard. The ruined church of St Kevin was first mentioned in historical annals dating from 1226. It was rebuilt in the 16th and 18th centuries but has lain in a ruinous state since it finally closed in 1912. The martyred Archbishop of Cashel, Dermot O'Hurley, is believed to have been buried here in 1584. He had been arrested the previous summer on groundless charges of plotting to overthrow the British Government in Ireland. The various gravestones, both of prominent people and of the lowly, have been carefully preserved, several on their original sites. There is something very peaceful and dignified about the way this graveyard has been transformed into a public park. The building dominating the rear of St Kevin's is the Dublin Institute of Technology, Kevin Street. Camden Row itself is largely a rather bleak street of commercial units. At the far end, opposite a cottage-style terrace, is the former Gasgoine Home, converted in 2000 to apartments. Colonel Trench Gasgoine opened the home in 1904 as the rather gloomily titled Home of Rest for the Dying. Enter New Bride Street and make for Bride Street, passing the junction with Kevin Street and the Iveagh Trust Buildings (the Iveagh trust was founded by Edward Cecil Guinness, Lord Iveagh).

The Bayno

When you come to railings fronting St Patrick's Park on Bride Street (named after the now-demolished church of St Bride) enter the first gateway, but keep walking along the railings until you reach the corner with Bull Alley. Diagonally across the road is a block of public housing flats built by Dublin Corporation to a standard that would make private apartment owners envious. Roundels set into brick walls depict, in terracotta, scenes from *Gulliver's Travels*, written by Jonathan Swift in 1726. Turn around to view the imposing St Patrick's Cathedral on the other side of the park, of which Swift was the Dean from 1713 to 1745. Flanking the other side of the park is the wonderfully restored Liberties Vocational School that started life in 1915 as the Iveagh Trust Play Centre. It had 11 classrooms, three large halls and an outdoor playground. It catered for the children of poor families and was very advanced for its day, with a curriculum that included practical and social subjects such as sewing, dancing, art, cookery, singing and swimming. The locals affectionately nicknamed the centre The Bayno (from beano, meaning feast) – a reference to the daily bun and cocoa given to the children. St Patrick's Park was first developed by Lord Iveagh in 1897 on a plot cleared of appalling slums, thanks to his munificence. Dublin Corporation took over the park in the 1920s. At the bottom of the steps leading down from the balustraded walkway that brought you into the park, turn to study the Literary Parade, a collection of 12 commemorative plaques, each contained in a recessed archway. The bronze plaques honour 12 Dublin-born poets, novelists and dramatists who have attained world-wide distinction in their field, three of whom have won no less than the Nobel Prize for Literature. For the record the names are: Jonathan Swift, Eilis Dillon, James Clarence Mangan, Oscar Wilde, George Bernard Shaw (Nobel Prize 1925), William Butler Yeats (Nobel Prize 1923), John Millington Synge, Sean O'Casey, James Joyce, Brendan Behan, Austin Clarke and Samuel Beckett (Nobel Prize 1969).

Walk into the centre of the park and again take in the surroundings. It is hard to believe that little over a century ago, this area was one of the most depressed slums in Europe, let alone Dublin. Back in the late 17th century, however, it was a bustling and rich district based on the local industries of the recently arrived Huguenots, who had fled their native France in the face of persecution. Their main activity here was weaving, and a thriving export business was established. Then jealous competitors in England petitioned Parliament and in 1699 cruel taxes were imposed, which literally shut down the weaving industry. By Dean Swift's time the Liberties had plunged into endemic unemployment and misery. As the years rolled on the distressful situation grew worse. The population kept increasing, forcing slum dwellings to be erected on every available piece of land – there were rickety houses built right up to the walls of the cathedral. The streets were narrow (due to their medieval origins), hygiene was virtually nonexistent, illness was rampant and mortality was amazingly high.

Into this scene came Lord Iveagh, one of the wealthy owners of the famed Guinness Brewery. In the late 1890s he began to clear away the worst slums in the immediate vicinity of the cathedral; he then built a complex of apartment-style flats to rehouse the dislocated poor, opened the above-mentioned play centre for the

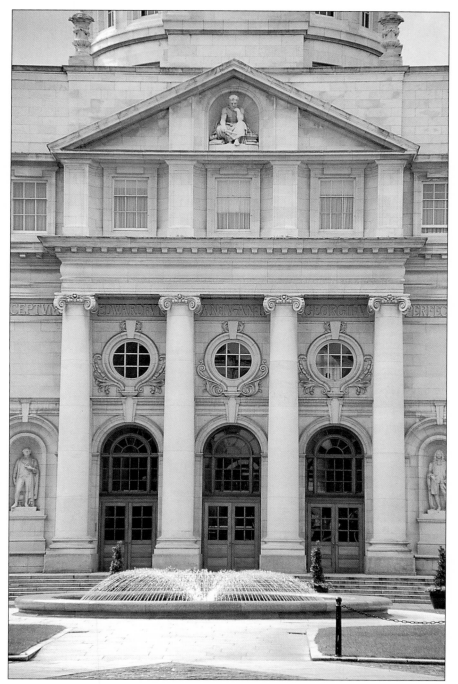

Plate 17: The Government Buildings complex on Merrion Street was the last major project completed by the British Government in Ireland before the creation of the Irish Free State in 1922 (see page 104).

Plate 18: One example of the decorative antique lamp-standards that adorn many of the city's streets. Several of the smaller columns found on bridges, on side and suburban streets, or in Merrion Square Park, were once lit by gas (see page 100).

Plate 19: Oscar Wilde, one of Dublin's most famous literary sons, is admirably commemorated by this memorial in Merrion Square Park (below; see page 101). The sculptor was Danny Osborne.

Plate 20: *Michael Collins, leader of the Provisional Government, was killed in an ambush during the Civil War of 1922–3. André Galland in* Le Petit Journal *(see page 101).*

Plate 21: *Hop shovelling at the Guinness Visitor Centre, which is housed in a huge industrial building that once served as the brewery's store house and fermentation centre (see page 115).*

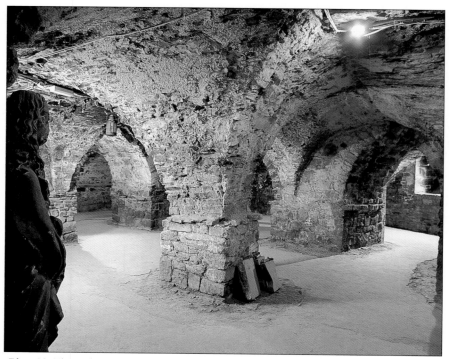

Plate 22: *The 12th-century crypt in Christchurch Cathedral, which contains a fascinating exhibition of ancient artefacts, is the oldest surviving structure in the centre of Dublin (see page 147).*

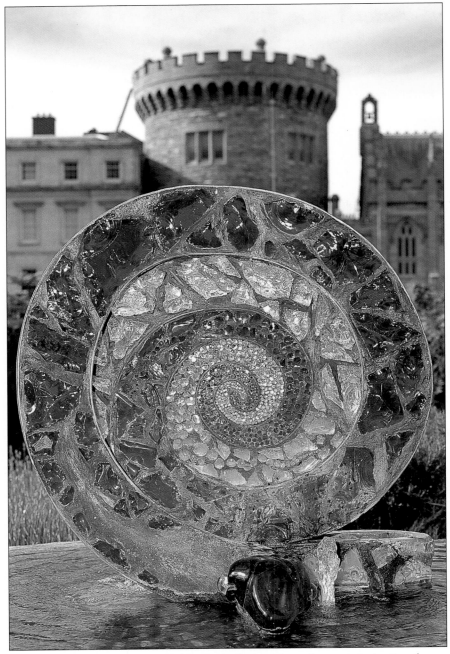

Plate 23: *Snake Fountain, Dublin Castle Gardens. The gardens mark the location of the original Dubh Linn (the Gaelic for Black Pool), which gave rise to the name of Dublin (see page 155).*

children, an indoor market to shelter the street traders and laid down the park for the enjoyment of all. The well-planned and executed projects of Lord Iveagh still stand as a testament to his vision and generosity. Forming a square behind the play centre are the Iveagh Flats. We shall visit the Iveagh Markets later. The park itself is managed by Dublin Corporation and, in season, has some of the richest floral displays in the city; its location is unique, with lovely backdrops such as St Patrick's Cathedral and Lord Iveagh's monumental buildings. Sculptures and fountains complete the picture.

An Antique Street

When you are ready to leave the park, exit by the far gate onto Patrick Street. Just before the gate is a small tablet surrounded by flowers. This commemorates the reputed baptism of converts in the vicinity by St Patrick himself, back in the 5th century. A holy well was revered here for centuries, the water presumably having something do with the River Poddle which still runs under the cathedral and the park. St Patrick's Close will take you past the cathedral, Marsh's Library and Kevin Street Garda Station. You may wish to visit these – they are dealt with in more detail in the walk entitled Some Great Interiors. Behind the opposite wall, along St Patrick's Close and around into Kevin Street, is the Deanery of St Patrick's. The great Dean Swift lived here amid his extensive and plentiful gardens, but the interior of the house itself was rebuilt following a fire in 1781. In the same block as the deanery is one of the last of Dublin's Dutch Billies. These were gable-fronted houses built in the style of indigenous Dutch architecture, which were quite common in Dublin in the late 17th and throughout the 18th centuries. Dutch settlers, who followed on after the victories of King William of Orange (King Billy), introduced this style in the 1690s.

Walk down the far side of Patrick Street. Opposite Bull Alley, climb the steps (there is also a ramp) under the arch of a modern apartment block, to emerge into Hanover Lane. This is a charming cobbled street lined with terraced cottages and town houses, many displaying colourful flower baskets. Other similar streets radiate out from Hanover Lane. Keep straight on until you come to Francis Street where there were no less than 18 antique shops at the last count. There are even specialist antique restoration shops. The street is named after St Francis of Assisi on account of the then nearby medieval Franciscan Abbey. The abbey (founded in 1235 and forcibly closed down in 1537) stood on the site now occupied by the church of St Nicholas of Myra (1834) on Francis Street. The latter has a striking interior including an altar made in Italy and a fine pieta by the famous Irish sculptor John Hogan. It is a strange fact that, for a period in the 19th century, the Isle of Man was once connected to the parish of St Nicholas of Myra. The Archbishop of Dublin, who then resided in Francis Street, was given temporary responsibility for the Roman Catholic Church in the Isle of Man. In recognition of this there is a commemorative design on the ceiling of the church featuring the triple-legged symbol of the Isle of Man. Across the road, at No.100, the world-wide apostolic movement, the Legion of Mary, was founded in 1921. Further up the street, at the corner with Dean Swift Square, is the former Iveagh Market. Funded by Lord

Iveagh, Edward Cecil Guinness, it was opened in 1907 to accommodate the street traders who had lost their pitches when the slums around Patrick Street were cleared. Dealers in old clothes and second-hand goods plied their trade here for generations. In early 2000 it was announced that it would be incorporated into a new development including a hotel, which may have been finished by the time you read this. In any case, look out for the bearded, winking face with the impish grin, one of the carved keystone heads, placed around the façade of the building (it is at the corner with Dean Swift Square). It is said to represent Lord Iveagh himself. The Tivoli Theatre at No. 135, although unpretentious on the outside, is one of Dublin's most successful theatres.

The Black Stuff

At the top of Francis Street turn left into Cornmarket, which was literally a corn market, established by a charter of King John in the 13th century. It affords a view down High Street towards St Audoen's and Christ Church. The spectacular frontage of the Augustinian church of St John the Baptist and St Augustine on Thomas Street sweeps up into a soaring tower and French chateau–like spire. The foundation stone was laid in 1862 but the building remained unfinished until 1911. The architects were Edward Welby Pugin and George Coppinger Ashlin. It stands on the site of a

St Catherine's Church, Thomas Street.

12th-century hospital founded by Ailred the Dane and dedicated to St John the Baptist. The statues around the tower were the work of James Pearse, the father of Padraig Pearse, a leader of the 1916 Rebellion. The Augustinians have been in Dublin since around 1280 and in this parish for over 300 years. The National College of Art and Design (NCAD), to the left of the church, resides in the former Power's Distillery. Almost next to the NCAD is one of the city's earliest fire stations, now occupied by a commercial concern. Vicar Street is the name of both a street and a bar/theatre standing alongside it. Turn left into Meath Street and right into Hanbury Lane. To the left of the lane is the site of the medieval St Thomas Abbey. When you reach a small park on the right, a converted graveyard, proceed up the adjoining St Catherine's Lane. This will bring you back to Thomas Street and the Doric façade of St Catherine's Church, built in 1765 and wonderfully restored in 1999/2000, after years of neglect, by CORE (City Outreach through Renewal and Evangelism), a movement within the Church of Ireland. The church was a silent witness to the execution of the leader of a failed rebellion, Robert Emmet. In 1803 he was hanged on a scaffold along with some of his fellow conspirators on the street facing the church.

Return via Thomas Court down the side of St Catherine's and turn right up Rainsford Street. The yellow brick houses at this corner, now privately owned, were the first to be built by the Guinness Trust (later the Iveagh Trust) in 1891. You are now in the industrial heartland of the Guinness Brewery. Large stone or brick warehouses rise from the cobbled streets. Railway tracks attest to the now defunct narrow-gauge line that criss-crossed the whole complex. The street is named after a former Lord Mayor, Sir Mark Rainsford, who at one time owned the lease of the property that was eventually sold to Arthur Guinness. Bear left at Vat House no. 11 into Crane Street and walk past the Hop Store, the Guinness Visitor Centre until the end of 2000. The brewery was founded in 1759 and went on to become, for a time, the largest in the world. Today it exports over 400 million pints per year – and this is in addition to what is produced by the 50 other Guinness breweries all over the world. A right turn into Bellevue (incorrectly called Belview on the street name plate) will bring you to Market Street and the magnificent new Guinness Visitor Centre in the huge storehouse. This was restored in 2000 at a cost of £35 million. Here you can experience the complete history of Guinness in a state-of-the-art exhibition and interpretative centre and, more importantly, taste the end product of all that effort at St James's Gate Brewery.

Charlemont Bridge
to Rathmines

Summary: Rathmines was an early suburb of Dublin that came into its own in the 19th century. It developed quite independently of the city and had its own Urban District Council until it was absorbed by the Dublin Corporation in 1930. You will wander through quiet terraced backstreets, Victorian squares, a park that witnessed Ireland's first balloon ascent, and a neighbourhood once known as Dublin's flatland because of the huge numbers of bedsits or flats let out to students and young workers in the area, particularly during the 1960s and 70s.

Start:	Stakis Hotel, Charlemont Place. Buses: 44, 44B, 48A, 62, 86. DART Station: none. Parking: only limited on street, disk parking subject to 3 hours maximum.
Finish:	Plaza Hotel or Charleville Hotel, Rathmines Road Lower. Buses: 14, 14A, 15B, 47, 47A, 47B. DART: none. Parking: only on-street parking subject to a maximum 3 hours.
Length:	3.2 km (2 miles).
Time:	1¼ hours.
Refreshments:	Take your pick from pubs, hotels and restaurants along the way.
Suitable for Bicycles:	Yes.
Pathway Status:	Street pavements and park paths throughout.
Best Time to Visit:	Any time, but parks close at dusk.
Connecting Walk:	Merrion Square to St Stephen's Green.

From the Stakis Hotel turn right, cross the Grand Canal over Charlemont Bridge and head down the pretentiously titled Grand Parade. The tree-lined Grand Canal forms the southern boundary of what is known as Dublin's Inner City. Similarly, the Inner City's northern boundary is delineated by the Royal Canal. Both waterways were built to carry commercial traffic between the capital and the hinterland during a time when roadways were either mere dirt tracks, unsafe or even nonexistent. Canal transport was surprisingly fast. The so-called 'fly boats' could carry 90 passengers in reasonable comfort and, because of their shallow draught, three or four horses could pull them, at a gallop, at up to 16 kph (10 mph). Hotels along the route provided comfortable accommodation for overnight stops. One of these hotels, the Portobello Hotel (1805), is just down the canal from here and is now part of Portobello College. This section of the Grand Canal was opened in 1791, although sections further west towards the River Shannon were in business from 1763. The canal is still fully navigable, but only pleasure craft use it, as commercial traffic ceased shortly after the Second World War. The waters have now been stocked with coarse fish, and dozens of swans have made it their home. This stretch of the road mixes modern office blocks with more traditional Victorian houses, the former thankfully disappearing as you continue along the route.

Balloon Travel

About 100 yards (90 metres) down Grand Parade, cross to the far side and enter Dartmouth Square via the six granite steps off the pavement. The houses here are solid Victorian red brick with granite basements, and while some serve as offices most are still lived in. Turn into Dartmouth Square North and enter the park through the gate, then walk to the opposite side underneath the magnificent pergola. There is something about the stately houses, the park and the tree-lined roads that exudes a great sense of time standing still. Next, saunter down into Dartmouth Road, which will bring you to Christ Church – an elegant stone building topped by a graceful steeple, now ecumenically shared by Anglicans and Methodists. A right turn will bring you into Leeson Street Upper, an amalgam of Georgian-style and Victorian houses. No. 29 is the headquarters of the St John Ambulance Brigade in Ireland. This part of Dublin developed in the early part of the 19th century and was a bastion of Englishness, as manifested by the names of the local streets – Sussex

Road, Chelmsford Road, Burlington Road, Waterloo Road, Wellington Road, Raglan Road and others. When you reach Appian Way, turn right and right again into Winton Road past the Fitzwilliam Lawn Tennis Club. Follow this quiet road onto Leeson Park and then switch left at the Molyneux Nursing Home into North-brook Road. Here, at No. 23, lived Henry Horatio Dixon (1869 – 1953), the first botanist to explain conclusively how sap rises in trees. Halfway up, on the left, you will pass an imposing stone mansion-like structure that is the Northbrook Clinic, the successor to the former St Anne's Hospital. Take the second left-hand turn and follow quiet Northbrook Avenue, a street of town houses and apartment blocks, until you reach Ranelagh Gardens Park.

Ranelagh Gardens Park takes its name from Lord Ranelagh in a roundabout way. He left Ireland around 1690 and settled in London. After his death, his lands in London were turned into the then famous Ranelagh Pleasure Gardens. Back in Dublin, a family called Hollister converted their grounds into a similar but more modest Pleasure Garden and also named it Ranelagh. This in turn gave its name to the whole district. One very significant historic event took place in Ranelagh Gardens. On 19 January 1785, Richard Crosbie, watched by 35,000 people, lifted off in Ireland's first hot-air balloon flight, a mere 14 months after the Montgolfier brothers became the world's first aeronauts.

Go around by the top end of the lake and walk along the path through the trees until you reach the archway of a bridge. This bridge once carried the Dublin to Bray railway, which was closed in 1959 and will again see service when the new light rail system, the LUAS, is opened around 2002. Amble under the bridge and onto Ranelagh Road, and turn right to walk past a Seventh Day Adventist church. After the bend in the road, cross via the traffic island towards the railings of Mountpleasant Square. Follow the railings to the left and go into the tranquil square itself. The line of terraced houses, mostly two-storey with basements, is neatly punctuated in the centre by a couple of three-storey houses. Some of the elegant lampposts have the words *Rathmines Urban District Council* emblazoned on their doors, a reminder of the days when this part of Dublin had its own autonomous local authority. The private park on your left is used mainly by the Mountpleasant Lawn Tennis Club. Turn left again at the top of the road and go under an open archway onto Mount-pleasant Avenue. Directly ahead and slightly to the right, you will see the green copper dome of Rathmines Church.

A Four-Faced Liar

Walk straight up Richmond Hill (which is actually quite level) until you reach the busy thoroughfare of Rathmines Road, then turn right towards the grey bulk of Rathmines Church. The Latin inscription above the tall Corinthian columns states that the church is under the patronage of Mary Immaculate, Refuge of Sinners. Enter and discover a beautifully proportioned building with classical ornamentation throughout. It was opened in 1854, but suffered a disastrous fire in 1920. Within the space of just five or six months, however, it was largely rebuilt and a new dome was added. This achievement was all the more incredible as it took place at a time of political and civil unrest, during the Anglo-Irish War.

Upon exiting the church, return back up Rathmines Road. Military Road, to the right, is so called because it leads up to a large military barracks established by the British Army in 1810. It was then called Portobello Barracks and was occupied by the cavalry of the Fourth Royal Irish Dragoon Guards. Windham Sadler, the son of England's first balloonist, James Sadler, not to be outdone by Crosbie's earlier ascent from Ranelagh Gardens, followed with his own spectacular elevation from the barracks square before an enthusiastic crowd of 100,000 in 1817. Portobello Barracks became the headquarters of the Free State Army in 1922, the year the Civil War broke

Former Town Hall, Rathmines.

out over the Anglo-Irish Treaty, which had ended the War of Independence against Britain a year earlier. It was from here that pro-treaty General Michael Collins, Commander-in-Chief of the army, departed on the fateful trip in August 1922 which ended in an ambush and his death at Béal na mBláth in County Cork. The barracks was later renamed Cathal Brugha Barracks in honour of one of the anti-Treaty leaders who also died in the war.

The buildings along the Rathmines Road are rather a hotchpotch and have not been enhanced by their modern additions and plastic signage, although there are some worthy exceptions. These include two new hotels and, in particular, the former Town Hall (now a college) and the Public Library directly opposite. The Town Hall, designed by Sir Thomas Drew, was opened for the Rathmines and Rathgar Urban District Council in 1899. The clock tower, a landmark in Rathmines, boasts four clocks that earned the tower the sobriquet 'the four-faced liar', as they used never to keep time with each other. Rathmines Library is believed to have been the first municipal library in Ireland to allow the public direct access to books rather than locking them away in bookcases. It was built in 1913 and was designed by Batchelor and Hicks in the Baroque style. Funding for the building came from the philanthropist Andrew Carnegie who, between 1897 and 1913, financially supported the opening of 80 libraries in Ireland.

You may now continue to wander around if the humour takes you, or rest in one of the hotels or bars. It is only a short bus ride back to the city or, heaven forbid, a 30-minute walk!

DARTing South

Summary: Like its companion journey in this book (DARTing North), this excursion is not a walk as such but a means of getting to one. However, there are so many interesting and scenic sights along the way that it merits its own description. Even commuters, who travel daily on the DART, will hopefully find a great many hidden treasures and nuggets of information that will enhance all their future trips. For visitors, there is no better way of seeing the backyards and the stunning panoramas that make Dublin such a unique city than from the comfort of a DART carriage.

Start:	Pearse DART Station, Westland Row. Buses: 1, 2, 5, 7, 8, 45, 46, 84. Car parking – limited on street. Disk parking for a maximum of three hours. There are multistorey car parks within 10–15 minutes' walk away.
Finish:	DART Station, Dalkey. Bus: 8. Car parking: limited in the centre but there should be plenty along the roads just outside the village.
Length:	12.9 km (8 miles).
Time:	25 minutes.
Refreshments:	Obviously you won't need any on this short journey. There are several good pubs and restaurants in Dalkey.
Pathway Status:	You will be staying in your seat. Incidentally you are not allowed to move between carriages.
Best Time to Visit:	Daylight hours are best if you want to enjoy the views.
Suitable for Bicycles:	Cycles are not allowed on the DART.
Route Notes:	It's best to sit on the left side of the carriage facing the direction of travel.

If you have arrived by road, enter Pearse Station and purchase your ticket to Dalkey, then head for the southbound platform. If you came by DART itself, alight at the station and wait for the next train (for a little background information on the DART system *see* the DARTing North route). While you are waiting, take in the surroundings and the old-world station. The line from Dublin to Dun Laoghaire (then called Kingstown) was first opened in 1834. Its purpose was to link the new steam-packet harbour of Kingstown with the city, and also to serve the small intermediate communities. The line thus became the world's first suburban railroad and was commercially successful from the very beginning. Initially called Westland Row Station, this mid-Victorian terminus (it was originally the end of line before the Loop Line connected it to Connolly Station) was renamed Pearse Station in honour of Pádraig Pearse, one of the leading patriots of the Easter Rising of 1916.

Waterline to the Railway Line

Board the next southbound train and try to sit on the platform side of the carriage, preferably facing in the direction you are going. Upon exiting the station you will notice that the tracks are laid on a raised embankment, punctuated by bridges crossing roads, a canal and a river. The train will pass quickly over the canal and the vast Grand Canal Docks, an 18th-century sheltered harbour complex. This area is undergoing major redevelopment and is now part of a huge dockland renewal programme. The new Barrow Street Station (opened in 2000) is the site of the old Grand Canal Street Railway Works where the rolling stock for the line was built in the early days. At that time, each railway company was an independent organization and usually built its own steam engines, carriages and wagons.

As you approach the next station you will notice that the line has returned to street level. This part of Dublin is predominantly composed of attractive Victorian housing (although only their less attractive backyards can be seen from the train) and many bland 1980s office blocks. Coming up on your left is the Lansdowne Road Rugby Stadium, the world's oldest international rugby ground; the first international was played here on 11 March 1878. The line travels under one of the stands before entering Lansdowne Road Station. Note the cabin at the level crossing. Until the level crossings were fully automated a few years ago, they were controlled from these cabins or signal boxes – a big wheel inside the cabin simultaneously opened or shut the four wooden gates. There were around seven of them, all built in the 1860s.

Just past the Dodder River, on the right, a spur branch line was opened in 1893 to curve into a two-platform siding for the Royal Dublin Society Showgrounds, where livestock and passengers were brought to the great agricultural shows. This branch line was closed only in 1973 when part of the land was sold for redevelopment. The next halt, Sandymount Station, was closed around the turn of the century due to lack of business, and was reopened in 1928 only to close again in 1933. It was recommissioned yet again, and largely rebuilt, for the commencement of the new DART services. The scenery along this stretch is mostly the back gardens of houses, the odd rugby pitch and lots of varied shrubbery. Sydney Parade, the next station, was

Dublin Bay

James Joyce Tower

Dalkey Village Centre

Bathing Shelter

West Pier

Stena Terminal

Salthill & Monkstown

Glenageary

Seapoint

Monkstown Centre

Dun Laoghaire Dart

Sandycove/ Glastule

Dalkey

also closed and reopened with the same frequency as Sandymount. Some remnants of the earlier station have been incorporated into the present structures, including the cast-iron pedestrian bridge.

So far, the line has been inland with no inkling that south of the Liffey River, most of it runs along the coastline; but prepare for a sudden and dramatic view of the open sea on your left. You will see the twin chimneys of Poolbeg Power Station and the Howth Peninsula, a 300 million-year-old landmass, on the other side of Dublin Bay; in the distance ahead, you can see Dun Laoghaire Harbour. If the tide is in, the sea is very close to the line, but if it is out, the waterline seems very remote indeed. It is rare to have such an extensive and relatively unspoilt beach area so close to a capital city. While the sea might look innocent enough today, in the days of sailing ships many came to grief here in the vicious winter storms. In November 1807 two ships, the *Prince of Wales* and the *Rochdale*, were driven ashore in a blizzard and over 385 perished, many of whom are buried in a nearby graveyard.

For the rail line to reach Booterstown Station, a causeway had to be built directly across the strand and this created the marshy inlet on your right. It has become a protected sanctuary for many birds including oystercatchers, lapwing, snipe, teal, linnets, herons and even kingfishers. The laying of the Booterstown Marsh/Sloblands sector of the line is thought to have caused the country's first industrial strike, when the labourers demanded higher wages for working under very difficult conditions in relatively hostile terrain. Booterstown Station has white painted walls, and used to have a canopy over the platform before the station was temporarily closed in the 1950s – a bad era for Irish railways, when many lines were discarded. When the DART was introduced, the original levels of most suburban platforms had to be raised. The old trains had steps (running boards) but DART carriages are flush with the platform for extra safety and speed of entrance and exit. At Booterstown you can spot the two levels, the original in stone and the more recent, raised level in concrete.

No Welcome for Napoleon

From this point on, the sea walls that protect the rail line from the sea are composed of rust brown granite. On the other side of the wall is a walk that will take you all the way to Dun Laoghaire and beyond. On the right is a Martello Tower, one of dozens built along the east coast in the early part of the 19th century to protect the coastline against threatened invasion by Napoleon Bonaparte. However, he never arrived. Some of these very strong but elegant stone towers have been converted into homes. Next in view on the right is Blackrock Park with its fountain and gracious pavilions. Beyond, you will begin to see the large and expensive Victorian and Edwardian sea-facing mansions that will be a feature of the landscape from now on.

Blackrock Station is a mixture of the old and the new. On the left are the whitewashed walls of the former outdoor swimming baths, which once made Blackrock famous as a bathing resort. The decorative railings along the station wall date from the 19th century. This and two of the next three stations (Seapoint and Dun Laoghaire) were designed by John Skipton Mulvaney, who also designed the Egyptian-style Broadstone Station on Dublin's north side. Blackrock is named after a large black rock that used to stand on the seashore, but was removed or dynamited in developments two centuries ago. Blackrock would be a good point to alight on the return journey for an exploration of the largely Victorian town and seafront.

When the railway was being built, not everybody welcomed its arrival with open

Town Hall, Dun Laoghaire.

arms. Two local landowners, Lord Cloncurry and the Reverend Sir Harcourt Lees, refused to let the railway cross their land. Negotiations followed, and they finally consented when they were each given cash settlements and their own private tower footbridge, pathway to the beach, a small private harbour and a bathing pavilion, among other sweeteners. You can still see the classical towers carrying Lord Cloncurry's personal footbridge and his temple-like bathing shelter on the rocky fore-shore. The quaint Seapoint Station building, first opened in 1863, still has its timber beams, stairway and canopy. The stone wall, capped by a balustrade and large port-hole-type windows, shows the hand of architect Skipton Mulvaney. This wall disguises a passageway to former stables belonging to William Osborne, on whose land the station was erected.

From this point on, the line moves slightly in from the sea and passes through Salthill Station, which was opened in 1984 using modern design and materials. This station is the gateway to Monkstown, a once atmospheric little town of grand mansions and lofty terraced houses, but now part of the greater conurbation of Dublin. On the left after Salthill, the rather elegant modern buildings in the grassy setting are in fact sewage pumping stations! The original 1834 railway line ended at this point, as it was the terminus for the old maritime village of Dun Leary (as it was called before being renamed Kingstown, and before it reverted back to the Irish name of Dun Laoghaire). This was also the site of the dún or castle of the 5th-century King of Tara, King Laoghaire – the Bord Lascaigh Mhara (the Fisheries Board) headquarters on the right is thought to be the exact site. On the left is the coal harbour, dating from 1767, which is now populated by flotillas of yachts; there are four long-established yacht clubs at Dun Laoghaire. Because of walls along the line, however, your view of the ferry terminals and the harbour itself will soon be restricted.

A Railway Run on Air

When Dun Laoghaire Harbour was built in the 1820s it was the largest man-made harbour in the world. For over a century, it was the main crossing point from Ireland to Holyhead in Wales. The new Stena Line terminal is on the left and some of the fastest large ferries in the world operate from here. Dun Laoghaire is now a vibrant town in its own right with parks, sea walks, hotels, restaurants, museums and shopping centres. A stopover here is a must. You can promenade along the West Pier, which is around 1.6 kilometres (1 mile) long; or on the East Pier, where you can walk outwards on the top level and return on the lower level.

Until the 1950s there was only one platform at Dun Laoghaire. A loop line allowed trains to use this platform whichever direction they were coming from. The many passengers for the ships, including hundreds and thousands of emigrants, did not get off at the station but at the wharf alongside the ships. This was served by a side or spur line, the passage for which is still visible to the left after the station. The station was modernized in the late 1990s, although the old architecture was allowed to merge with the new state-of-the-art facilities.

This section of the track, from here to Dalkey, was laid in 1844 as the once world-famous Atmospheric Railway. The outward uphill journey was propelled by suction, the return by simple gravity (although a strong wind might prevent the train from actually reaching the station itself!) The line was abandoned after 10 years, partly due to rats eating the tallow that sealed the leather covering the valve openings on the suction pipe. The pumping station was located at Dalkey, the end of the line. From Dun Laoghaire until you reach Glastule the line is lower than the road and the cutting is lined on both sides by stone walls. After the next short tunnel the track is laid on concrete slabs. There are several antique bridges along this section that did not offer enough clearance for the electric power cables, so rather than raise or demolish the bridges the line was lowered and the tracks set into a bed of concrete. While all this work was going on, one line always stayed open, and the service never closed, not even for one day.

The next station, Sandycove and Glastule, was originally built on a hill above the line and was a rather crude structure of corrugated iron and wood. This is the stopover point if you want to visit the James Joyce Museum in the Martello Tower in Sandycove. From here, shrubbery takes over from stone walls on either side of the line. The speed of the train is somewhat slower along this stretch due to gradations and curves. The pedestrian walk above and on the right is called the 'metals', a reminder that it was once the rail line used to bring the quarried granite from Dalkey Hill down to Dun Laoghaire when the harbour was being built in the early 1800s. Note the Irish place names on the station signboards. Usually the English form is a direct Anglicization of the original Irish – for instance, Glenageary in Irish is Gleann na gCaorach or 'the glen of the sheep'. Glenageary Station was built by the Dublin and Wicklow Railway Company (D & WR) – unlike the line from Dublin to Dun Laoghaire – and is a fine example of the company's granite and brick architecture. The platform height here did not have to be altered. Still on the route of the old Atmospheric Railway, you are now climbing up towards Dalkey, the destination of this tour. Dalkey Station's waiting room is typical of the Dublin & South East Railway Company (DSER), the successor to the D & WR. The standard features are a semi-elliptical roof, a straight series of windows at a fixed height and latticed beams inside.

The section of the line from here to Bray was built by the D & WR and the same company, for reasons best known to itself, also built a competing second line from Dublin's Harcourt Street Station to Bray, taking an inland route. This second line joined the coastal track further along at Shanganagh Junction. The Harcourt Street Line, as it came to be known, closed down on 1 January 1959. With increased suburbanization and traffic congestion the closure turned out to be a big mistake, but a large part of the line is now being reused for LUAS, the new light rail transit system.

Dalkey Station is the ideal point to jump off and tour the old town itself. The indigenous population has, in recent years, been swollen by hundreds of new residents, many of whom are famous in the literary, sporting, commercial and entertainment worlds. Exotic and expensive period mansions line the coast and the hills between Dalkey and Killiney. There are several pubs, restaurants and small hotels to cater for your needs before you undertake the return journey by DART to Dublin.

Lanes Beside the Tracks

Summary: This is the shortest walk in the book (it could easily be fitted around other walks based in the area) but it will take you down streets and lanes usually frequented only by locals, and there is an interesting little surprise or two along the way. If you have time, you can also visit the National Print Museum and the Irish Labour Museum, two museums not generally on the tourist trail, but nonetheless intriguing.

Start:	Barrow Street DART station. Buses: 1, 3. Car parking: there is plenty of on-street parking at meters (maximum 3 hours).
Finish:	Sandymount DART Station (you have the option of finishing in Sandymount village (*see* Dry Greens to Wet Sands). Buses: 7, 7A, 8, 45. Car parking: there is some along residential streets, but it can be in short supply. There are meters in Sandymount village.
Length:	2 km (1¼ miles).
Time:	1 hour.
Refreshments:	Take something with you if you wish, but the walk is short enough for you to wait until you return to the city or enter Sandymount village. Along the route there is only the occasional shop or pub (apart from two luxury hotels – *see* below).
Pathway Status:	Footpaths throughout.
Best Time to Visit:	Anytime, but check the opening hours of the museums if you want to visit them.
Suitable for Bicycles:	Yes.
Connecting Walks:	From DARTing South (just walk the bit between Barrow Street Station and Sandymount Station) and on to Dry Greens to Wet Sands.

Barrow Street DART Station, on the site of the old railway works owned by the Dublin and Kingstown Railway (*see* DARTing South), was opened for the first time in 2000. The building of the station was justified by the growth of new businesses and residences in the area – see for example, the attractive blocks of new apartments overlooking the tracks on the south side. Turn left, cross the road, and walk down Barrow Street. This was laid down in about 1795 and is named after the River Barrow, which is directly navigable from the nearby Grand Canal. Barrow Street is wide but usually not too busy. The wall running down the right-hand side (if it is still there) closes off the yards where the city gas was once manufactured. The site is due for major redevelopment but the ground has to be cleared first, as it is badly contaminated from the manufacture of town gas. Two high flour mills rise above the rooftops on your left, another legacy of the area's former industrialization. It is also quite possible that, by the time you read this, at least one of the mills will have disappeared to make way for more new offices and apartments. The mills and the apartments facing you at the end of Barrow Street overlook the huge docks of the Grand Canal (*see* 'Pearse Street to the Great South Wall'). This part of Dublin is presently going through massive change. Barely five years ago only a few thousand people lived here. By 2005 several tens of thousands of new residents will be accommodated in the vast new developments now underway.

Turn right at the next junction into Gordon Street, a road lined with closely-packed cottages and terraced houses. This whole area was reclaimed from the sea, work that began in the early 18th century but was mainly completed a century later. To give you a feel for life in this well-kept little enclave, the route now weaves in and out of the tidy little streets. The houses are relatively small and many owners have converted their attics to create extra space. Carry on down the left-hand side, passing Gerald Street and Howard Street. Ahead, to the right, the existing elaborate external ironwork of a demolished gas tank is clearly visible over the roofs of the houses. You will see this decorative object close up a little later on. Turn left into Hope Street and take a few minutes to soak up the atmosphere of this close-knit community. From here, take the next right into South Dock Street, turn right into Joy Street, left along Doris Street, and right into Ormeau Street. Back at Gordon Street, turn left before emerging onto South Lotts Road. Turn right. This road is so named because when the land was reclaimed, Dublin Corporation divided it into lots, or lotts as they were termed in the 17th century, to sell as building plots. At this point you are very close to the lofty iron columns and connecting tracery of the former expanding gas storage tank. This elegant giant is on the preservation list and will form the central feature of some future imaginative apartment block. Depending on when you read this, you may even be looking at the finished article.

Silent Cannons

Walk the full length of the road, passing under the railway bridge, right up to the junction with Shelbourne Road. Cross over to the far side, to Haddington Road, originally called Cottage Terrace but later renamed in honour of the Earl of Haddington, Lord Lieutenant 1834–1835. Walk along the footpath, which is separated from the grass verge by chained bollards. These are no ordinary bollards but the full complement of cannons from a Royal Navy frigate. They date back to 1760. Go through the gate of the walled compound into the grounds of the former Beggars' Bush Barracks. The British military opened these barracks in 1827 as a recruiting depot, and also as a base for a Royal Artillery regiment. During the Anglo-Irish War of 1919–1921 a large number of troops and paramilitary police, including the infamous auxiliaries, were stationed here. Several executions were carried out within the walls. It was the first Dublin barracks to be taken over from the British by the Irish

National Army after the signing of the Treaty in 1921. Erskine Childers, writer (he was author of *Riddle of the Sands*, a pre-First World War spy story) and patriot (*see* page 67) was executed by pro-Treaty forces in Beggars' Bush in 1922. His son of the same name became a popular President of Ireland in 1973, but he sadly died in office only a year later. The barracks are no longer a military establishment, and the barrack houses have mostly been tastefully converted into apartments. The Garrison Church is now the excellent National Print Museum, which has an amazing collection of old printing machines, still in full working condition, along with other artefacts from this ancient craft. The central building opposite the entrance to the barracks now houses the Irish Labour Historical Society's Museum and Archives. The large red brick building, so out of scale and place in the otherwise historic and atmospheric barracks, is home to the Department of Public Enterprise and the Labour Court.

Return to Shelbourne Road and meander along the outer wall of Beggars' Bush, noting the slits or rifle loopholes along its length. Towards the end, there is an inclined private road leading back into the barracks. Go up here and stand just inside the gates to take a look. In 1997, the old army quarters were restored and converted into senior citizens' flats by Dublin Corporation, and they are now in pristine condition. As you carry on up Shelbourne Road, the houses become larger and grander. You are now at the periphery of the swanky suburb of Ballsbridge. Several of these large houses have been turned into guesthouses, a tradition in this part of Dublin that has led to the building of many hotels. Two of these, the luxurious Berkeley Court and the Towers, are situated on Lansdowne Road near its junction with Shelbourne Road. These hotels stand on the site of the former Trinity College Botanic Gardens and some trees from that period are still growing in the grounds. When you reach the Lansdowne Road junction, turn left and head for the railway crossing. On the left are the world-famous Lansdowne Road rugby grounds, which are also home to the Wanderer's

Football Club. The stadium is not a hi-tech, modern construction but a stalwart from the mid-1890s with some later additions. In fact, the grounds at Lansdowne Road saw their first international rugby match in 1876. The road itself is named after the 4th Marquis of Lansdowne (a place in Somerset, England) who died in 1866. It was laid down in around 1855. Incidentally, Shelbourne Road was named after the Earl of Shelbourne, one of the titles of the Marquis of Lansdowne.

Thundering DARTs

Walk over the level crossing to the far side of Lansdowne Road DART Station, noting the old signal cabin on the way, and cut into the narrow lane that runs directly alongside the southbound platform. Walk along with stone walls on either side until you arrive at a metal pedestrian bridge over the River Dodder. Around here there was once a distillery on the banks of the river, one of many then operating in Dublin, but it was demolished in the mid-19th century and its rubble was used for the foundations of two new roads, Herbert Road and Newbridge Avenue. The River Dodder rises in the Wicklow Mountains only a short distance from the source of the River Liffey. Unlike the Liffey, which meanders for 125 kilometres (75 miles) before reaching the sea, the Dodder plunges straight down to meet the Liffey at Ringsend. Until properly managed in more recent years, the normally tranquil river was often transformed into a destructive raging torrent after downpours of rain or when snow

Railway Cottages off Lansdowne Road.

melted in the mountains. When you cross the bridge you can wander along the river for a while to enjoy the local scenery. You can choose between the right- or left-hand paths, but whichever you take you must return to this spot and continue through a gateway in the wall into Railway Cottages, the next lane. Here you will pass by twelve charming cottages built for railway workers and which gave their name to the lane. At the time of writing, planning permission was being sought to build more houses on their extensive gardens. This is a recurring sight around the city as it responds to the pressure to provide homes for a burgeoning population. You are now only a few strides away from the railway line, which will stay alongside you until the end of the walk. When you come out onto Serpentine Avenue, look to the right and you will see part of the headquarters of Allied Irish Banks, Ireland's largest bank group. Cross over into Oaklands Park, a quiet suburban street of Victorian houses. As you are now away from the bustle of traffic, you may well hear the twittering of bird song or sounds of people gardening.

Continue on through a barrier into another lane. You are now very close to the railway line (it is fenced off for safety) and it is worth waiting here until a DART train comes thundering by. The first warning of a train's approach is the eerie whistling from the overhead power lines. Even more dramatic is the rush and clatter at close (but safe) quarters from a speeding intercity express train. The lane comes out onto Holyrood Park. At the corner with Sandymount Avenue you reach Sandymount DART Station, your destination. You can return to the city by DART or walk to Sandymount village for refreshment (*see* 'Dry Greens to Wet Sands' for directions).

Dry Greens to Wet Sands

Summary: Sandymount Village still exudes a late Victorian atmosphere, which is enhanced by its tiny village green, the occasional antique shop front and streets of Victorian houses. Some of the scenes in James Joyce's *Ulysses* are taken from around Sandymount and its hinterland. As its name might suggest, it is located near the open sea and much of this walk is along the shores of Dublin Bay. The walk ends at Booterstown Marsh, a wildlife reserve especially important for its wading birds and rare plants.

Start:	Sandymount Village. Bus: 3. DART: Sandymount Station. Car parking: metered parking around the green; otherwise look for spaces elsewhere.
Finish:	Olde Punch Bowl, Booterstown. Buses: 7, 7A, 8, 45. DART: Booterstown Station. Car parking: use the Park and Ride car park beside the station. There is usually a charge if you are not using the DART. Otherwise, try to find on-street parking, but watch for clearways (zones of no parking during rush hours).
Length:	3.7 km (2¼ miles)
Time:	1¼ hours.
Refreshments:	Try one of the pubs in Sandymount Village or the Doyle Tara Hotel near the finish; or wait until you reach your final destination, the Olde Punch Bowl pub.
Pathway Status:	Public footpaths or tarmac promenades form the main part of the walk. There is also an optional beach walk.
Best Time to Visit:	Any time of the year during daytime.
Suitable for Bicycles:	Yes, but there are no bicycle lanes.

If you have arrived by DART, walk up Sandymount Avenue, past the Cerebral Palsy Ireland Centre, and take the left turn into Gilford Road. This will bring you straight into Sandymount Village, the jumping-off point for anyone arriving by bus. The Green, a little triangular park, is precious to the villagers and is the general rendezvous point, where friends meet and chat. Its shape also has the effect of drawing the flanking streets into an intimate relationship with each other and with the Green itself. Cross over the road and onto the Green. Ahead of you is a pharmacy, which still has an exquisite and relatively unaltered Victorian shop front. Nearly two centuries ago, Sandymount was a tiny isolated village of thatched houses crowded around the Green. Then the nobility and gentry, who had recently discovered that swimming in the sea was good for one's health, came to try the waters off Sandymount Beach. Business boomed and guesthouses multiplied. To keep the rabble out, the residents charged bathers two pence for beach facilities, double the rate of neighbouring Irishtown. Sandymount became posh. When, from 1840, the horse-drawn omnibus clattered out to Sandymount, the influx of desirable visitors grew and so did Sandymount. Served by railway and tram, it became a much sought-after suburb of Dublin.

In the Footprints of *Ulysses*

Head down Newgrove Avenue, a street of 19th- and 20th-century houses, which dramatically opens out to reveal a panoramic view of Dublin Bay. With the aid of the traffic roundabout, cross over to the beach side and turn right to walk along either the sand or the pathway. You are in good company – Stephen Dedalus, in James Joyce's *Ulysses*, took the morning air on Sandymount Strand to muse about his life and allow his mind to wander. His view was not much different from yours almost a century later. What is different are the tall chimneys of Poolbeg Power Station, the reclaimed land around it and the large cargo ships queuing to be piloted into Dublin Port. Like Stephen Dedalus, you can let your mind wander as you take the sea air and head to where the railway line meets the sea, a little over a mile away. You will pass a Martello tower, a Victorian baths (now derelict), along a choice of beach, promenade or footpath. Near the end of Strand Road, you will need to take the footpath to follow this itinerary.

When you reach the railway, you will find a level crossing called the Merrion Gates; until recently, the crossing had wooden gates that were opened manually. The railway line runs between Dublin and Dun Laoghaire and other points further south. Before you cross the tracks, you may wish to take a small detour to the left through the opening on the strand. Ahead, stretching into the distance, is the raised embankment of the railway line, which was built in 1834 (*see* DARTing South).

Carefully cross the busy Merrion Road with the aid of the traffic lights and the centre island (there are no pedestrian lights as such here). Once on the footpath opposite turn left, passing an archway with 'St Mary's Home for Female Blind' carved into it. This institution is now more appropriately named St Mary's Centre for the Visually Impaired, and the modern complex shares its ground with the Caritas Convalescent Centre. On your left you will pass the old red brick house built for the level crossing gatekeeper. Where the railings of the convalescent centre ends, an old relic still in everyday use is set into the wall – a wall-mounted post box dating back to the reign of Queen Victoria, with her insignia VR (Victoria Regina) emblazoned on it. Note the tall lamp standards along the road. These were erected in pairs facing each other instead of being spaced alternately, as is usually the case. This is because they were not originally lampposts at all, but poles holding up the electric wires for the former tramline.

Pass the Doyle Tara Hotel (unless you feel like pausing here for refreshments) and turn right immediately after it onto a side road. A very short distance up, enter a small cemetery that is located directly behind a petrol garage. This little graveyard has been largely forgotten, but still has its own dignity. Burials date from the 14th century. Some of the tombstones have quite poignant inscriptions. A tiny marker on the grave just inside the gate tells us that Mary Rennik, who died in 1799, was aged a mere 14 years. Disease, poverty and poor medical knowledge resulted in high mortality among children and young adults in Ireland's not-too-distant past. Another gravestone emphasises this sad fact: its inscription reads, 'This stone was erected by Charles Dunn of Bride Street in memory of his beloved wife Catherine Dunn who departed this life 3 July 1816 aged 35 years. Also three of his children who died young. *Requisescat in pace*,' (rest in peace). The cemetery is mainly renowned as the final resting-place for the many who perished in the shipwrecks of the troopships *The Prince of Wales* and *The Rochdale* during the vicious storms of November 1807.

Birds of a Feather

When you have completed your tour of the cemetery, leave the grassy compound (don't forget to close the gate), and return to the main road. Cross Trimlestown Avenue, go past the lovely cut stone walls of Trimlestown Lodge and onto Rock Road. On your left side the Booterstown marsh and bird sanctuary comes into view, which you will visit later. A sign will now remind you that you are leaving the jurisdiction of Dublin Corporation and entering the Borough of Dun Laoghaire and Rathdown, one of Dublin's three County Councils. On the wall of a house called Rosmore is a later version of a wall-mounted post box, this time dedicated to King Edward Vll. Another house, Glena, complete with turret on the left gable, was once the home of Count John McCormack (1884–1945), Ireland's greatest tenor and a legend in his own lifetime.

After Booterstown Parish Club building and Grotto Avenue you will approach a set of traffic lights. Cross back here to the seaward footpath and proceed through the car park towards the DART station and Booterstown Marsh. At the station end of the car park have a look through a break in the trees towards the marsh itself and view the shallows for signs of bird life. Booterstown Nature Reserve, to give the 4-hectare (10-acre) salt marsh its official name, is an extraordinary wetland and bird sanctuary that is managed by An Taisce, the National Trust for Ireland. Originally an open inlet from the sea, it was cut off by the building of the railway. During the

'Glena', Booterstown.

135

Second World War the marsh was drained and turned into allotments for growing vegetables, but this activity stopped after the war. The marsh did not dry out completely, however, as it was fed by an incoming stream. Today, a system of sluice gates allows the tides to fill and flush out the reserve, although there is a current concern that this may not be sufficient to sustain a healthy and balanced marsh without the intervention of a supportive management plan. A rare plant, *Puccinellia fasciculata*, a salt-marsh grass, is abundant here. The birds that you might see include a colony of herons as well as redshank, snipe, pied wagtail, teal, mallard, kingfisher, curlew, moorhen and black-headed gull.

On the opposite side of the car park is the inlet from the sea, which feeds into the marsh via the controllable sluice gate. To the right of the station is a footbridge, which you can climb to reach the beach on the other side. From here you can enjoy an unrestricted view for miles. If you are still feeling energetic, you can launch out on another embracing walk in any direction you wish. At this point, decide if you want to take the DART or the bus back to your destination. You can always regain some lost energy in the nearby and welcoming Olde Punch Bowl.

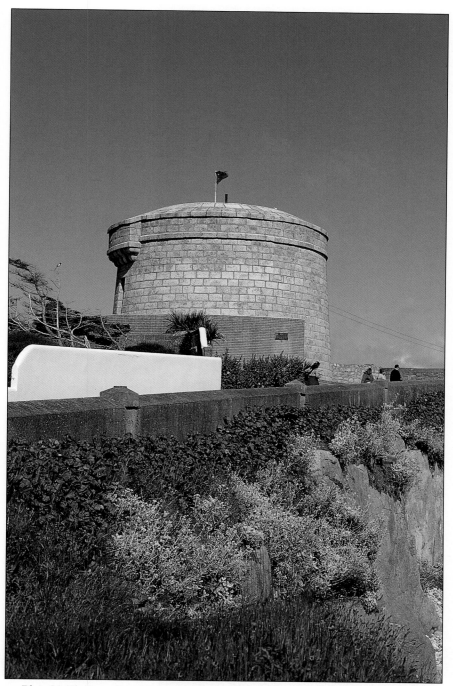

Plate 24: *The James Joyce Museum at Sandycove is housed in the Martello Tower where Joyce himself once lived and which featured in the opening chapter of* Ulysses *(see page 126).*

Plate 25: *Decorative cast-iron frame, which used to enclose an immense expanding tank of town gas, awaits integration into a new building development on Barrow Street (see page 128).*

Plate 26: *Booterstown Marsh, created 160 years ago by the building of a railway embankment, is now an important bird reserve (see page 135).*

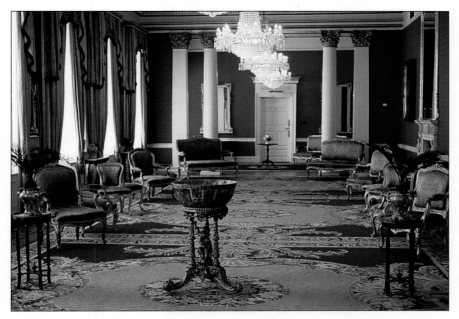

Plate 27: *The Blue Room (or Drawing Room), Dublin Castle (above; see page 155). This room forms part of the exquisite 18th-century State Apartments built to house the Lord Lieutenant (Governor of the British Government in Ireland) and to provide entertainment such as the Grand Balls of the so-called Castle Season.*

Plate 28: *Three- and four-hundred year old bodies, mummified in the preservative atmosphere, are on view in the crypt of St Michan's Church on Church Street (see page 147).*

Plate 29: *From around the 8th to the 10th century, Irish monks produced intricately illustrated manuscripts, several of which have survived to this day and are now considered to be priceless world treasures (see page 155).*

Pearse Street to the Great South Wall

Summary: This is truly a walk of contrasts, starting in the middle of busy city streets with the noise of traffic thundering all around, and finishing on a very narrow finger of land with the sea crashing in on three sides. The journey will take you through booming new apartment areas, traditional residential districts, vast dockland zones and a power-generating complex. All this will gradually yield to wild scenery and a sea wall, which, when it was built, was the longest in the world. And the wonder of it all is that few people seem to know about walking the Great South Wall – so when you have completed it, keep it a secret!

Start: Holiday Inn Hotel, Pearse Street. DART: Pearse Station. Bus: 3. Car parking: some on-street metered parking available.

Finish: First option – Poolbeg extension. Bus: 1. Unless things have improved since writing, there are only one or two services a day and none on a Sunday, so you really need access to a car.

Second option – Walk to Irishtown Road and pick up Bus 3 to the city centre, or take a DART from Lansdowne Road Station.

Third option – follow the outward route by car as far as, say, the Ringsend waste water treatment plant, and walk the round-trip from there.

Length: First option – 10 km (6¼ miles); second option – 12.5 km (7¾ miles); third option – 6.4 km (4 miles).

Time: 2½ hours (first option), 3 hours (second option), 1½ hours (third option).

Refreshments: There are some options at the beginning, but then nothing along the way, so you need to bring your own food and drink.

Pathway Status: Street pavements and roadside footpaths until you reach the granite blocks of the Great South Wall.

Suitable for Bicycles: Ideal except for the Great South Wall itself, which is slightly dangerous for cycling as it is narrow, with pedestrians walking along it.

Best time to Visit: Daytime during any moderate weather, but do not walk along the Great South Wall if it is very windy or when waves are breaking over it.

Connecting Walk: None convenient.

Route Notes: During the writing of this book the Great South Wall was closed to the public for improvement works. It is due for reopening by the end of 2000, and should then offer a better surface.

Pearse Street is named after Padraig Pearse, principal leader of the 1916 Rising, who was born in No. 27 when it was still known as Great Brunswick Street. When the Holiday Inn group opened its first Dublin hotel on this street in 1998, some thought it had made an unwise choice of location. Pearse Street and the whole surrounding area were very down-at-heel and psychologically, the hotel seemed too far away from the city centre. In fact, it is only 800 metres (½ mile) from Trinity College, and in the following years the perception of the location radically improved. Far-reaching developments have and are about to be launched; modern offices and apartment blocks are burgeoning in the streets radiating away from Pearse Street. The adjacent Grand Canal Docks, themselves undergoing rehabilitation, are proving to be a catalyst in the rejuvenation of the area.

Safe Havens

Turn left outside the hotel, and head towards the Ringsend Road passing, on your left, Pearse Square Park. One of the other catalysts in the regeneration of Pearse Street must be Pearse Square Park. Formerly known as Queen's Square, it dates from 1839 but by the mid 1990s it was in a poor condition. Dublin Corporation and the residents of the charming terraced houses surrounding the park got together in 1996 and agreed to restore it to its original formal layout. Some new features were installed including the bronze sculpture *Harmony* by Sandra Bell. Continue straight on, crossing the metal MacMahon Bridge built in 1857 to replace a wooden structure of 1791 called the Draw Bridge. The present bridge can be opened to allow high-masted vessels to enter the southern half of the Grand Canal Docks. From the bridge, there is a good view of both sides of the docks, including, on the right, the excellent Waterways Visitor Centre. Turn left after the bridge and onto the dockside wharf, walking past some marina jetties. When you come to Charlotte Quay you can browse around looking at the odd assortment of boats moored there, from small yachts to aged island ferries. Charlotte Quay was named after Queen Charlotte, wife of George III, and is opposite Hanover Quay, named after the English royal dynasty. The docks were built between 1791 and 1796, and the two main basins, containing 10 hectares (25 acres) of water 4.8 metres (16 feet) deep, could accommodate 600 ships. Even though they were built to provide what Dublin Port always lacked up until then, deep-water anchorages, the docks failed to reach their potential; there were never more than a few dozen ships berthed here at the same time. It seems that the inconvenience of negotiating the complex entrance locks was too much of a bother for captains who preferred to work their schedules around the tidal changes. As a commercial enterprise the docks failed, and they became quite desolate. Now their true value to urban regeneration has been recognized and exciting times lie ahead. By the time you read this, it may be possible to walk the whole length of Charlotte Quay and come out at the other end of Ringsend Road. If not, you may have to return the way you came in.

At the junction with the South Lotts Road you will be able to see, on the right, Shelbourne Greyhound Racing Stadium. Another bridge, in this very watery part of Dublin, will carry you over the River Dodder and into the suburb of Ringsend. Ringsend Bridge was built in 1803 and was specially designed to hold firm against the periodic onslaughts unleashed by a river that, until controlled by engineering works, used to surge down in torrents from the Wicklow Mountains when swollen by rains or melting snows. St Patrick's, the parish church of Ringsend, lies on the far side of the bridge and was built in 1912. There has been a settlement at Ringsend from Celtic times, and for the next 1,000 years a fishing community thrived here, selling their catches of herring, oysters, cockles and mussels in the markets of Dublin. The name probably comes from the Irish word, *Rinn*, which means a point or spit of land, referring to the finger of gravel built up along the Dodder estuary.

Turn left into Thorncastle Street and right onto York Road. It was at approximately the meeting of these two roads that a small harbour was built in the latter half of the 16th century. Its purpose was to replace Dalkey, which was excessively far away, as a deep-water port for Dublin. It was to Ringsend that Oliver Cromwell came in 1649, followed by a 4,000-strong cavalry force and 8,000 infantry. His thorough and ruthless conquest of Ireland was achieved in the remarkably short time of nine months.

From this vantage point there is an excellent view of Dublin Port and all the shipping. Directly ahead is the North Quay extension, built in 1871, with its roll-on, roll-off cargo facilities. Behind it is Alexandra Basin, named after the Princess of Wales who opened the dock in 1885 in the company of her husband, the future Edward VII. Over the 20th century, land reclamation continued to extend the port eastwards; the Port authorities are currently seeking a further extension, which is being vigorously opposed by the residents of Clontarf on the northern shoreline. For a closer look at the waterside, it is possible to pass through an opening in the perimeter wall and onto the road that leads to the East Link Bridge, but it would be unwise to cross the busy road at this point. Continue along York Road, which soon becomes Pigeon House Road. Before subsequent reclamation, this road was the starting point of the Great South Wall, but more about that later. The toll road running parallel to your left was built to service the East Link Bridge, which was opened in 1984. As part of the deal the development company had to install double glazing free of charge in all the charming cottages lining Pigeon House Road. At the pedestrian lights leave this section of Pigeon House Road to cross the toll road and climb down the steps to the continuation of Pigeon House Road. Two boat clubs, Stella Maris and Poolbeg, soon give way to the first of several container depots.

The Power of Cannons and Megawatts

On the far side of the roundabout, over to the right, you can see Dublin Corporation's main lift pumping station, a facility that pumps the city's waste water to the treatment works further downriver. Turn left into South Bank Road, flanked on one side by another container yard and on the other by a large factory, owned by the Irish Glass Bottle Company. Take the next left, then the next right, to return once more to the interrupted Pigeon House Road. On the side facing the river is the entrance to Dublin Port's only ferry terminal on the south bank of the River Liffey. On the right is an older-generation power station, now being fitted with new gas turbines with a 400-megawatt output.

The last portion of the walk has been through a fairly dilapidated area, and two waste metal yards do little to enhance matters. The low wall running along the left side of the road was once the sea wall. In fact, until the middle of the 20th century, the sea lapped right up to both sides of the road from a point east of where you crossed the first section of Pigeon House Road. You have now reached the huge new Ringsend waste water treatment plant, part of Dublin Corporation's massive Dublin Bay Project. With a capital expenditure of over £200 million, this project (which includes an undersea pipeline to bring waste water from the north bay area) will dramatically improve the water quality in the whole of Dublin Bay.

Over the low wall on the left is the old Pigeonhouse Harbour, opened in 1793 as a cross-channel passenger port. In the last century it was taken over to be used as settling tanks for waste water treatment until it was replaced by the new plant. Following the rebellion of 1798, the government requisitioned the harbour and turned it into a military strongpoint. Its purpose was twofold: it could receive reinforcements from Britain or provide a last ditch defence and escape route if the English were to lose control of the country. The military stayed until 1897, and little remains of the fort today except part of the West Gateway (opposite the second entrance to the treatment plant) and the adjoining perimeter wall with its gun loopholes. The gateway was protected by two drawbridges. The soldiers' handball court stands on the other side of the road.

Straight ahead is a group of buildings of very different vintages. Still looking as new as the day it was built is the granite-faced Pigeonhouse Hotel, erected 1793–95 and designed by Robert Poole. It was used to accommodate passengers before and after the ordeal of the sea crossing. When the military took over, it became the officers' quarters. The name Pigeonhouse is derived from John Pidgeon, who from 1761 was caretaker of the storehouse on the South Wall. He was allowed to supplement his meagre income by supplying food and drink to weary sea travellers, and his house became known as Pidgeon's House, later shortened to Pigeon House. In 1902 the Dublin Corporation Lighting Committee laid the foundation stone of the Pigeonhouse Electricity Station, the empty red brick building standing to the left of the old hotel. The station ceased operation in the mid-1970s. By then, since 1969 in fact, the replacement Poolbeg Station was up and running. This is the large complex forming the backdrop to the other two buildings. This plant can produce almost 1,000 megawatts of electricity. The twin stacks, the tallest structures in Dublin, are each 207 metres (680 feet) high and it takes maintenance men about an hour to climb to the top. At the entrance to the gates of Poolbeg Station are three mounted cannons that were placed here in 1992. They are part of the armament of Pigeonhouse Fort and are long-barrel 12-pounders, made between 1770 and 1776. At the rear of each gun is the gun weight mark, 34-0-1, being 34 hundredweights, 0 quarters and 1 pound (1.7 tonnes). Further up are two arrow markers known as Blomfield Proof Markers. Blomfield designed a test for cannons that involved firing double the normal charge of gunpowder. If the cannon survived the shock it was proof of its integrity. The guns could fire a 12-pound (5.4 kilogram) cannon ball a distance of up to 1,829 metres (2,000 yards). On top of the barrels is the coat of arms of King George III. Walk around the perimeter of the station, which will bring you past Irishtown Nature Park, a habitat and nature conservation park, and a beach that was formed after the closing of a landfill site used for

Poolbeg Lighthouse.

domestic refuse in the 1970s. It is estimated that 750,000 tons of sand were dredged from Dublin Harbour (a good thing anyway) to fill the 36.4 hectare (90 acre) site at Poolbeg.

The Great South Wall

This is the time for brisk walking, both to get to your destination, the Great South Wall, and to breathe in the bracing sea air. When you arrive at the Liffey again, you are almost in the very mouth of Dublin Harbour. You now proceed along the Great South Wall, which once stretched from the mouth of the River Dodder to the lighthouse you can see in the distance. While the history of its construction is interesting, perhaps you should not read about it while walking along the parapet lest you plunge into the water. The Ballast Office (the then Port Authority) decided in 1715 to drive piles (a line of heavy stakes) into the south side of the shipping channel to afford shelter for ships lying in the harbour, and to prevent sand from the South Bull Sand Bank from encroaching into the channel. Work began in 1716 with the laying of timber piles. This proved not to be a long-lasting proposition and in 1759 the directors of the Ballast Office decided to build a stone wall. This consisted of two parallel walls of granite filled in between with sand and stone rubble, then topped again with granite. The blocks, each weighing around 1 tonne, were ingeniously interlocked so that no form of bonding material was necessary. Work was not completed until 1792. Much of the granite came from quarries on the south Dublin hills, including Dalkey. Three harbours near Dalkey were built to ship stone over in barges – Coliemore, Bullock and Sandycove. When completed, the 5-kilometre (3-mile) long wall was one of the longest sea walls in the world. It had been hoped that the retreating tides, pressed in by the wall, would scour a deeper channel, but this did not happen until the North Bull Wall was completed in 1824.

A short distance before the wall turns slightly inwards is the intriguingly-titled 'Half Moon' swimming club. This refers to the gun battery emplacement built in 1793 in the shape of a half circle. At the end of the wall is Poolbeg Lighthouse. In 1761 it was decided to build a lighthouse to coincide with the construction of the stone wall. It was commissioned in 1768 and was one of the first to use candles as its light source. Various modifications were made to the lighthouse itself and its lighting mechanisms over the years. The rocks protecting its foundations were often carried away by winter storms until large blocks of mass concrete in cast-iron bindings were added in the mid-19th century. Since 1968, Poolbeg Lighthouse has been automated and unattended.

No doubt you are a little tired after this longish walk and now you must return. Facing again toward the port, you might like to reflect on the people who built this wall and on the hardships they had to endure, often in the foulest weather. Thanks to them, countless thousands of mariners and their passengers have enjoyed greater safety when negotiating the treacherous sandbars and contrary winds at the entrance to Dublin Port.

Dublin Underground

Summary: Dublin is essentially not an underground city. The many revolutions in the city were never serviced by runners using the sewers, as were those in Paris or Warsaw. Few houses even possess a cellar, although those built in the Georgian period had basements to contain the kitchen, pantry, wine cellar and the coal supply. The city has no metro or underground railway, but there is talk of one being constructed sometime in the mid 2000s. There are, of course, sewers – some very large indeed – and culverted rivers criss-crossing the city underneath your feet. Subterranean places such as these are usually closed to the public, but you will stand over them and let your imagination and some facts transport you into their depths; and there are still many opportunities for going 'down under' for the intrepid underground walker.

Start:	Gresham Hotel, O'Connell Street. DART: Connolly Station. Buses: most city centre buses are within a few minutes' walk. Car parking: use the Gresham Hotel multistorey car park, or any one of several others in the neighbourhood.
Finish:	The Cellar Bar, Merrion Street. DART: Pearse Station. Buses: 10, 11, 13. Car parking: adequate on-street metered spaces.
Length:	6.8 km (4¼ miles). You can rearrange the route and shorten it to suit yourself, if you wish.
Time:	2 hours.
Refreshments:	There is no shortage of refreshment points along the route.
Pathway Status:	Wear comfortable and flat shoes for easy walking on steps and stairs.
Best Time to Visit:	Only during the opening hours of the selected sites.
Suitable for Bicycles:	Only if the bicycle has a good lock, because you won't be able to take it into any of the underground venues.
Route Notes:	All the underground sites are dry and clean.
Connecting Walk:	Talbot Street to the North Docklands or A Basin at Blessington.

Upon leaving the Gresham Hotel, turn left and take a look at the Eircom building standing at the corner with Cathal Brugha Street. These premises replaced the once-famous Alex Findlater & Company, Grocery, Wine and Spirit Merchants.

Findlater's was established in 1823 and opened in O'Connell Street (then called Sackville Street) 12 years later. At this time, O'Connell Street was lined on both sides with Georgian mansions – the only survivor today is No. 43, directly across the road and now part of the Royal Dublin Hotel. All these mansions had extensive cellars, but when Findlater's started business they excavated a huge extension to their cellars that reached right under the street itself. So huge were their cellars, or so the local lore would have us believe, that they could store more hogsheads of wine than could be loaded on four Atlantic liners. Parts of these cellars still exist. If you look towards the top of the street at the Parnell Monument, you will see four cast-iron bollards on the traffic island in front of it. On close inspection you will see that they are punctured with holes – the air holes for the cellars below. These vaults had to be built with great skill, not only to withstand the trundling traffic overhead but also to stop the River Liffey from seeping in. Even though the river is some distance away, it must be remembered that this is all land reclaimed from the estuary, and during high tides the river shoots streams of water through the substratum. Several buildings on the street are without the benefit of watertight cellars and have to keep pumps going day and night. Now walk down O'Connell Street in the direction of the river. Evidence of cellars can often be spotted along the pavement. Steel trapdoors (usually outside pubs) allow access to underground stores, and glass squares set into a frame (called pavement lights) let light into cellars. Next, turn left into Cathedral Street, but before doing so look over to the central island on O'Connell Street to where a set of railings guard steps going down. This is not the entrance to a metro (that day will come!) but to a public toilet.

Meet the Mummies
Once on Cathedral Street, mount the steps onto the podium of the Pro-Cathedral (completed 1825). Halfway along, straddling another set of steps, is a small blockhouse, the entrance to the crypt. In here a number of Dublin's Archbishops are buried, along with over 900 benefactors of the church. The vaults are vast, and until the church was finally completed they were leased to the Commissioners of Inland Revenue as bonded storage space for spirits. Unfortunately, except on rare occasions, the vaults are closed to the public. The city's retail sector has its own crypts, the department store basement. Two of the city's largest, Clerys on North Earl Street (the next turn right, first onto Marlborough Street and right again onto North Earl Street) and Arnotts in Henry Street (a continuation of North Earl Street on the opposite side of O'Connell Street) have famous basements, but Roches Stores, also in Henry Street, is perhaps the most celebrated. As you walk along Henry Street, passing Moore Street on your right, you might like to know the origins of their names. These streets were first laid down in the 1720s by the developer Henry Moore, the Earl of Drogheda. In his pursuit of immortality the good earl named five streets after his name and title: Henry Street, Moore Street, (North) Earl Street, Of (now Moore) Lane and Drogheda (now O'Connell) Street. St Mary's Church, now a pub, on the corner of Mary Street (an extension of Henry Street) and Jervis Street, had a small crypt but most burials took place in the adjoining graveyard, now a public park. Walk down Jervis Street and cross over to the Ormond Quay wall. Look over towards the Clarence Hotel (owned by the band U2) and search for a tunnel-like opening in the lower half of the river wall. If the tide is high you might not see it, but hopefully you will be in luck. This is the main outfall, not for sewage, but for the Poddle River. For 4 kilometres (2½ miles) the Poddle is culverted before becoming part of the city sewer network, and so is sadly hidden from view. It was once the lifeblood of the medieval walled city; it also filled the moat around Dublin Castle and formed a pool at its rear, offering safe anchorage to the Viking boats. Its name in Irish – *Dubh Linn*, the Black Pool – led to the city's present name. Next, you make your way to another St Mary's by walking upriver along Ormond Quay and turning right into Capel Street. St Mary's Abbey is itself underground, or at least the Chapter House is, having been swallowed up by centuries of construction. You will find the entrance up Meeting House Lane, which is reached by turning left off Capel Street into a street called St Mary's Abbey and right again into the short lane. The abbey was founded by the Benedictines in 1139 and was taken over shortly afterwards by the Cistercians. It then became the most important religious institution north of the River Liffey until its suppression in 1539. It was then largely demolished, but somehow the Chapter House survived by being buried under future building work. It is a fascinating place to visit, but first check its limited opening hours under *Further Information*. Proceed along Mary's Abbey and Chancery Street, passing the Bridewell Garda Station with

its underground cells connected by tunnels to the nearby courtrooms, before arriving at the Church of St Michan on Church Street. This was the first parish church north of the Liffey, having been founded by the Vikings in 1096. A highlight of a visit to the church must be a tour of the vaults and their rather macabre contents: the exposed mummified remains of several bodies that were buried three or four centuries ago. They have been preserved by the constant temperature, the limestone walls and various chemicals present in the dry air. You may need a little light relief after this, so head down Church Street, cross the River Liffey and onto the right-hand side of Bridge Street Lower, and take a break at Dublin's oldest pub, the Brazen Head. The building may date from 1668, but a tavern of this name is believed to have existed here since 1198.

Continue up Bridge Street Upper and turn left into High Street. You are now entering the heart of medieval Dublin. A remarkable visitor centre has recently opened in St Audoen's Church, the entrance to which is on your left at the end of the railings. The church itself, established in 1181 and the city's oldest continuously-used parish church, is exposed but it is way below present street level. Within the church is an underground cobbled laneway dating from the 12th century. Continue along High Street and around to Christ Church Cathedral. You can, of course, visit the Cathedral itself, but the purpose of this walk is to see the crypt, one of the largest of its kind in Ireland or Britain. Dating from at least the 12th century, the crypt, which holds the massive weight of the cathedral above, is the city centre's oldest structure. It was restored to its full glory in 1999/2000. The many artefacts on view are explained on site. A quick detour around to Exchange Street Lower will bring you to Isolde's Tower, one of the main defensive bastions around the medieval city walls. You can only see its foundations behind a large specially designed grill underneath a modern building. Walk from Exchange Quay to Essex Quay to the corner with Parliament Street. The real reason for bringing you to this corner is to view the magnificent terracotta reliefs running around the façade of the Sunlight Chambers. These charming sculptures depict the manufacture and use of soap and were commissioned by Lever Brothers who built the Sunlight Chambers in about 1900. You will see much more than foundations of another medieval tower and part of the city wall in the undercroft of Dublin Castle, though you will need to visit the State Apartments of Dublin Castle to do so (*see* 'Some Great Interiors'). Turn right into Parliament Street and at its other end swing into Dame Street. As you pass the Olympia Theatre on your left you are also passing over the aforementioned Poddle River, which runs directly under the theatre. Continue along Dame Street and into College Green.

Heroic Policeman

The building standing on the corner of College Green and Foster Place used to be the 18th-century Daly's Club, a notorious gentleman's gambling den. It had a tunnel connecting it directly to the Houses of Parliament (now the Bank of Ireland). Tunnels (remnants of which were recently uncovered) also used to connect the Custom House to the brothels near the present-day Connolly Station. Wind your circuitous way to the corner of Burgh Quay and Hawkins Street via Westmoreland Street.

You have now reached a memorial consisting of a square base surmounted by a pillar and a Celtic cross. Under this section of road, at the corner of Hawkins Street and Burgh Quay, lies a network of connecting sewers. On Saturday 6 May 1905 at about 3.00pm, a worker named John Fleming opened a manhole cover and descended into the 7.3-metre (24-foot) deep sewer to investigate a broken pipe. He was almost immediately overcome by deadly sewer gas, as were two of his colleagues who rushed to assist him. A small boy witnessed the scene and sprinted to a policeman standing near O'Connell Bridge. Constable Patrick Sheahan, aged 29, was a member of the College Street 'B' Division of the Dublin Metropolitan Police. A giant of a man – 1.92 metres (6 feet 4 inches) tall and 114.3 kilograms (18 stone) in weight – Sheahan was already a legend in the town. Reckless of his own safety, he had once snatched an elderly couple from their collapsing house. On another occasion he had single-handedly stopped a runaway bull in Grafton Street. Without a moment's hesitation, Constable Sheahan climbed into the shaft and hauled out two of the victims before succumbing himself. By this time more volunteers had arrived and for the next hour a grisly circus of would-be rescuers requiring rescue themselves ensued. Eventually, in addition to the deaths of Sheahan and Fleming, 12 other men were taken in a serious condition to hospital. The heroism of all concerned, embodied in the sacrifice of Sheahan, caused a great wave of emotion across the city. Thousands of mourners attended Sheahan's funeral and medals for gallantry were presented to two fireman and 30 civilians. The Lord Mayor opened an appeal to collect funds for a memorial to the memory of Constable Sheahan and the other rescuers. As a result the present monument was erected on Burgh Quay in 1906.

From here, cut through Trinity College to Nassau Street, passing through the Arts Building and its underground Douglas Hyde Gallery on your way through. Next door, the college's newest library has vast underground library storage and workspace. The Provost himself can commute from his elegant 18th-century residence to the college proper via his own personal tunnel. Near the top of Dawson Street on the right-hand side is that rare breed of animal, an underground pub. Not only is the Dawson Lounge underground, it is also the smallest pub in Dublin. You can hardly pass by this sanctuary without paying your respects. Then, stride up St Stephen's Green West and into Harcourt Street until you reach the old railway station on your left. To its left is the arched entrance to Findlater's Wine Merchants (a descendent of the Findlater's mentioned at the beginning of this walk). Your legitimate excuse to enter is to visit its wonderful museum, and also to gaze at the seemingly endless series of huge vaults (21 in all) that were built under the station over 140 years ago. Return down Harcourt Street and cut right into Hatch Street, passing on the corner a hot-spot night club, The PoD (Place of Dance), which also resides in a couple of vaults. A little south of here is the Grand Canal (which is not on this itinerary) alongside which is the 4.8-kilometre (3-mile) long tunnel of the Greater Dublin Drainage Scheme. Its internal diameter is 3.66 metres (12 feet) so it is relatively comfortable to walk through. The tunnel is divided into two compartments, one for storm (rain) water and the other for foul water (sewage), and was opened in 1984 to cater for the new towns of Blanchardstown, Lucan and

Constable Sheahan Memorial.

Clondalkin and for the relief of flood-prone areas in Rathmines, Harold's Cross and Crumlin. The tunnel, which is buried 9.1 metres (30 feet) underground, tracks alongside the Grand Canal until it reaches the Grand Canal Docks, into which it discharges the storm water. The foul water continues on to the Ringsend waste water treatment works. Hatch Street is not named after a hatch that might allow you underground, but after John Hatch, a prominent resident of Harcourt Street. At the junction with Leeson Street turn left and cross over to the other side. Look over the railings into the basement areas of the buildings lining Leeson Street, especially on the right-hand side. Many of the basements are occupied by late-night venues, making Leeson Street the night-club strip of Dublin. Carry on down by the Green again and into Hume Street. On the pavements along here and along the next street, Ely Place, look for the small round metal covers outside each house. These are coal-hole covers, covering the entrances for deliveries of coal direct into the cellars in bygone days. The holes themselves were designed to be too small for burglars to enter. Next cross over Merrion Row, turn right and left again into Merrion Street, and cross to the right-hand side.

At last you have arrived at your underground refuge, the Cellar Bar, part of the luxury Merrion Hotel. Have a well-earned drink in the cellar, where food for the baby that was to grow up and defeat Napoleon at Waterloo was once prepared: the house above you, Mornington House, was the birthplace of Arthur Wellesley, the Duke of Wellington.

Some Great Interiors

Summary: Dublin was never a rich city, so architectural and artistic embellishments both to the outside and inside of buildings are necessarily relatively modest. Nonetheless, within the confines of scale, the city possesses some very fine or elaborate interiors dating from medieval days right through to the Georgian and Victorian eras. Some modern examples are also well worth looking at and are therefore not ignored. While there are a fair share of important interiors north of the River Liffey, they are more widely spread out, so for the sake of visiting a collection in close proximity the walk is centred on the south side. Commercial, institutional, religious and entertainment venues are all included in the itinerary.

Start:	Bewleys Restaurant, Westmoreland Street. DART: Tara Street Station. Buses: all city centre bus routes are within a few minutes' walk. Car parking: use the Fleet Street multistorey car park.
Finish:	Café en Seine, Dawson Street. DART: Pearse Station. Buses: it is only a 5–10 minutes' walk to most services, but specifically the numbers 10, 11, 11A, 11B, 13, 15A and 46A pass the door. Car parking: Kildare Street or Setanta multistorey car parks.
Length:	4.8 km (3 miles)
Time:	1½ hours
Refreshments:	There are refreshment options within some of the interiors.
Pathway Status:	City paths all the way.
Best Time to Visit:	During business hours, but only if you want to enter all the mentioned buildings.
Suitable for Bicycles:	Yes, but they could be an encumbrance if you are hopping in and out of premises.
Connecting Walks:	From The Northside Pub Crawl, and to Mount Street Bridge to Merrion Square.

Ernest Bewley opened his Westmoreland Street café in 1896 and offered a simple menu: tea, coffee, rolls, rich cakes, sticky buns and eggs (boiled, poached or scrambled). Bewley knew how to charge – his motto was, 'Give the public what they want, and let them pay for it.' Admittedly his café was top class and the rich aroma of roasting coffee beans was all the temptation anyone needed. 'Anyone' included James Joyce, who was partial to a 'nice cup of black coffee in a nice small cup'. Westmoreland Street was handsomely decorated in a style typical of the end of the

19th century, with mahogany counters, plush alcoves, marble-topped tables and stained glass windows. Unfortunately the shop was severely damaged by fire in 1977. Apart from a restoration after the fire, a more recent revamp was carried out in 2000. Now quite a large enterprise, the interior is split into various sections, each with its own atmosphere and theme.

Priceless Treasures

Exit Bewleys, turn right and work your way up to the nearby Bank of Ireland, and enter by the Westmoreland Street portico. Follow the signs to the House of Lords. When the bank bought the old House of Parliament (Parliament had been dissolved in 1800 as a result of the Act of Union), it was obliged to destroy all internal vestiges of the previous legislature. To satisfy the watching authorities, the bank appeared to follow this instruction with gusto – it secretly intended to preserve the House of Lords but to do this, it had to remove the House of Commons to show willing. As a result, the Lords' chamber remains much the same today as it was when designed by Sir Edward Lovett Pearse in 1728. Of all the furnishings, the pair of tapestries are the most notable, hung in 1733. They were woven by Dutch craftsmen living in Dublin and depict the *Glorious Battle of the Boyne* and *the Glorious Defence of Londonderry*. Also still in place is the original carved oak mantelpiece. The 1,233-piece chandelier dates from 1788. The Mace of the House of Commons, made in England in 1765, is the building's only link with that assembly. Before leaving the bank, visit the magnificent Cash Office. It was constructed on the site of the former Hall of Requests and the lobby of the House of Commons.

Another bank worth visiting is the Allied Irish Bank (AIB) in College Street. To reach here cross Westmoreland Street into College Street and the bank is just beyond the Westin Hotel. Opened in 1868 as the head office of the Provincial Bank of Ireland (a bank later absorbed into AIB) the interior is lofty and impressive. The purpose of such grandeur in banks was to keep customers in awe and to show that their money was obviously safe. Now set your compass for Trinity College and head for the Old Library by crossing College Street, turning right and walking along by the railings of the college until you meet the main entrance gates opposite College Green. Follow the direction signs within the college for the Old Library. This is where the priceless *Book of Kells* is on show in its own room, but apart from viewing this and other accompanying treasures, the main purpose of your visit here is to see the glorious interior of the library. The library proper starts on the first floor. The ground floor was originally an open arcade so that the priceless books could be kept safely out of reach of the damp caused by the River Liffey's constant underground seepage: after all, Trinity was built on land reclaimed from the estuary. The foundation stone was laid for the library in 1712, and when it was finished it was thought to have the largest reading room in Europe. At that time the library, containing rows of oak book compartments, extended to single floor height only. The ceiling was also flat. In the 1860s architects Thomas Deane and Benjamin Woodward doubled its size by constructing upper-level compartments and converting the flat ceiling into a high barrel-vaulted one. This is the great space that you can see today. Over 200,000 volumes are stored here. Before leaving Trinity College visit the Museum Building, the hub of the Engineering faculty. To reach it leave the library by Library Square (where the Campanile stands), turn right and the Museum Building is the next building in line with the Old Library. Also by Deane and Woodward, this masterpiece is meant to evoke a Venetian palace. The central interior space is certainly reminiscent of a palazzo, with a columned vestibule leading to a magnificent stone staircase. While there you can enjoy a number of permanent engineering exhibits that are on display.

Leave Trinity College by the exit through the Arts Building (behind the Old Library), turn left along Nassau Street and continue on a straight line to Leinster and Clare Streets, turning right into Merrion Square. A visit to the National Gallery will reveal not only an art collection of international standard, but an interior space to match the hangings. The modern simplicity of the north wings contrasts dramatically with the more decorous rooms of the original south wing, built in 1864. The most splendid room in the gallery, a work of art in itself, is the Baroque Room. If it is a Saturday morning, buy a ticket for visiting Government Buildings from the gallery desk. Next, visit the Natural History Museum on the other side of Leinster Lawn. The Natural History Museum and the south wing of the National Gallery are identical on the outside. This is because the gallery's first designer, Sir Richard Griffith, a surveyor who had never designed a building before, copied the earlier museum (built 1856–57). The plain exterior of the Natural History Museum does little to prepare the visitor for the extravaganza of displays on several floors and tiers of galleries within. It breaks every rule of modern display techniques by vastly overcrowding every available space, including hanging whale skeletons from the ceiling – and yet it is this cramming that gives this extraordinary institution its appeal. In terms of research, the museum is world-renowned as a major entomological centre (in other words, for its study of insects).

Unless it is a Saturday morning and you have your visitor's ticket obtainable from the National Gallery, you can only admire Government Buildings, the next building to the left of the Natural History Museum, from the outside. However, it is certainly the most imperial of Dublin's buildings and was the last major British undertaking. In fact, it was not competed until 1922 when Ireland was already independent. For decades it housed government offices in its wings, while the central block was given over to University College Dublin. Since 1990, after a lavish restoration, this central section houses the offices of an Taoiseach (the Prime Minister), the Department of an Taoiseach and the Cabinet. The Press Conference Room, some Government Departments and offices for TDs (Teachtaí Dála or Members of Parliament) are also accommodated here. The works of Irish artists and artisans are prominently displayed throughout the halls, stairways, corridors and meeting rooms within the building. The public tour visits most of the main rooms including the Taoiseach's suite.

Interesting Conversions

Merrion Square has by now given way to Merrion Street along which you should continue until you can turn right into Merrion Row and, next, St Stephen's Green North. At the corner of Kildare Street drop into the sumptuously designed Shelbourne Hotel (founded 1824), built to its present design in 1867. The hotel still retains most of its Victorian embellishments. A morning coffee or an afternoon tea in the elegant drawing-room will not go amiss. From the Shelbourne turn right into Kildare Street and walk two-thirds of the way down until you arrive at the National Library on your right. The main reading room of the National Library, which opened in 1890, is well worth a visit, but you will have to negotiate with the receptionists downstairs if you don't need to carry out research. A beautiful barrel-vaulted ceiling with classical trimmings overlooks the rows of reading desks and the exquisitely carved woodwork. The downstairs rotunda-shaped vestibule will not disappoint either, and you don't need permission to visit it. Cross directly over to Molesworth Street and call into the Freemasons' Hall. If you cannot call during the official visiting hours, you might still be lucky if the receptionist or librarian have a free moment to show you around.

The various meeting and ceremonial rooms are quite stunning, and exhibit very elaborate and themed decorations. Erected in 1867, the Freemasons' Hall is rich in history and the Dublin Lodge of the Freemasons is, after London's, the second oldest in the world. Follow Molesworth Street to Duke Street and turn right into Grafton Street. Pop into Marks and Spencer (at the corner of Duke and Grafton Streets) to view the grand marble staircase. The present owners bought the former Brown Thomas store, retained only the street façade and completely rebuilt the interior. In doing so they resited the marvellous staircase, which previously led to the basement. Next, walk up Johnston's Court and into the Powerscourt Centre. This was originally a backyard, and its transformation, first completed in 1981 and modified in the late 1990s, is impressive. Walk straight through the centre and into the ground floor of Powerscourt House, a Georgian mansion built in 1774, to exit into South

William Street. Turn right and continue to Andrew Street which will bring you to the Dublin Tourism Centre. Drop in for a minute and view the excellent conversion carried out in the mid 1990s to the former St Andrew's Church (built 1873). Turn into Church Lane and call into the National Irish Bank on the corner with College Green. This is another sumptuous bank interior which has an exceptional vaulted ceiling. If the bank is closed it is still possible to see the ceiling from the outside as it is usually floodlit. It was built for the Union Bank in 1867 and designed by William Murray and Thomas Drew.

Continue into Dame Street and take a well-earned break in the Mercantile Bar on Dame Street, a former bank converted into a several-tiered bar and restaurant. Its interior is certainly not a traditional Irish bar. The elaborate bank fittings and decorations were manipulated and augmented to create a theme based on ancient Greece: classics and clarets under one roof. City Hall, on your left at the end of Dame Street and opened by the Guild of Merchants as the Royal Exchange in the 1770s, has been the meeting place for the City Council since 1851. In 2000 it was completely restored, and the rotunda and ambulatory are now a magnificent space. The lower ground floor houses a collection of the city's municipal treasures going back nearly 900 years. On the other side of City Hall is the entrance to Dublin Castle. It would be impossible to explain here, even briefly, the history and magnificence of the State Apartments in Dublin Castle, and in any case the only way to see them is to take the official tour. Dublin Castle was first built in 1204 and the luxurious State Apartments were erected and embellished for the court of the Lord Lieutenant during the 18th and 19th centuries. A second tour visits the Royal Chapel, which is noted for its internal plasterwork, oak and stone carvings and the stained glass coat-of-arms of all past Viceroys. Walk to the rear of the castle to visit the Chester Beatty Library Galleries. A restored 18th-century clock tower building, linked to an ultramodern wing, displays one of the world's most important collections of Oriental and early European art and manuscripts. You can have a break on the very serene roof garden.

The Saint of Love

A good brisk walk is now in order. Follow the map to St Patrick's Cathedral. Founded in 1192, it had reached a state of near collapse by the 1850s. Sir Benjamin Guinness of the illustrious brewing family funded a complete restoration which was carried out between 1860 and 1864. St Patrick's and the features of its interior have a rich history that is fully explained in an excellent free leaflet available at the door. A short distance further up St Patrick's Close is Marsh's Library. Opened by Archbishop Narcissus Marsh in 1701, this is Ireland's oldest public library. Larger inside than you might expect – it holds over 25,000 volumes which date from the 15th century onwards – the layout has hardly changed in three centuries. A group of 'cages', that readers used to be locked into while examining rare books, are still in situ. Another place that you might prefer not to be locked in is Kevin Street Garda Station, even if it is situated on the remnants of a 13th-century Archbishop's Palace – you will pass this on your way to Aungier Street to visit the Carmelite Church of Our Lady of Mount Carmel. This church is commonly referred to as Whitefriar Street Church, as its original entrance was from that street

Marsh's Library.

when the building was only a third of its present size. It was built in 1825, on the former site of a Carmelite Abbey that was founded in 1280 and confiscated in 1539 by decree of King Henry VIII. There are excellent presentations on the history and the interior displayed in the entrance porch. One thing you should not miss is the casket containing the earthly remains of St Valentine, the patron saint of lovers, situated under a side altar to the right of the church. Turn left down Aungier Street, taking the next right into Stephen Street Lower, and continue into South King Street until you pass the Gaiety Theatre. You can really only see the resplendently colourful Victorian-style auditorium of the Gaiety if you attend a show, so you could perhaps drop into the box office and take it from there. Call into the Stephen's Green Centre (on the opposite side) to view its conservatory-like interior, which some people have denigrated by comparing it to a Mississippi steamboat. That's a bit unkind, but it does have a very bright and showy atmosphere.

At last, you are almost there. Cross into St Stephen's Green North, take the next left into Dawson Street and seek out Café en Seine (quarter of the way down on the left). Converted in 1994 from dull insurance offices (in a previous life it was a church hall), this was Dublin's first café-style bar to break away from the traditional-type bar and to focus on the food and coffee culture that now has become the norm. Wallow in its Parisian-style surroundings and let me tell you about some great interiors on the north side, especially... zzzzz!

Further Information

Opening Times

In a city that is rediscovering and developing its tourist and heritage infrastructure at a rapid rate, times of opening can change without notice, but hopefully on the more generous side. However, all the present growth and redevelopment may also mean that some places, open at the time of writing, may be temporarily closed for refurbishment or enhancement when you arrive. It may be advisable, if you have to go out of your way to visit a particular site, to telephone in advance to confirm the current hours of opening. Unless they are designated as specific visitor sites, e.g. St Patrick's Cathedral, St Michan's etc., churches may only open during service times. In the centre of Dublin, Roman Catholic churches tend to be open all day but in the suburbs they may close in the afternoons and evenings, except for Mass and religious ceremonies. Public houses (pubs) generally open daily 10.00–23.30. Department stores and shopping centres are usually open Mon–Sat 09.00–18.00/19.00 (Thu until 21.00), Sun 12.00/13.00–18.00. Banks are open Mon–Fri 10.00–16.00 (Thu until 17.00).

TALBOT STREET TO THE NORTH DOCKLANDS (pages 18–23)

CONNOLLY STATION
Amiens Street, Amiens Street, Dublin 1. Tel: Train enquiries 836 6222; fax: 836 4760.
Open the station is open for mainline trains 07.00–22.00 approximately.

FAIRVIEW PARK
Fairview, Dublin 3. Tel: 833 6262; fax: (Dublin Corporation Parks Dept.) 670 7332.
Open accessible all times but avoid at night.

ROYAL CANAL WAY – NEWCOMEN BRIDGE TO ASHTOWN AND ROYAL CANAL WAY – ASHTOWN TO LEIXLIP (pages 24–35)

The Royal Canal towpath is open at all times. Avoid at night.

ASHTOWN TO A CHIMNEY TALL (pages 36–40)

PHOENIX PARK VISITOR'S CENTRE
Phoenix Park, Dublin 8. Tel: 677 0095; fax: 820 5584.
Jan–mid Mar: Sat/Sun 09.30–16.30, mid–end Mar: daily 09.30–17.00, Apr–May: daily 09.30–17.30, Jun–Sep: daily 10.00–18.00, Oct: daily 10.00–17.00, Nov–Dec: Sat/Sun 10.00–16.30.
Admission free.

THE CHIMNEY
Chief O'Neill's, Smithfield, Dublin 7. Tel: 817 3800.
Open daily all year (except Christmas Day and Good Friday) 09.30–18.00.
Admission charge.

CEOL
Irish Music Interactive Centre, Smithfield,

Dublin 7. Tel: 817 3800.
Open all year (except Christmas Day and
Good Friday) Mon–Sat 09.30–18.00, Sun
10.30–18.00.

A PLACE APART – ST ANNE'S
PARK (pages 41–46)

ST ANNE'S PARK
Clontarf, Dublin 3. Tel: 833 1859; fax:
(Dublin Corporation Parks Dept.) 670 7332.
Open accessible at all times but avoid at night.

RED STABLES
St Anne's Park, Dublin 3.
Awaiting confirmation of specific phone
numbers and opening times. In the mean-
time enquire at the main St Anne's telephone number given above.

A BASIN AT BLESSINGTON
(pages 47–53)

JAMES JOYCE CENTRE
35 North Great George's Street, Dublin 1.
Tel: 878 8547; fax: 8788488.
Open all year: Tue–Sat, 10.00–16.30, Sun
12.30–16.30.
Admission charge.

BLESSINGTON BASIN
Blessington Street, Dublin 7. C/o Dublin
Corporation Parks Department Tel: 672
3305; fax: 670 7332.

KING'S INNS
Henrietta Street, Dublin 1. Tel: 874 4840;
fax 872 6048.
Open business hours.

GARDEN OF REMEMBRANCE
Parnell Square East, Dublin 1.
Open daily 09.00–dusk or until 18.00.

DUBLIN WRITER'S MUSEUM
18/19 Parnell Square, Dublin 1. Tel: 872
2077.
Open mid Mar–Oct: Mon–Sat 10.00
–17.00, Sun and Public Hols 11.30–18.00,
Nov–Mar: telephone for details.
Admission charge.

HUGH LANE MUNICIPAL GALLERY
OF MODERN ART
Parnell Square North, Dublin 1. Tel: 874
1903; fax: 872 2182.
Open Tue–Fri 09.30–18.00, Sat
09.30–17.00, Sun 11.00–17.00. Closed
Mon. Most Sundays at 12.00 there is a free
concert in the Gallery.
Admission free to all Gallery events. Guided
tours should be arranged two weeks in
advance.

PYRAMIDS AND CYLINDERS
(pages 54–58)

ST MOBHI'S CHURCH & GRAVEYARD
Church Avenue, Dublin 9. Tel: 842 8596.
Open for church services only. A key can be
borrowed from no. 3 Church Avenue.

DUBLIN CITY UNIVERSITY
Glasnevin, Dublin 9. Tel: 704 5000; fax: 836
0830.
Open daytime and evenings.

CARMELITE MONASTERY OF THE
INCARNATION, HAMPTON HERMITAGE
Gracepark Road, Dublin 9. Tel: not available to the public.
Open the church is open 12.00–14.00,
15.00–16.45 except the first Friday of each
month and during Lent and Advent.

ALL HALLOWS COLLEGE
Gracepark Road, Drumcondra, Dublin 9.
Tel: 837 3745; fax: 837 7642.
Open at all times, but check with reception
before touring around.

GRAVEYARD OF ST JOHN THE BAPTIST
Church Avenue, Drumcondra, Dublin 9.
Tel: 837 2503.
Open 10.00–16.00.

DARTing NORTH (pages 59–62)

DART STATIONS
Iarnród Éireann passenger information Tel:
836 6222.
Open 07.00–23.00.

HOWTH (pages 63–67)

HOWTH PIERS
Open at all times.

IRELAND'S EYE (pages 68–72)

Boats operate from the East Pier. Tel: 831 4200 or mobile 087–267 8211.
Departures: Summer: at regular intervals from 11.00. Off season: call by telephone to check.

MALAHIDE TO SWORDS
(pages 73–77)

FINGAL COUNTY COUNCIL HEADQUARTERS
Main Street Swords, Co. Dublin. Tel: 872 7777.

SWORDS CASTLE
Swords, Co. Dublin. Tel: 840 0891.
Open Mon, Wed, Thu 10.00–12.00, 13.00–16.00; Fri 10.00–12.00, 13.00–15.00.
Admission charge.

SWORDS TO NEWBRIDGE DEMESNE (pages 78–81)

NEWBRIDGE DEMESNE
Donabate, Co. Dublin.
Open daylight hours all year.

NEWBRIDGE HOUSE
Donabate, Co. Dublin. Tel: 843 6534
Open April–Sep: Tue–Sat 10.00–13.00, 14.00–17.00; Sun & Bank Hols 14.00–18.00;
Oct–Mar: Sat, Sun & Bank Hols 14.00–17.00.
Admission charge.

SWORDS TO DUBLIN AIRPORT
(pages 82–86)

SWORDS CASTLE
Swords, Co. Dublin. Tel: 840 0891.
Open Mon, Wed, Thu 10.00–12.00, 13.00–16.00; Fri 10.00–12.00,

13.00–15.00.
Admission charge.

SWORDS ROUND TOWER
Swords, Co. Dublin.
Open restricted hours, but ask the caretaker if it is convenient to admit you.

DUBLIN AIRPORT
Co. Dublin. Tel: 814 1111; fax: 844 4534
Open: daily except Christmas Day.

THE NORTHSIDE PUB CRAWL
(pages 87–91)

OLD JAMESON DISTILLERY
Bow Street, Dublin 7. Tel: 807 2355.
Open Mon–Sun 09.30–18.00, last tour at 17.00.
Admission charge (this includes a glass of whiskey). No alcoholic beverages to under 18s.

ST MICHAN'S CHURCH
Church Street, Dublin 7. Tel: 872 4154.
Open Mon–Fri 10.00–17.00, Sat 10.00–13.00.
Admission charge.

FOUR COURTS
Inns Quay, Dublin 7. Tel: 872 5555.
Open 10.00–16.00 approx. The public may attend most court cases.

ZANZIBAR
34–35 Lwr Ormond Quay, Dublin 1. Tel: 878 7212.
Open Mon–Fri 16.00–late, Sat/Sun 12.00–late.

ABBEY THEATRE
26 Lower Abbey Street, Dublin 1. Tel: 878 7222; fax: 872 9177.
Open foyer open Mon/Sat daily. Shows daily, usually at 20.00.

THE SOUTHSIDE PUB CRAWL
(pages 92–96)

NATIONAL PHOTOGRAPHIC ARCHIVE
Meetinghouse Square, Temple Bar,
Dublin 2. Tel: 603 0200.
Open Mon–Fri, 10.00–17.00.

GALLERY OF PHOTOGRAPHY
Meetinghouse Square, Temple Bar,
Dublin 2. Tel: 671 4654.
Open Mon–Sat, 11.00–18.00.

IRISH FILM CENTRE
6 Eustace Street, Dublin 2. Tel: 679 5744;
fax: 677 8755.
Open offices and shop open during normal
office hours. Cinemas and bar open until
late evening.

MOUNT STREET BRIDGE TO MERRION SQUARE (pages 97–102)

PEARSE SQUARE PARK
Pearse Street, Dublin 2. C/o Dublin
Corporation Parks Department. Tel: 672
3305; fax: 670 7332.
Open daylight hours.

MERRION SQUARE PARK
Merrion Square, Dublin 2. Tel: 661 2369.
Open daylight hours.

NATIONAL GALLERY OF IRELAND
Merrion Square, Dublin 2. Tel: 661 5133;
fax: 661 5372.
Open Mon–Sat, 10.00–17.15 (Thu until
20.00), Sun 14.00–17.00.
Admission free but donation appreciated.

MERRION SQUARE TO ST STEPHEN'S GREEN (pages 103–109)

NATIONAL GALLERY OF IRELAND
See Mount Street Bridge to Merrion Square.

ST STEPHEN'S GREEN PARK
St Stephen's Green, Dublin 2. Tel: 475
7816.
Open: Mon–Sat 08.00–dusk, Sun
10.00–dusk.

NATIONAL CONCERT HALL
Earlsfort Terrace, Dublin 2. Tel: 671 1533;
fax: 671 2615.
Open for buffet lunches and pre-concert
meals. Lobby and booking office open
10.00–19.00. Concerts most evenings and
often at lunchtime.

IVEAGH GARDENS
Earlsfort Terrace, Dublin 2. C/o Dúchas,
The Heritage Service. Tel: 647 2453; fax:
661 6764.
Open 09.00–18.00, until dusk during the
winter.

THE LIBERTIES (pages 110–115)

ST CATHERINE'S CHURCH
(CHURCH OF IRELAND)
Thomas Street, Dublin 8.

ST KEVIN'S PARK
Camden Row, Dublin. C/o Dublin
Corporation Parks Department. Tel: 672
3305; fax: 670 7332.
Open daily during daylight hours.

MARSH'S LIBRARY
St Patrick's Close, Werburgh Street, Dublin
8. Tel: 454 3511.
Open weekdays 10.00–12.45, 14.00–17.00;
Sat 10.30–12.45. Closed Tue, Thu and Public
Hols.
Admission donation appreciated.

ST PATRICK'S PARK
Patrick Street, Dublin 8. Tel: 454 3389.
Open daily during daylight hours.

ST PATRICK'S CATHEDRAL
Patrick Street, Dublin 8. Tel: 475 4817; fax:
454 6374.
Open Tue–Fri 09.00–18.00, Sat
08.30–17.00, Sun 10.00–16.30. Closed
daily 13.00–14.30. Afternoon service on
Sundays at 15.00.
Admission donation requested.

GUINNESS VISITOR CENTRE
Market Street, Dublin 8. Not yet open in
late 2000.

CHARLEMONT BRIDGE TO RATHMINES (pages 116–120)

DARTMOUTH SQUARE PARK
Dartmouth Square, Dublin 6. C/o Dublin Corporation Parks Department. Tel: 672 3305; fax: 670 7332.
Open daily during daylight hours.

RANELAGH GARDENS PARK
Ranelagh, Dublin 6. C/o Dublin Corporation Parks Department. Tel: 672 3305; fax: 670 7332.
Open daily during daylight hours.

DARTING SOUTH (pages 121–126)

DART STATIONS
Iarnród Éireann passenger information. Tel: 836 6222.
Open 07.00–23.00.

LANES BESIDE THE TRACKS
(pages 127–131)

IRISH LABOUR HISTORY SOCIETY
MUSEUM & ARCHIVES
Beggars Bush Barracks, Dublin 4. Tel: 668 1071.
Open Mon–Fri 10.00–13.00, 14.00–16.00.
Admission free.

NATIONAL PRINT MUSEUM
Beggars Bush Barracks, Dublin 4.
Open Tue–Thu, Sat, Sun 14.00–17.00.
Admission free.

DRY GREENS TO WET SANDS
(pages 132–136)

BOOTERSTOWN CEMETERY
Booterstown, Co. Dublin.
Open daylight hours.

PEARSE STREET TO THE GREAT SOUTH WALL
(pages 137–143)

PEARSE SQUARE PARK
Pearse Street, Dublin 2. C/o Dublin Corporation Parks Department. Tel: 672

3305; fax: 670 7332.
Open daylight hours.

WATERWAYS VISITOR CENTRE
Grand Canal Quay, Dublin 2. Tel: 677 7510; fax: 677 7514. *Open* Jun–Sep: daily 09.30–17.30; Oct–May: Wed–Sun 12.30–17.00.
Admission free.

DUBLIN UNDERGROUND
(pages 144–150)

ST MARY'S ABBEY
Chapter House, Meetinghouse Lane, Dublin 1. Tel: 872 1490.
Open mid Jun–mid Sep: Wed & Sun 10.00–17.00.
Admission charge.

ST MICHAN'S VAULTS
Church Street, Dublin 7. Tel: 872 4154.
Open Mon–Fri 10.00–17.00, Sat 10.00–13.00.
Admission charge.

ST AUDOEN'S
Near Christchurch, Dublin 8. Tel: 677 0088; fax: 670 9431.
Open Jun–Sep: daily 09.30–17.30.
Admission charge.

CHRIST CHURCH CRYPT
Christchurch Place, Dublin 8. Tel: 677 8099; fax: 679 8991.
Open May–Sep: daily 0930–17.00; Oct–Apr 09.30–16.30.
Admission donation requested.

THE FINDLATER MUSEUM
On the corner of Harcourt Street and Hatch Street, Dublin 2. Tel: 475 1699.
Open Mon–Sat 10.00–17.30.
Admission charge.

UNDERCROFT, DUBLIN CASTLE
Dame Street, Dublin 8. Tel: 679 6111.
Open Mon–Fri 10.00–12.15, 14.00–17.00; Sat, Sun and Public Hols 14.00–17.00.
Admission charge.

SOME GREAT INTERIORS
(pages 151–156)

CITY HALL
Cork Hill, Dublin 8. Tel: 679 6111.

HOUSE OF LORDS
Bank of Ireland, College Green, Dublin 2.
Tel: 677 6801.
Open Mon–Fri, 10.00–16.00, Thu
10.00–17.00.

DUBLIN TOURISM
St Andrew's Centre, Suffolk Street, Dublin 2.
Tel: administrative only: 605 7700;
tourist info, Ireland: 1850 230 330.
Fax: 605 7749.
E-mail: dublintourism@msn.com
Open 2 Jan–15 Jun, 15 Sep–30 Dec:
Mon–Sat 9.00–17.30 (Tue open 9.30), 16
Jun–14 Sep: Mon–Sat 08.30–19.30, Sun
11.00–17.30, Public Hols 11.00–17.30.

OLD LIBRARY
Trinity College, College Green, Dublin 2.
Tel: 677 2941; fax: 677 2694.
Open Mon–Fri 09.30–16.45, Sat
09.30–12.45.
Admission charge.
The College itself is open during daytime
hours (entrances from College Green,
Nassau Street, Lincoln Place and Westland
Row) and most evenings through the main
entrance on College Green only.

MUSEUM BUILDING
Trinity College, College Green, Dublin 2.
Tel: 677 2941; fax: 677 2694.
Open during daytime college hours.

NATIONAL LIBRARY
Kildare Street, Dublin 2. Tel: 661 8811.
Open Mon 10.00–21.00, Tue & Wed
14.00–21.00, Thu & Fri 10.00–17.00, Sat
10.00–13.00. Closed Sun.
Admission free, but readers have to register.

NATIONAL GALLERY
See Mount Street Bridge to Merrion
Square.

NATURAL HISTORY MUSEUM
Merrion Street, Dublin 2. Tel: 677 7444.
Open Tue–Sat 10.00–17.00, Sun
14.00–17.00.

GOVERNMENT BUILDINGS
Merrion Street, Dublin 2. Tel: 662 4888.
Open Sat mornings only.

MASONIC LODGE
17 Molesworth Street, Dublin 2. Tel: 676
1337.
Open Daily guided tour at 14.30, Mon–Fri,
Jun–Aug only.
Admission charge.

STEPHEN'S GREEN CENTRE
St Stephen's Green, Dublin 2.
Open normal shopping hours, 09.00–18.00.
Thu & Fri 09.00–20.00.
Open Sunday afternoon.

GAIETY THEATRE
South King Street, Dublin 2. Tel (admin):
677 1717.
Open box office Mon–Fri 10.00–17.00.
Shows generally start at 20.00.

MARSH'S LIBRARY
See The Liberties.

ST PATRICK'S CATHEDRAL
See The Liberties.

CBL GALLERIES
Dublin Castle, Dame Street.
Open Mon–Fri 10.00–17.00, Sat & Sun
14.00–17.00.

STATE APARTMENTS & CHAPEL ROYAL,
DUBLIN CASTLE
Dame Street, Dublin 8. Tel: 679 6111.
Open Mon–Fri 10.00–12.15, 14.00–17.00;
Sat, Sun and Public Hols 14.00–17.00.
Admission charge.

Bibliography

Bennett, D., *Encyclopaedia of Dublin,* Dublin, Gill and Macmillan, 1991.

Cowell, J., *Where They Lived in Dublin,* Dublin, O'Brien Press, 1980.

de Breffny, B., *Ireland: A Cultural Encyclopaedia*, London, Thames and Hudson, 1983.

DeCourcy, J.W., *The Liffey in Dublin,* Dublin, Gill and Macmillan, 1996.

Farmar, T., *The Legendary Lofty Clattery Café,* Dublin, Riversend Ltd, 1988.

Gilligan, H.A., *The History of the Port of Dublin,* Dublin, Gill and Macmillan, 1989.

McCready, C.T., *Dublin Street Names,* Dublin, Carrig Books, 1994.

Mulligan, F., *One Hundred and Fifty Years of Irish Railways,* Belfast, Appletree Press, 1983.

O'Donnell, E.E., *The Annals of Dublin,* Dublin, Wolfhound Press, 1987.

Pearson, P., *Dun Laoghaire,* Dublin, O'Brien Press, 1981.

Summerville-Large, P., *Dublin, The Fair City,* London, Hamish Hamilton, 1979.

Williams, J., *Architecture in Ireland 1837–1921,* Dublin, Irish Academic Press, 1994.

Note: Much of the information was also sourced from the author's own body of published work and from his own extensive collection of primary source material.

Index

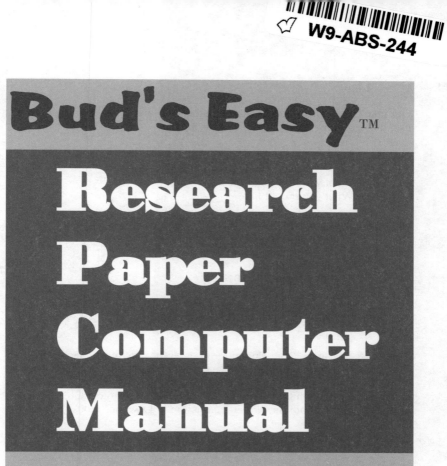

Bud's Easy™

Research Paper Computer Manual

For Macintosh

SECOND EDITION

ALVIN BARON, PH. D.

LAWRENCE HOUSE PUBLISHERS
NEW YORK

User's Input

Our goal is to improve this book continuously to make it easier for you to use. Here's your chance to give us your input.

Tell us:
- How you think the book can be improved.
- What you like about the book.
- What you do not like.

Send comments with your name, address, and phone number to:
Research Director
Lawrence House Publishers
500 East 77th Street
New York, New York 10162
or E-mail to:
budbooks@mindspring.com
Thanks.

Bud's Easy Research Paper Computer Manual for Macintosh Second Edition
Copyright © 1999 by Lawrence House Publishers. All rights reserved. No part of this book may be stored, copied, reproduced, or transmitted in any form or by any means including but not limited to photocopy, photograph, magnetic or other record without the written permission of Lawrence House Publishers.

ISBN 1-891707-02-7

First Printing, June 1998
Second Printing, December 1999 Enlarged library research section

Trademarks

Trademarked names appear in this book. The publisher states that it used trademarked names only for editorial purposes and to the benefit of the trademark owner with no intention of infringing on those trademarks.

Every effort has been made to make this book as complete and accurate as possible, but no warranty or fitness is implied. The publisher assumes no responsibility for errors or omissions, or for damages resulting from the use of the information contained herein.

Published by Lawrence House Publishers
New York

Contents

Part 3   Using the Publication Manual of the American Psychological Association to Write Research Papers

FOREWARD TO THE SECOND EDITION

In just a few years the Internet has become the richest source of information in the world. Not since the invention of the printing press has there been a such a powerful medium to spread knowledge to all humankind. While there are refinements to be made and problems to be solved, the Internet offers the scholarly and skilled researcher tremendous opportunities to explore vast stores of knowlege.

Our aim in this second edition is to provide the student with the latest and most effective techniques for searching the Net. In addition, we have incorporated the latest Modern Language Association and American Psychological Association standards for citing electronic sources.

HOW TO USE THIS BOOK

First, read **Chapter 1. Bud's Easy Task Method for Research Papers, Theses, and Reports** from beginning to end in order to get an overview of the planning, research methods, outlining and drafting which are necessary for writing a scholarly paper.

Second, decide, with your instructor if required, which citation style you will use to document your paper. The **MLA Handbook** and the **Publication Manual of the American Psychological Association** are the two most frequently assigned style manuals in colleges, universities and high schools. **Part 2** of this book provides details for the **MLA Handbook** and **Part 3** does the same for the **Publication Manual of the APA.**

To avoid confusion, this book is color coded. All of the tabs for the **MLA Handbook** are in shades of blue while the tabs for the **Publication Manual of the APA** are in shades of black. Once you decide to use one of the manuals, you need use only the part of the book you need.

Third, if you are a beginning computer user, read **Chapter 3. Basic Macintosh Instructions** to get started with the computer. Here you will find help with turning your computer on and starting your program. You will also find instructions for basic word processing.

Fourth, locate the word processing program you will be using in either **Part 2** or **Part 3.** Tabs along the edge of the pages, color coded as noted above, will help you locate your program. Once you begin writing you will be assisted with all the mouse clicks and keystrokes you need for formatting title, bibliography, and other special pages as well as specific instructions for page numbering, setting margins, and preparing tables.

Go to it and good luck with your project!

Part One

Researching and Writing the Term Paper

Basic Macintosh Instructions

Part One

Researching and Writing the Term Paper

Basic Macintosh Instructions

Bud's Easy Task Method For Research Papers Theses And Reports

Research or term papers are assigned because writing them will enable you to:

- **learn the skills to do library research**
- **gather facts and ideas on a specific subject**
- **hone your writing skills**
- **report accurately what you have discovered**
- **provide the reader with your sources**
- **evaluate and select from among many ideas**
- **develop a thesis and defend it**
- **improve your thinking skills**

The ability to do all of these tasks will prove valuable in many future school, college, and work activities. Although writing the research paper or even the more comprehensive thesis is a challenging and demanding job, you will find that you derive much satisfaction when you submit a carefully crafted paper to your instructor.

Bud's Easy Task Method breaks the seemingly monumental assignment into a series of relatively simple tasks and provides clear instructions which make it easy to succeed. If you follow the directions you will gain confidence as you complete each task knowing that you are moving along steadily. Remember the old adage, **"The longest journey begins with a single step."** Come along now and let's take the first step toward success!

THE RESEARCH PAPER

TASK 1: GET STARTED

This task is simply to get moving. Procrastination is an unhealthful way of dealing with a job you don't like. Many people delay because they are afraid of failure. You may later ease your ego pangs over a D grade by claiming, "If I'd given it more time, I'd have gotten at least a B." Don't kid yourself! Be a responsible person. Get started now. Your instructor has given you directions about subjects, length, format, and due dates. Be sure you understand the assignment.

Divided into a series of tasks, the writing of a term paper is not as difficult as it first appears and it can even give you lots of satisfaction. You may even enjoy it. Let's go, right now! Continue reading all of Chapter 1 to get an overview of the whole job. Then go back and complete all of the separate tasks.

TASK 2: SELECT A GENERAL TOPIC

This task is to select a general topic which will be refined to a thesis statement later. Study the **Topic Checklist** below. Then select your own general topic. Keep working until it passes all **Topic Checklist** criteria. When you and your instructor are satisfied, go on to **Task 3.**

TOPIC CHECKLIST	
• **Not too broad**	"Preparations for D-Day" **not** "Causes and Results of World War II"
• **Not too narrow**	"Impact of Foreign Car Imports **not** "BMW Mag Wheels"
• **Interesting to readers**	"Ocean Tides - Alternative Fuel" **not the obvious** "Should We Seek Other Fuels?"
• **Not too technical**	"Chemotherapy For Cancer" **not** Carcinoma of the Pancreas" (unless required).
• **Scholarly**	"Influences on Coleridge's 'Kubla Khan'"
• **Interesting to you**	Opens a new, challenging area to you
• **OK with Instructor**	Meets subject, length or other criteria

My General Topic is _____

_____

Time For Task 2: One Hour

TASK 3: SEARCH FOR INFORMATION

SEE IF THERE IS ENOUGH DATA ON YOUR TOPIC

This task is to see if there is enough information of the highest quality on your topic. As you begin your search, use the **Source Quality Checklist** below to help you screen potential material.

S O U R C E   Q U A L I T Y   C H E C K L I S T

Primary Sources:	First hand material such as letters, documents, novels, news stories. Excellent material.
Secondary Sources:	Material written about primary sources, events, or ideas.
• **Copyright date**	Most recent unless historically significant.
• **Author's reputation**	Well-known in field, prolific, university scholar.
• **Scholarship**	Material footnoted, detailed, accurate. Not from sensational, "low-brow" books or magazines.
• **Relevance**	Relates closely to topic.
• **Objectivity**	Clear point of view. Recognizes ideas of others.
• **Bibliography**	Extensive, scholarly sources.

BEGIN BIBLIOGRAPHY COLLECTION

Today's reference search may involve as much non-print and electronic material as print material. As you search through card catalogs, reference books, online computer catalogs, and CD-ROMs, you must copy the applicable **bibliographic information,** the **call numbers,** and **locations** for each book, journal or magazine article, database, or electronic source containing information on your topic. You will need this information to compile your final bibliography or to find the material in the library if necessary.

You may use 3 x 5 inch cards, computer printouts, or your computer for your bibliography file. The entry must contain as much bibliographic data as necessary for the type of reference as listed on the following pages. Assign each source a **code number** and write it on the **upper** right corner of each card or computer printout or type it alongside the entry in your computer list. **A sample bibliography card and sample computer bibliography file entry for a book is shown on page 1-4.**

THE RESEARCH PAPER

Computer Bibliography File

If you are working with a computer, open a file named, **"Bibliography."**
Begin typing in alphabetical order and for each source include:

1. **All the bibliographic data needed for the type of source.**
2. **The library call number and location to find it later.**
3. **Your code number.**
4. **Page numbers of pages with good information.**
5. **Your comments on the content and value of the source.**

Your bibliography can be modified by deleting or adding sources as
you search. Remember to back up this file to disk frequently.

Sample Bibliography Entry in Your Computer File

```
                          Bibliography
Code Number  ──────────────────────────►   Code # 3
Bibliographic        Noyes,  Russell.   William Wordsworth.
    Data     ────►      New York: Twayne Publishers,
                           Inc., 1971.

Call number  ────►   Call# 821.7   Stacks
Page numbers ──────► See pages 68, 71, 105, 106
Your comment─►  Comment: Good info on "Tintern Abbey"
                       and nature themes.
```

Handwritten Bibliography Cards

Use 3 x 5 inch cards. Include the five items listed above for the
computer file.

Sample Handwritten Bibliography Card

Your code number ────────────────────────────────► ③

Call number ────────────────────────────────► 821.7
                                    N

Author ────► NOYES, Russell

Title ────► WilliAM WORDSWORTH

Publication city ────► NEW YORK

Publisher ────► TWAYNE PUBLISHERS, INC

Date ────► 1971

Page numbers ────► pp. 68, 71, 105, 106

Your comments ────► GOOD INFO ON "TINTERN ABBEY"
AND NATURE THEMES

THE RESEARCH PAPER

BIBLIOGRAPHIC INFORMATION REQUIRED FOR VARIOUS SOURCES

BOOKS
> Author's name
> Title of the book part (an introduction, essay or poem, etc.)
> Title of the book
> Name of editor or translator
> Edition
> Number(s) of volume(s)
> Series name
> Publication city
> Publisher
> Publication date
> Page number(s)

PERIODICALS - MAGAZINES AND JOURNALS
> Author's name
> Title of article
> Periodical name
> Series number
> Volume number
> Issue number
> Publication date
> Page number(s)

CD-ROMS BASED ON A PRINTED DATABASE
> Author's name
> Publication information for the printed database.
> Database title underlined
> Publication medium (CD-ROM)
> Vendor's name if relevant
> Electronic publication date

CD-ROMS NOT BASED ON A PRINTED DATABASE
> Author's name
> Title of material in quotation marks
> Date of material
> Database title underlined
> Publication medium (CD-ROM)
> Vendor's name if relevant
> Electronic publication date

BIBLIOGRAPHIC INFO

DISKETTE OR MAGNETIC TAPE

Author's name
Title of part of work in quotation marks
Title of product underlined
Edition, release, or version
Publication medium (Diskette or Magnetic tape)
Publication city
Publisher
Publication date

MATERIAL FROM COMPUTER SERVICES BASED ON A PRINTED SOURCE

Author's name
Publication information for the printed source
Title of database underlined
Publication medium (Online)
Computer service name
Access date

MATERIAL FROM COMPUTER SERVICE NOT BASED ON A PRINTED SOURCE

Author's name
Title of material in quotation marks
Date
Title of database underlined
Publication medium (Online)
Computer service name
Access date

ELECTRONIC JOURNALS, NEWSLETTERS, AND CONFERENCES

Author's name
Title of article or document in quotation marks
Title of journal, newsletter, or, conference underlined
Volume or issue number
Publication date in parenthesis
Number of pages if given or *n. page.*
Publication medium (Online)
Computer network name
Access date

ELECTRONIC TEXTS
>Author's name
>Text title underlined
>Publication information for printed source
>Publication medium (Online)
>Repository of the electronic text
>Computer network name
>Access date

TELEVISION OR RADIO PROGRAMS
>Title of episode in quotation marks
>Program title underlined
>Names of pertinent performers, writers, directors, producers.
>Series title if any
>Network name
>Station call letters and city
>Broadcast date

CONDUCTING RESEARCH IN THE LIBRARY

Libraries have changed dramatically and will continue to change as a result of the electronic and computer revolution. Research has become easier and faster since we can use computers to find sources. We can search many reference tools without having to schlep piles of books from dusty stacks only to discover that most are useless to us. Most important, more and more data is being recorded electronically, so the amount of material available on all subjects is increasing dramatically.

Today we are beginning to speak of the "virtual library" because we can go beyond the walls of the traditional library to access data in distant libraries, in commercial databases, and in other computers around the world from our computer terminals. Nevertheless, many of the tools of research remain the same whether we access them in print or electronically.

EXPLORING YOUR LIBRARY

Begin by visiting your library and reading any student handbooks available or attending an orientation lecture. You will save time and avoid missteps if you are familiar with your library's facilities and the location of its various departments.

THE RESEARCH PAPER

If yours is a traditional library with card catalogs and a reference section, the search should be straightforward. You will be using 3 x 5 cards for your bibliography. Just be sure to ask the librarian(s) for help. They love to be of assistance and are specially trained in research techniques.

On the other hand, if you are at a college or university or a more modern high school library, you will have to become acquainted with the electronic tools available. You will be able to access separate library collections and even reach into the catalogs and resources of other libraries. You probably will not even have to go to the library very often. You should be able to do research and possibly even access library resources from your computer at home, in your dorm, or computer center. The library itself will be equipped with many terminals.

A good place to begin after your initial orientation is at a computer screen. If you are in the library, hitting the Esc or Enter key will usually bring up the **library's home page**. If away, get on the **Internet** and type the URL (internet address) of your library and its homepage will appear. If you are unfamiliar with the Internet see pages 1-22 to 1-24 for help. Typically, you will see **"links"** to the following: a **student handbook, instructions for the online catalog, descriptions of special collections such as reference, connections to other libraries within and outside your school, and possibly Internet services.** Clicking on any of the underlined links will bring up the corresponding page.

SEARCH TOOLS

Libraries are filled with special search tools. Be sure to use as many as possible to help you in your search for information.

Powerful tools for library research include:
- ◆ **General Catalogs - Online and Card**
- ◆ **Reference Section**
  - ■ **Encyclopedias**
  - ■ **Indexes**
  - ■ **Bibliographies**
  - ■ **Abstracts**
  - ■ **Research Guides**
  - ■ **Dictionaries**
  - ■ **Biographies**
  - ■ **Yearbooks**
  - ■ **Statistical Information**

SEARCH 1: SEARCH THE ONLINE CATALOG

Most libraries have begun cataloging their collections online, gradually eliminating the old card catalog. Systems vary so you will have to learn your library's procedures by following the instructions on the terminal, attending orientation lectures, or reading instructional pamphlets. Most screens have easy to follow directions. The first screen may offer options such as restricting the search to holdings at one library building or extending the search to other libraries. Some systems allow you to search within a range of publication years or by type of source such as films or electronic journals. You can choose these options by clicking on boxes.

Typical Online Catalog - First Screen

The catalog in this illustration offers indexes beginning with **General Keyword.** Begin your search by selecting the index you want to search. In the example below, the student selected General Keyword from among the choices in the list. This system outlines the index selected in blue. Under the index list the screen describes what the selected index contains. In this case, it is **"General Search of Major Fields."**

Typical First Screen of Online Catalog

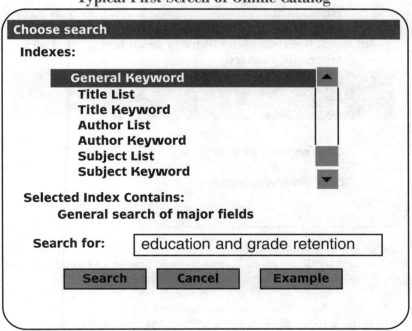

Choose search

Indexes:

> **General Keyword**
> **Title List**
> **Title Keyword**
> **Author List**
> **Author Keyword**
> **Subject List**
> **Subject Keyword**

Selected Index Contains:
> **General search of major fields**

Search for: education and grade retention

[Search] [Cancel] [Example]

THE RESEARCH PAPER

Most systems allow you to refine searches with **Boolean logic (see Internet Search pages 1-26 to 1-28 for details)** which uses the words, *and, not,* and *or.* For example, this student was researching the topic, **"social promotion,"** the practice of promoting failing students to the next grade. She entered **"education and grade retention"** as keywords in the **Search for: box.** The student then clicked on the **Search Button** at the bottom of the screen. The computer searched its database to find all the books in the collection which have information on both keywords. As you can see, the screen also offers options to cancel the search and to view an example of a source. **See the Typical First Screen of Online Catalog on page 1-9.**

Typical Second Screen of Online Catalog

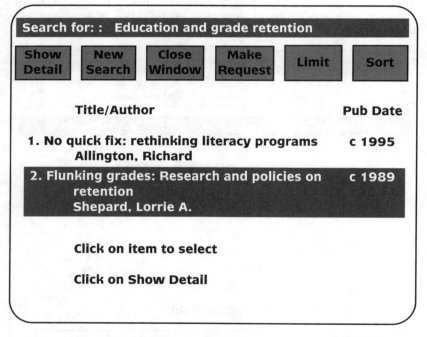

Search for: : Education and grade retention					
Show Detail	**New Search**	**Close Window**	**Make Request**	**Limit**	**Sort**

Title/Author	Pub Date
1. No quick fix: rethinking literacy programs Allington, Richard	c 1995

2. Flunking grades: Research and policies on
   retention
   Shepard, Lorrie A.
	c 1989

Click on item to select

Click on Show Detail

This online catalog yielded two titles, *No Quick Fix* and *Flunking Grades.* See the illustration, **Typical Second Screen of Online Catalog** just above.

The student noted the instruction on the bottom of the screen: **Click on item to select.** She clicked on the book that looked very good,

Flunking grades: research and policies on retention. She also clicked on **Show Detail** to get more information.

The third screen appeared with the following information about the book: **Call number**
Status showing that the book has been checked in
Full tile
Publisher
Description showing volume, number of pages, illustrations, and book size.
A note that the book is part of a series.
A note that the book contains a bibliography and index
A note showing other related subjects.

Typical Third Screen of Online Catalog

Bibliographic Detail: Title 1 of 2

Call Number: LB3063.f57 1989   **Status:** Checked in

Title: Flunking grades: Research and policies on retention/edited by Lorrie A. Shepard and Mary Lee Smith

Publisher: London; New York: Falmer Press, 1989

Description: viii, 243 p.: ill; 24 cm

Series: Education policy perspectives

Bibliography: Includes bibliography and index

Subjects: Promotion (School-United States)

The information about the series and other subjects is underlined, which indicates that these are "links." Clicking on the underlined words will open more pages with further information. See the illustration, **Typical Third Screen of Online Catalog** just above.

THE RESEARCH PAPER

Once you have located several sources, the next job is to prepare the bibliography "cards." You can copy the data longhand on 3 x 5 inch cards, obtain a printout from the computer, or download to a disk. Obtaining a printout or downloading will save you much copying and avoid errors in transcribing. Be sure you have all the information required for the source as shown on pages 1-5 to 1-7. Be certain to assign each source a code number and indicate the location in the library.

Now retrieve all the books from the stacks or wherever they are located. Skim the tables of contents and indexes to find information on your topic. Write the page numbers on which you find relevant material on the bibliography "cards" or printouts and jot comments describing the material. Try to find at least five good sources.

If abstracts or full text printouts are available, skim to see if the information is of value. Make appropriate notes on the bibliography "card" printout for the source. Put the abstracts or full text printouts aside for **Task 7.**

SEARCH 2: SEARCH THE CARD CATALOG

Some libraries have not yet switched to online catalogs while others still retain part of their collections in card catalogs. Ask the librarian to ascertain the status of your library's cataloging.

Look through the subject and author-title catalog drawers. Try to locate at least five sources on your topic. Complete a 3 x 5 inch bibliography card for each book. Locate the books in the stacks or other location. Skim the tables of contents and indexes to find information on your topic. Write the page numbers on which you find good material and jot a comment describing the information. Remember to assign each book a code number. See the **Sample Bibliography Card on page 1-4.**

SEARCH 3: SEARCH THE REFERENCE SECTION

For an overview of your subject begin with standard reference works. Every field has specialized reference books such as encyclopedias, indexes, bibliographies, research guides, biographical indexes, and statistical summaries. Librarians love to help with research so don't be shy about asking for assistance. They can steer you to the best reference sources.

THE RESEARCH PAPER

Reference works will be found in **print,** in **CD-ROMs**, in **online data bases** or in **microform.** Print material is generally arranged by subject with encyclopedias and dictionaries about the same subject shelved together. Annual publications like bibliographies and indexes like the *Reader's Guide to Periodical Literature* are usually shelved in one place.

CD-ROMs may be inserted into your personal computer or may be installed in the library's online system. Online databases are accessed through the library's computer. Databases from other libraries or commercial vendors can also be retrieved, but some suppliers charge fees for this service. Remember that you may be able to access CD-ROMs and databases from your own PC through the Internet. More on this later in the chapter.

CD-ROMs and online databases have the advantages of being more current and more inclusive than corresponding print material. In addition, you may be able to download data directly to a disk and or to your PC. Some libraries even sell blank disks for a minimal charge if you forget your own.

SEARCH 3. 1: SEARCH ENCYCLOPEDIAS

General encyclopedias are OK for preliminary research to give you an overview of your topic. They provide good overall coverage of most important persons, events, and topics, but you must go beyond them. Some encyclopedias are available in CD-ROM format or online. They may or may not be in your library database.

GENERAL ENCYCLOPEDIAS
Encyclopedia Americana
New Encyclopedia Britannica

Special encyclopedias for most specific disciplines are published. Check with your librarian for the encyclopedia(s) in your field.

TYPICAL SPECIAL ENCYCLOPEDIAS
Encyclopedia of Asian History
Encyclopedia of the Biological Sciences
Encyclopedia of World Art

SEARCH 3. 2: SEARCH INDEXES

Indexes contain alphabetically arranged information from magazines, scholarly journals, newspapers, and other sources. They are published periodically and are usually bound in volumes containing a range of dates. General indexes catalog articles from popular newspapers and magazines. Specialized indexes catalog articles from journals within a discrete discipline. Many indexes are now on CD-ROM and are included in most library databases. If so, both the general and special subject indexes will be available, frequently with abstracts and full text printouts. Ask your librarian for help in finding print special indexes.

POPULAR GENERAL INDEXES
Expanded Academic ASAP
Infotrac
National Newspaper Index
New York Times Index
Reader's Guide to Periodical Literature
Wilson Select

TYPICAL SPECIAL INDEXES
Art Index
Education Index
General Science Index
Literary Criticism Index
Medline

SEARCH 3. 3: SEARCH BIBLIOGRAPHIES

Bibliographies contain lists of publications. There are bibliographies of bibliographies, bibliographies of general subjects, and bibliographies of special fields. There are even bibliographies of reference books - a good place to start.

As with other reference works, some are available on CD-ROM and in online databases and some are not.

POPULAR GENERAL BIBLIOGRAPHIES
Bibliographic Index: A Cumulative Bibliography of Bibliographies
The New York Times Guide To Reference Materials

THE RESEARCH PAPER

TYPICAL SPECIAL BIBLIOGRAPHIES
American Women and Politics
Bibliographic Guide to Black Studies
Bibliographic Guide to Business and Economics
MLA Bibliography
Political Science: A Bibliographic Guide to the Literature

SEARCH 3. 4: SEARCH ABSTRACTS

Almost every discipline publishes volumes which summarize articles from the journals in the field. If you find an abstract which looks valuable, get the journal and read the full text. If the journal is not in the library, it is permissible to cite information from an abstract as long as you use the appropriate citation. Many abstracts are now on CD-ROM and in online databases with full text available. Ask your librarian for the abstracts which are published in your field and check the online database in the library.

TYPICAL SPECIAL SUBJECT ABSTRACTS
Art Abstracts
Biological Abstracts
Education Abstracts
Historical Abstracts
Newspaper Abstracts
Periodical Abstracts
Psychological Abstracts
Sociological Abstracts

SEARCH 3. 5: SEARCH RESEARCH GUIDES

Research guides usually contain reference tools and other sources available for research in a particular discipline. Ask your librarian for the latest research guides in your area of research. Check to see if any are available on CD-ROM or in online databases.

TYPICAL RESEARCH GUIDES
Information Sources in Economics
Library Research Guide to History
Literary Research Guide

SEARCH 3. 6: SEARCH DICTIONARIES

Dictionaries contain alphabetically arranged brief definitions within specific disciplines. Excellent for obtaining precise meanings of unfamiliar terms in your area of research. Check with your librarian for a dictionary in your subject. Check your library's online database for electronic dictionaries.

TYPICAL DICTIONARIES
Black's Law Dictionary
Dictionary of Botany
Dictionary of Philosophy
Dictionary of the Social Sciences

SEARCH 3. 7: SEARCH BIOGRAPHICAL SOURCES

Volumes of biographical data are published for persons living and dead. In addition, some disciplines publish biographical data on prominent persons in specific fields. If your research deals with a person, these sources will provide brief biographical summaries which can serve as a starting point before going on to full biographies. Some biographical sources are available in electronic format.

POPULAR BIOGRAPHICAL SOURCES FOR LIVING PERSONS
Biography Index
Current Biography
Who's Who in America
International Who's Who

POPULAR BIOGRAPHICAL SOURCES FOR DEAD PERSONS
American National Biography
Webster's New Biographical Dictionary

TYPICAL BIOGRAPHICAL SOURCES IN SPECIFIC DISCIPLINES
Who's Who in Religion
American Men and Women of Science

SEARCH 3. 8: SEARCH YEARBOOKS

Yearbooks contain information about specific personalities, discoveries, inventions, or other events which occurred during a specific year. To locate such current information use one of the following yearbooks.

POPULAR YEARBOOKS
Americana Annual
Britannica Book of the Year

SEARCH 3. 9: SEARCH STATISTICAL SOURCES

Statistical data is available from many sources, particularly government agencies. If your research deals with such data, ask your librarian for help finding specialized statistical information.   Much statistical information is available in electronic format.

STATISTICAL DATA PUBLICATIONS
Demographic Yearbook
Statistical Abstract of the United States
Statistical Yearbook

SEARCHING WITH CD-ROMs OR ONLINE DATABASES

You will have to learn the way to access your library's CD-ROM collections and its databases since systems vary. To search CD-ROMs or online databases follow the instructions in your library's handbook, on the terminal, or ask a librarian for help.

Electronic encyclopedias and dictionaries are usually the easiest to use. A nice feature of electronic encyclopedias is the incorporation of graphics and sound so you can actually hear famous speeches and see color photos of things. Some electronic dictionaries provide correct spoken pronunciation of words.

CD-ROM or online indexes hold much more information and are quicker and easier to use than print indexes. Many indexes contain abstracts and full-texts of articles, so you can quickly tell whether the article will be of use in your research. Remember, too, that every library cannot afford to purchase every index or every journal in each index so don't be surprised if you cannot retrieve some sources.

Follow the instructions on the terminal. The first screen will usually provide a list of databases by subject These may include abstracts, indexes, bibliographies, and other reference tools. The collection within each database will vary from library to library.

THE RESEARCH PAPER

**Typical First Screen of Online Databases
Showing Databases by Subject**

Databases by Title
Databases by Vendor

Databases by Subject

Databases by Subject
Table of Contents
Art & Humanities
Biography
Biology & Marine Science
Business
Education
General
General Science
Government
Law
Library Science
Literature
Medical
Music
News
Political Science
Psychology
Social Sciences

☞ **Available only from library workstations**
⊞ **Indicates full-text available**

(Click on underlined links to access databases)
GENERAL

- Article1st ☞ ⊞
- Contents1st ☞
- Expanded Academic ASAP ⊞
- FactSearch ☞
- FastDoc ☞ ⊞
- FirstSearch ☞ ⊞
- GPO (Government Printing Office)
- GPO *(for Windows 95 and higher)*
- Infotrac ⊞
- A Matter of Fact
- A Matter of Fact *(for Windows 95 and higher)*
- NetFirst ☞
- PA Research II Periodicals ⊞
- Periodical Abstracts ☞ ⊞
- Periodical Contents Index ☞
- Readers' Guide Abstracts ☞ ⊞
- Wilson Select ☞ ⊞

The illustration above shows a typical first screen of an online database collection. On the left is a list of databases by subject. In this illustration, a student writing a paper on the **Kosovo war** was interested in **President Clinton's role.** She clicked on the **General link** in the **Databases by Subject** list on the left side of the screen.

From the list of databases under the **General** heading the student decided to search the **Readers' Guide Abstracts.** This is a database which contains abstracts of articles which appear in the magazines and newspapers which the **Readers' Guide** indexes. She clicked on the **Readers' Guide Abstracts link**. The second page opened which described the type of periodicals, dates of publication, update periods, and availability of full texts in the database.

At the top of the screen is a **search box.** Our student typed **"Kosovo and Clinton"** in the **Search for** box and clicked on the **Start Search** button. See the illustration of the second screen on the next page.

THE RESEARCH PAPER

**Typical Second Screen of Online Databases
Showing Selected Database**

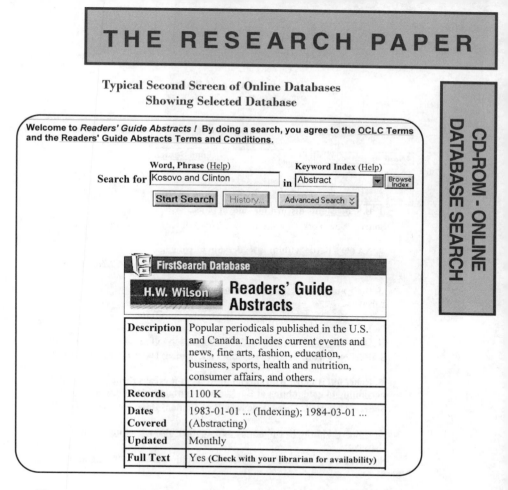

The screen opened showing the search results. **See the illustration on page 20 showing the third screen.** At the top of the screen you can see the results of the search which found 161 records. The page will usually show the first ten sources (only six are shown in this illustration) which contain the keywords entered in the Search box.

Our researcher clicked on **Number 2. NATO's battle within: is leadership missing?** to open the next screen with an abstract of the article and full bibliographic data. **See the illustration of the fourth screen on page 21.**

A note at the top indicates that this library owns the item. Clicking on the **Get/Display Item** will open the full text of the article. In most libraries you will be able to print out the abstract page or the full text pages and/or download to your own disk. The **Libraries with Item**

**Typical Third Screen of Online Databases
Showing Initial Search Results**

| **Database**= Readers' Guide Abstracts | **Search**=ab:(Kosovo and Clinton) | **Results**= 161 records

| ⏬NextPage | ⏫PrevPage | Go To Record: | 1 | | Limit Search |

Tagged Records (Help)
| Show | Clear |

1. U.S. discounts discord for sake of talks..
Source: New York Times (Late New York Edition) **Date:** 1999 *Tag Record* ☐

2. NATO's battle within: is leadership missing?..
Source: New York Times (Late New York Edition) **Date:** 1999 *Tag Record* ☐

3. Blair under domestic pressure on ground forces. Kosovo).
Source: New York Times (Late New York Edition) **Date:** 1999 *Tag Record* ☐

4. On a wing and a prayer?. (B. Clinton and use of ground forces; op-ed).
Source: New York Times (Late New York Edition) **Date:** 1999 *Tag Record* ☐

5. Relief bill is laden with special projects as it creaks through committee. pertaining to gold mining at Buckhorn Mountain in Washington State).
Source: New York Times (Late New York Edition) **Date:** 1999 *Tag Record* ☐

6. Upheaval in the Kremlin may add another obstacle to finding peace (Kosovo).
Source: New York Times (Late New York Edition) **Date:** 1999 *Tag Record* ☐

button will yield a list of local libraries which have the article. The **E-Mail Record** button will open a screen that asks you to which e-mail address you want the item sent!

You can use the abstract printout as your bibliography card since all the bibliographic information is there and you eliminate any chances of error in copying. Be sure to add your code number in one corner of the printout.

SEARCHING MICROFORM SOURCES

Microforms are print materials which have been photographically reduced to very small size on film to save much needed space. These films are known as **microcard, microfilm**, and **microfiche** (*microfeesh*) depending on the technology used. The library maintains special machines which are called "readers" which enlarge the print and enable you to read the material.

THE RESEARCH PAPER

**Typical Fourth Screen of Online Databases
Showing The Abstract of the Selected Source**

```
[ Database= Readers' Guide Abstracts | Search=ab:(Kosovo and Clinton) | Results= 161 records | Record=2]
[Libraries with Item] [Get / Display Item] [E-Mail Record]

[⍯ NextRec] [⍠ PrevRec]

Ownership: FirstSearch indicates your library owns this item or magazine.
      NUMBER: BRGA99032713
      AUTHOR: Gordon, Michael R.
       TITLE: NATO's battle within: is leadership missing?.
      SOURCE: New York Times (Late New York Edition) (May 20 '99) p. A14
 STANDARD NO: 0362-4331
        DATE: 1999
 RECORD TYPE: art
    CONTENTS: feature article
    ABSTRACT: President Clinton continues to wrestle over the question of
              whether to dispatch combat forces to Kosovo, and without clear
              direction from Washington, NATO's strategy for bringing the
              war to a successful close has begun to unravel.  The British,
              Germans, and Italians are all on separate pages with regard to
              the issue of ground troops in Kosovo, and this confusion
              within NATO is undoubtedly welcome news for President Slobodan
              Milosevic of Yugoslavia, whose strategy from the start has
              been to survive the air war, encourage divisions within the
              Western alliance, and attempt to negotiate a Kosovo settlement
              on his terms.
     SUBJECT: Kosovo (Serbia)  - History - Civil War, 1998-  - American
              participation.Kosovo (Serbia)  - History - Civil War, 1998-  -
              Ground troops.Kosovo (Serbia)  - History - Civil War, 1998-  -
              NATO participation.

[⍯ NextRec] [⍠ PrevRec]
```

Typically, libraries use microform for old copies of newspapers, magazines, or journals which because of age would dry up and fall apart if left in their original states. If you are doing historical research and need information that is very old, you will probably find it in the library's microform collection. Ask your librarian for help.

CONCLUDING LIBRARY RESEARCH

When you have searched all the library's resources for information on your topic, you should have a large stack of bibliography cards and/or printouts or you should have a fairly lengthy list of bibliographic entries in your computer "Bibliography File." Be sure each entry has your code number, the library's call number, the location in the library, and, most important, your notes about the information you found on your topic. You should be thoroughly immersed in the subject and have a good idea of how other writers have dealt with the topic.

The next step is to search the Internet if you have a modem.

WHAT IS THE INTERNET?

The Internet is a network of millions (and the number is increasing daily) of interconnected computers worldwide. No one owns the Internet and it has no central facility. Nevertheless, this remarkable electronic communication network enables users to:

- **Send and receive electronic mail**
- **Join special interest groups**
- **Discuss common topics in real time**
- **Search for information on a wide range of subjects**
- **Download text, graphics, sound, and software.**

HOW THE INTERNET WORKS - INTERNET PROTOCOLS

Communication is established between computers through special systems called **protocols.** Usually the name of the protocol forms part of the address. The most frequently used protocols are:

E-mail: Send and receive messages worldwide, usually in seconds, to individual mailbox addresses. Photos, text and other files may be attached.

Listserv: Participate in e-mail discussions on specific subjects, frequently academic, conducted by organizations. You must subscribe by sending an e-mail to a *listserver* which transmits messages to and from subscribers.

Usenet News: Participate in discussions in newsgroups. Messages about many topics are exchanged among *newsgroups* on electronic bulletin boards. Different from *listserv* in that messages are stored on computers and users must log on to read messages. Some newsgroups are academic but topics vary widely. Newsgroups are definitely not recommended as sources for serious research because it is difficult to assess the quality of information or the authority of the writer.

FTP: **File Transfer Protocol** is used to transfer computer files including pictures, sounds, software, and text to your computer. Many sites are restricted to those who have an account which allows users to access and download information. However, most public agencies allow free access to anyone using the username, *anonymous,* to log on and download files.

Gopher: With the rapid growth and technological development of the World Wide Web, gopher sites have gradually begun to disappear, but they can be accessed on the Internet. Gopher is more like a regular library subject catalog and it will search the holdings of many computers for your subject.

Telnet: Telnet is a protocol which enables you to log on to another computer and use it as your own. Connections in some schools and universities allow students to use large computers from their homes or dorms.

THE WORLD WIDE WEB

As the Internet grew, scientists developed an umbrella shell called the World Wide Web which provides easier access to the Internet protocols described above. The Web uses an interface based on **hypertext** which is a technique of linking words or pictures to other files. Information is retrieved on the Web through **hypertext documents** which are capable of holding text, graphics, and sound. Hypertext documents use a special language called **HyperText Markup Language** or **html.** To access a hypertext document on the Web you must use the letters **http** for *HyperText Transfer Protocol.*

The first hypertext document you see when you reach a site is called a **"home page."** Each page contains **underlined** and **highlighted words** or **graphics** which are links to other Internet sites. By clicking on the links, the user opens the next page which can contain images, video, sound, and text. The whole is a "web" of links which can produce an amazing array of information.

URL: UNIFORM RESOURCE LOCATOR OR INTERNET ADDRESS

The **URL** is the address of sites on the Internet. Internet addresses are similar to regular mail addresses, but look more complicated. The **protocol name** always begins a URL whether it is an **http, gopher,** or **FTP** site. The URL contains a series of network names separated by dots (.), slashes (/), and tildes (~).

URLs are very specific. Some are case sensitive, which means if some of the letters are capitalized, the user must be sure those are capitalized when typing the address. An extra space, period, or other miscue will make it impossible to reach the site.

INTERNET SEARCH

INTERNET ADDRESS DOMAINS:

com........commercial and business
edu.........educational institutions
gov.........government agencies
mil..........military organizations
net..........network resources
org..........other organizations

For example, *http://starburst.uscolo.edu* means there is a sub-network called **starburst** connected to a network at the **University of Southern Colorado** and it is an **educational institution**. A two letter country abbreviation usually ends the address when a country is designated. The address, *http://www.ed.gov,* is the **U.S. Department of Education Online Library**. **E-mail** user's names are placed at the beginning and followed with the @ sign. Thus, *kwilliams@delaware.udel.edu* is the address of **K. Williams** at the **University of Delaware**.

IMPORTANT: Internet addresses, URLs, frequently change, move, or disappear. Don't be surprised if you cannot access a URL. If stymied, your best bet is to use the major part of the URL at the left of the address followed by the domain. The home page should open with links to the site you are trying to reach.

INTERNET SERVICE PROVIDERS

Internet service providers are the organizations, usually commercial, which hook you up to the Internet via a modem which dials your telephone. Popular ISPs are **America Online, Compuserv**, and **Mindspring**, but there are many more. Most charge a monthly fee or a fee based on usage.

Once connected, the ISP's home page appears. The home page will resemble a typical **windows application window** complete with a **Menu Bar** and a **Tool Bar.**

WEB BROWSERS

Several "browsers" or programs for accessing the Internet are available such as **Netscape Navigator, Microsoft Explorer, and Mosaic.** The browser is the device which lets you access the Internet. Learn the uses of your browser's **File, Edit, Favorites** or **Bookmark, Back, Forward, Help,** and other buttons on the **Button Bar.**

CONDUCTING RESEARCH ON THE INTERNET

Information consisting of articles, graphics, video, sound, and software resides in the millions of computers which make up the Internet. This information can be obtained with amazing speed as compared with research in a conventional library. However, the Internet is like a vast library which has no regular system of cataloging such as the Dewey Decimal System or the Library of Congress Catalog. Therefore, finding the material you need requires some special knowledge of the Internet.

The good news is that advances in search techniques are rapidly making searching simpler, faster, and more precise. The following pages will empower you to get the most out of this vast, rich, and valuable information resource.

SEARCH TOOLS

Conducting a thorough search will require you to use all of the search tools available on the Internet. You should use each systematically to insure that you have made an exhaustive search for all the significant material on your topic.

Powerful tools for searching are available including:
- **Search Engines**
- **Meta-Search Engines**
- **Subject Directories**
- **Periodical Guides**
- **Book Guides**
- **Guides to Other Library Collections and Resources**
- **Listserv Mailing Lists Guides**
- **E-mail Address Guides**
- **Usenet Newsgroups Guides**

SEARCH 1: SEARCH WITH A SEARCH ENGINE

Read the entire section on search engines to learn about them before you begin to use this tool.

Search engines can access most of the Internet protocols including gopher and FTP, but each differs in the manner of searching and in the files which it searches. All search engines will present a list of files based on the **key words** you use in the query. The list will include hypertext links which are underlined and highlighted. Moving the cursor over the link will change its shape. Clicking on the links will bring new files to your computer.

Each search engine has slightly different "rules" for searching and you must follow these rules to obtain the most effective search. When you open the home page of an engine, click on the **Help, FAQ (Frequently Asked Questions)**, or **special searching files** for specifics.

> **HINT:** It is a good idea to print out the Help, FAQ, and special searching files and keep them at hand because they will explain the intricacies of each engine and spell out the best ways to formulate your searches.

Most search engines are commercial and profit oriented so their home pages will be filled with advertising, but the searches are usually free. The best search engines on the Internet are constantly being improved so check the Help and FAQ files regularly for changes.

Click on the **Search Button** of your **ISP's home page**. The **home page** of one of the search engines will open. You can change engines by typing its **URL** in the **Address Box** at the top of the home page and pressing **Enter** or clicking the mouse.

To initiate a simple search, type **key words** which represent the concepts of your topic in the blank **Search Box** of the engine and click **Search**. Remember, you may have to modify your key words for each engine. Search engines also offer **advanced searches** and other refinements to focus the search.

> **HINT:** Try each engine in turn to see how it works and compare the results.

Refining the Search Engine Search

The success of your search depends on four factors:

- the way the search engine conducts its search
- the database of the search engine you are using
- your choice of the best key words for each engine
- your skill in using the special "operators" for each engine

Because of the vast number of documents available on the Internet, a simple one word query to a search engine can produce thousands of documents each of which has links to others. The result is confusion and frustration, because it is impossible for you to examine all of the files. And how would you know whether you have obtained the best ones?

For example, if you were to enter the key word, Clinton, in the search box, the search engine will produce thousands of documents related to President Clinton, but also thousands of files for towns named Clinton, inventors named Clinton, schools named Clinton, Clinton *ad nauseum*.

Therefore, you have to use the **special searching rules** of each engine. Being very specific with key words and using **Boolean** and other **"operators"** will help refine the search.

Some people think **Boolean logic** is a fancy computer term intended to intimidate users. Actually, it is named after the 19th century English mathematician, Boole, who believed that language could be expressed algebraically. A series of **"operators"** based on Boolean mathematics is used to refine searches.

Boolean Operators

AND Use AND between two words. Only files containing both words will appear.
President Clinton AND Gore

OR Use OR between two words. Only files containing at least one of the words will appear.
President Clinton OR Gore

NOT Use NOT before a word. No files containing the word following NOT will appear.
President Clinton NOT Gore

ALL is the same as AND

ANY is the same as OR

Non-Boolean Operators

Some search engines use other non-Boolean operators.
+ is the same as AND. Place the **+** before the term.
- is the same as NOT. Place the **-** before the term.

Proximity Operators

NEAR Use NEAR between two words. Only files in which the two terms occur within 10 words of each other will appear.
Clinton NEAR Gore

FAR   Use FAR between two words. Only files in which the two terms occur 25 or more words apart will appear.
President Clinton FAR Gore

Phrase Searching Operator

"   "   Use quotation marks to narrow the search.

> **"bilingual education"** will yield specific files about bilingual education. **Bilingual education** without quotation marks will yield many separate files with the word, **education**, and many separate files with **bilingual**. **Organization names** and **proper names** will work as phrases without quotation marks in some search engines.

Truncation Operator

*   Use an asterisk * after a root word to generate files with all variations of the word.

> **human*** will yield **humanist, humanism, humane, etc.**

How to Refine Key Words to Improve Your Searches

STEP 1. **Examine your topic and identify the key words which are most likely to produce the best results. Try to be as specific as possible.**

Topic: Effectiveness of Workfare Programs in New York State
Possible Key Words:
> workfare, welfare, workfare legislation, welfare reform, workfare effectiveness, New York State

STEP 2. **List the possible combinations which may narrow the search and use appropriate Boolean or other operators.**

Possible Key Search Words and Phrases:
> welfare AND Pataki, workfare AND "New York State," welfare AND Pataki, welfare AND "New York State Laws", "welfare reform" AND "New York State", "welfare reform," welfare, workfare, "workfare effectivness", etc.

If not successful, try different key words. Learn which operators each engine expects. Some engines allow plain language questions, such as **"How effective is workfare?"** and give hints for refining the search.

HINT: PRINT OUT THE FIRST PAGE of each search to keep the URLs of "good" files. Stick with one search engine trying different key words until you are satisfied that you have exhausted all possibilities. Then try each engine in turn using its special search "rules" and compare the results.

HINT: USE BOOKMARKS. Open a new folder for this project in the Bookmarks or Favorites list of your browser and place all of the good sites in it.

When you locate a file which you think you will use repeatedly, click on the Bookmark Button in the Menu Bar. Click on Add and the file will be saved. To access later, click on Bookmarks. A drop down list will appear with the file in the list. Click on the file and the page will open. At the end of the session, delete the ones you do not want to save.

Trouble Shooting Search Problems

Unrelated documents in results?
- ➜ Use correct spelling of all key words.
- ➜ Use proper capitalization if engine is case sensitive.
- ➜ Use the proper syntax for the engine.

Too many documents or documents not related to your topic:
- ➜ Use Boolean AND logic to be sure each term appears.
- ➜ Use Boolean NOT logic to eliminate irrelevant terms.
- ➜ Use advanced search procedures of the search engine.

Too few documents:
- ➜ Use Boolean OR to broaden search.
- ➜ Use less specific and fewer keywords.
- ➜ Link important terms with Boolean AND.
- ➜ Use the truncation operator.

Advanced Searching

To refine the original search, engines will provide forms of **advanced searching** such as *sub-searching* which is a search within the results of a previous search. *Results ranking*, the order in which results appear, is also offered by most engines and also refines the search. Some engines offer *"More like this?"* options to retrieve sites similar to the ones presented. Detailed descriptions of these refinements will be found in the **Help, FAQ** or other files of the engine. New and specialized search engines as well as improved search techniques are being developed all the time. Maintain a lookout for them in online or print publications.

INTERNET SEARCH

POPULAR SEARCH ENGINES

AltaVista
http://altavista.digital.com

Infoseek
http://www.infoseek.com

Lycos
http://www.lycos.com

Yahoo
http://www.yahoo.com

Excite
http://www.excite.com

Hotbot
http://www.hotbot.com

Webcrawler
http://www.webcrawler.com

Northern Light
http://www.nlsearch.com/

SEARCH 2: SEARCH WITH META-SEARCH ENGINES

Using a meta-search engine is a good way to search. Meta-search engines search several of the search engines mentioned above at the same time and display files from all of the engines it has searched. However, meta-search engines differ in the way they report the results of searches. Some list the results by individual search engine in sequence while others provide a single list. One permits the user to sort results by domain while others offer other options for reporting results.

Meta-search engines also differ in the way they search and in the special instructions you must give them so you will have to study the **Help** and **FAQ** files of each carefully. However, it is important that you become thoroughly familiar with the individual engines first so you will be able to evaluate the results produced by the meta-search engine.

HINT: Study and print out the meta-search engines Help and FAQ files.

POPULAR META-SEARCH ENGINES

Dogpile
> **http://www.dogpile.com**

Inference Find
> **http://www.inference.com/infind**

MetaCrawler
> **http://www.metacrawler.com**

Metafind
> **http://www.metafind.com**

SEARCH 3: SEARCH SUBJECT DIRECTORIES

In an effort to bring some order to the Internet, many universities, libraries, search engine companies and other organizations are producing subject directories arranged like the subject catalogs of regular libraries. Most of the search engines listed above maintain subject directories. Directories range widely in quality and content. Some are carefully evaluated by experts who write annotations while others are not very scholarly.

A subject directory is a good place to search because it will give you a good overview of the general topic in which you are interested. Many subject directories will lead you to the home pages of organizations, universities, and libraries which can provide specific information on your topic. Searching subject directories is a good way to find sources which you may not have known existed. For example, you may find journals and magazines, organizations, and even full text material related to your subject.

Subject directories or indices are usually organized like the branches of a tree so the user can search from general to increasingly more specific topics. As with search engines, read the **Help files** carefully to get clear directions for using specific subject directories.

Each subject directory will look different, but in general you will see a list of major topics on its home page. For example, the **Yahoo** home page has a directory which begins with **Arts** and **Humanities, Business, Computers, Education**, etc. If you continued a search for information on **welfare reform in New York State**, clicking on **Sociology** under the **Social Science heading** and entering **"welfare reform"** in the search box yields a list of 23 sites.   Several are excellent such as the the **Welfare Policy Center** of the Hudson Institute which has a rich mine of material under its own index of **Articles, Best Practices**, etc.

If you enter the **Scout Report Signpost** subject directory and click on the letter **W, Welfare** will appear in a list of topics begining with W. Clicking on **Welfare** will yield six good sites.

> **HINT: Just as with search engines, it is a good idea to try each directory, print out valuable sites and bookmark the sites which look promising in your special Bookmark Folder.**

POPULAR SUBJECT DIRECTORIES

Search engines
> http://search engine name.com

Argus: The Clearinghouse
> http://www.clearinghouse.net

WWW Virtual Library
> http://www-sul.stanford.edu/

INFOMINE: Scholarly Internet Resource Collections
> http://lib-www.ucr.edu

Yahoo!'s Indices
> http://www.yahoo.com

Librarians' Index to the Internet
> http://sunsite.berkeley.edu/

UCB Library and Internet Resources by Subject
> http://lib.berkeley.edu

Scout Report Signpost
> http://www.signpost.org/signpost/

Brittanica Internet Guide
> http://www.ebig.com/

BUBL Link
> http://www.bubl.ac.uk

Magellan
> http://www.mckinley.com

THE RESEARCH PAPER

SEARCH 4: SEARCH GUIDES TO PERIODICALS

Just as you used the print copy of the *Reader's Guide to Periodicals* in the library, so you can use several online periodical guides to find magazines or journals related to your subject. Some magazines and journals provide indexes to their publications. You may be able to access full text articles from some magazines or articles.

Continuing your search for information on **welfare reform**, you might open the **Excite** search engine: **http://www.excite.com.** If you type **"welfare reform" AND journals** in the search box, many sites will appear including one leading to the **University of Chicago's** *Social Science Review* and an article titled, **"Welfare Reform and the Revival of Ideology - An Essay Review."**

POPULAR GUIDES TO PERIODICALS

Many journals and magazines have their own home pages.
> http://www.title of magazine or journal.com

Use a search engine with a key word search
> **Type: The name of the periodical or journal in the search box and click Search.**
> > or
>
> **Type: The subject AND journals or periodicals in the search box and click Search.**

Use a search engine subject directory or other directory
> **Click on a subject such as "Business" and type the word, journals, in the search box and click Search.**

Use one of the following Internet periodical guides

Ecola Newsstand
> http://www.ecola.com

Ejournal Site Guide: Academic
> http://www.library.ubc.ca/

Internet Public Library Reading Room Newspapers
> http://www.ipl.org/reading/news

Internet Public Library Reading Room Serials
> http://www.ipl.org/reading/serials

UC San Diego Library Directories of Electronic Journals
> http://gort.ucsd.edu/

SEARCH 5: SEARCH GUIDES TO BOOKS

Although the Internet has no catalog, a few Internet sites are beginning to catalog books. Full text is available at some sites. Each site has different resources and each has different rules for accessing material.

The **Internet Public Library**, for example, offers searching by **Dewey Decimal Classification.** Clicking on the **300 Social Sciences** classification, and narrowing the classification to **362.5** will produce a possible source for the topic, Welfare Reform, a book titled, *Necessary Poverty: A New Approach.*

POPULAR GUIDES TO BOOKS

College or University Libraries
> **http://Internet address of college or university.edu**
> The home page may contain links to the library and then to collections of books.

Internet Public Library Reading Room Texts
> **http://www.ipl.org/reading/books**

Literature Online
> **http://lion.chadwyck.com/**

Digital Books, Images, and More
> **http://sunsite.berkeley.edu/**

Online Books Page
> **http://www.cs.cmu.edu/books.html**

SEARCH 6: SEARCH LIBRARIES AND LIBRARY REFERENCES

Many university and other major libraries allow users to access their catalogs via the Internet. Some enable you to download text. The following sites will provide information on libraries and their collections.

POPULAR LIBRARY GUIDES

Search Engines
> **Type: libraries in the search box and click search.**

Libweb
> http://sunsite.berkeley.edu/Libweb

Internet Public Library
> http://www.ipl.

SEARCH 7: SEARCH ACADEMIC MAILING LISTS IN LISTSERVS

Many academic organizations conduct discussions on specific subjects. You may find information by locating a mailing list which deals with your subject. There are a number of mailing list finders, but as with search engines each differs in the manner in which it searches. Read the **Help files** for specific instructions.

POPULAR LISTSERV MAILING LIST GUIDES

For a print book with the addresses of listservs, see the ***Directory of Electronic Journals, Newsletters and Academic Discussion Groups*** by Lisbeth King, Diane Kovacs, and others.

Search Engines
> **Type: listservs or listservs AND your subject in the search box and click Search.**

Kovacs' Directory of Scholarly E-lists
> http://n2h2.com/KOVACS/Sindex.html

Liszt
> http://www.liszt.com

Catalist
> http:www.lsoft.com/lists/listref.html

To Subscribe to a Mailing List

1. Open your Internet connection. Click on your e-mail software. Eudora and Netscape Messenger are examples.
2. Click on New Message. The message box will appear.
3. Type the listserv subscription address at the To: prompt.
4. Tab down to the message area. Type SUBSCRIBE (name of listserv) (your name). Click Send.

INTERNET SEARCH

To Send a Message to a Mailing List

1. Obtain the mail address of the mailing list. It is usually different from the subscription address.
2. Follow the above directions for subscribing, except type the message you want to send in the message area.

To Unsubscribe from a Mailing List

1. Follow the instructions for subscribing above, except type SIGNOFF (mailing list subscribe address).

SEARCH 8: SEARCH E-MAIL SOURCES

You may want to locate an important researcher or source for your research. You can use one of the E-mail address finders below.

POPULAR E-MAIL ADDRESS GUIDES

Bigfoot
> **http://www.bigfoot.com**

Four 11
> **http://www.four11.com**

SEARCH 9: SEARCH USENET NEWSGROUPS

Newsgroups use electronic bulletin boards to exchange messages about many topics. While most are not scholarly, a few academic forums do exist. Be extremely cautious before accepting and citing any information received from a newsgroup. Newsgroups can be accessed on the Web, but Listservs are accessed through e-mail.

You may need special software which many ISPs now provide to access newsgroups. Methods for accessing newsgroups vary. Use the Help file of your ISP or search engine.

POPULAR USENET FINDERS

Use a search engine.
> **Type: Newsgroups, Usenet, or Newsgroups AND your subject in the search box and click Search.**

DejaNews
> **http://www.dejanews.com**

EVALUATING INTERNET SOURCES

Information which appears in print form has usually been subjected to careful editing based on long established journalistic standards. Publishers are usually diligent in checking the facts in articles which they publish. The editors of scholarly journals are most judicious in selecting and editing research articles. Nevertheless, the careful researcher will scrupulously evaluate print material for accuracy, point of view, and bias.

If print material needs careful evaluation, information obtained on the Internet needs even more intensive scrutiny before being accepted. Responsible online publishers and writers maintain the same standards as those for print media, but others do not. With very little expense, anyone can become an electronic publisher, set up a home page, write articles for Usenet or Listserv discussion groups, send e-mail, and enter chat rooms. In many cases, it is impossible to determine exactly who the writer is or whom he or she represents. As you obtain information, use the **Internet Source Evaluation Checklist** below to screen material.

INTERNET SOURCE EVALUATION CHECKLIST

Site	Is the site an **edu, org, gov**, or **mil** site? These are most reliable and maintained by colleges and universities, professional organizations, the military, and governmental agencies. Be cautious of **com**, or commercial sites. They usually are heavily weighted with advertising. They may contain information for which payment has been made for publication. Check **Listservs** carefully and be wary of **Usenet** discussion groups and **chat rooms**. **E-mail** should be carefully evaluated and accepted only if it is a personal communication from a known expert which can be verified.
Author	Is the author **well-known, expert, qualified**? Is there an **association** with an established, recognized institution?
Publisher	Is the publisher an establishment such as a **university, professional organization, government agency, or well-known publisher**? Be careful of

publishers which exist only on the Web. Check these carefully. Find out who they are and their qualifications to publish on the subject.

Links   Do **hypertext links** take you to **educational** or other solid sites which can lead to further reliable research and not to commercial sites?

Bibliography   Is there a **bibliography** which attests to **scholarship** and leads to quality sources?

References   Are quality sources cited which you can locate and check? Since paragraphs and page numbers are rarely given, **retrieve** the **file** by **typing** its **URL** in the **address box** of your browser. When the file appears, click on **Find** in the **Edit Menu**. A **Find Dialog Box** will appear. **Type** the **word(s)** or **phrase** you want to verify and click **Find** or press **Enter**. The browser will **locate** and **highlight** the **word(s)** or **phrase** you typed.

Currency   Is information current with **recent publication date**? Internet documents are frequently updated.

Point of View Are **facts** rather than **opinion** presented? Much on theInternet is highly opinionated without grounding in facts. Is author's **point of view** clear and supported by facts? Is **purpose** to persuade, explain, or inform?

Audience   Is information intended for **mature, serious readers**? Reject material which is frivolous or chatty.

COLLECT INTERNET BIBLIOGRAPHY CARDS AND DOWNLOAD INTERNET FILES INTO YOUR WORKING DOCUMENTS

You have been accumulating bibliography cards from your library search. Now add the Internet bibliography cards.

With a file on the screen, prepare an **Internet bibliography card** with all the information required for an **Internet bibliographic entry**. **See page 1-5 for details.** Be sure to assign a **code number** and place it in the upper right corner of the card.

THE RESEARCH PAPER

Highlight the sentences, phrases, or paragraphs you may want to use in your paper. Click on **Copy** in the **Edit Menu** of your **browser**. **Open** a **new document** in your word processor and **save** it as **Outline** or **Notes**. You will need to re-organize this document later when you work on **Task 7. Organize and Classify Notes. See page 1-47** for details on the computer method of organizing notes. Place the **cursor** where you want the copied material to appear in your **Outline** or **Notes Document. Click** on **Paste** in the **Edit Menu** of your word processor. The material will be copied to your document. **Type** the **code number** you assigned to the material in **bold type** near the material so you will be able to properly cite it in the body of your paper and in the bibliography.

GET AN OVERVIEW TO SEE HOW OTHERS TREATED YOUR TOPIC

After researching several articles in magazines, journals, books, and the Internet, you should have some idea of how others have dealt with your topic. You should have identified significant issues. Look through the notes on your bibliography cards or computer printouts. What are the points of view? Are there many or a few? What are the major issues? Jot down a few ideas. Now set the material aside for a day and let the information percolate in your mind.

DECIDE HOW YOU WILL DEAL WITH THE TOPIC

Now is the time to bring your own ideas into the project. Through your reading of sources have you developed your own point of view? Do you agree or disagree with your sources? Has some new or original approach leaped into your mind? Could you apply the information in the sources in a new way? What do you think about this topic? Write down your thoughts. Let them flow. This is the most important part of the research paper project because it will lead directly to your writing the **THESIS STATEMENT** in **Task 4.**

Time for Task 3: 4-8 hours

INTERNET SEARCH

1-39

THESIS STATEMENT

TASK 4: DEVELOP A THESIS STATEMENT

This task is to refine your ideas and develop a thesis which can be "proved" or supported by your research. Read through the following list of **Thesis Approaches** to see which fits your thinking. You may want to re-read your bibliography cards or printouts once more. Note that the examples are all in declarative sentences which can be "proved" with facts.

THESIS APPROACHES

Chronology—	The rise of the Imagist Movement can be traced over a period of twenty years.
Procedure—	Five steps are required to produce liquid oxygen.
Cause/Effect—	Economic factors caused deterioration in Sino-Soviet relations in 1950.
Problem—	Differing Moslem ideologies make Israeli-Palestinian peace difficult.
Solution—	The energy crisis can be solved by solar and nuclear power.
Comparison—	Acupuncture is a better anesthetic than malothane.
Similarity—	TV and motion picture writing are similar in several respects.
Difference—	Marriage rites differ among Far Eastern, Middle Eastern, and Western families
Relationship—	Hemingway's life experiences influenced his work.
Analysis—	Three major issues are related to the crisis in Iran.
Literary Theme—	Romantic themes prevail in two major works of Wordsworth.
Pro—	Kennedy's handling of the Cuban missile crisis was good foreign policy.
Con—	Four medical theories oppose radical mastectomy in breast cancer.
Category—	Several ethnic populations in America grew during the past ten years.

Now write your thesis statement in a declarative sentence. Identify which thesis approach you are using. Think the words, "I believe..." just before you write your thesis statement. This will insure that **YOU** and **YOUR** ideas are in the paper. Check your thesis against the following checklist.

THESIS CHECKLIST

My thesis statement is:
(I believe)_____
_____

The thesis statement:

- uses the (select from list above) thesis approach.
- is not too broad.
- is not too narrow or technical unless required.
- can be proved with the material I have found.
- is scholarly
- is OK with my instructor.

If your thesis statement meets all the above criteria, go on to **Task 5.** If not return to **Task 4** and write a new thesis statement.

Time For Task 4: 1-2 Hours

TASK 5: WRITE A TOPIC OUTLINE

This task helps you organize the information you have found to prove your thesis statement. The thesis approach will suggest the outline.

OUTLINING HINTS

Organize and classify ideas under major headings which support and prove the thesis statement. Do not include your introduction and conclusion in this outline. They will be written as part of **Task 9.**

Plan at least two subdivisions under each major heading. If you cannot, your outline is faulty. Subheads should also have at least two subdivisions.

The **Preliminary Outline** will tell you what information is lacking and send you back to the library to search for it. If you cannot find the material, revise your outline. Do not stretch or pad insufficient information.

Use the Harvard outline or the more modern decimal outline in which all information introduced by the same first numeral relates to the same major topic.

THE RESEARCH PAPER

HARVARD OUTLINE	DECIMAL OUTLINE
I.	1.
A.	1.1.
B.	1.2.
1.	1.2.1.
2.	1.2.2.
a.	1.2.2.1.

SAMPLE OUTLINES

DIFFERENCE THESIS APPROACH

If you selected this approach, you have to identify the elements which differ and then show how they differ.

    Thesis Statement: *Marriage rites differ among Far Eastern, Middle Eastern, and Western families.*

    1. **Marriage Rites in the Far East**
        1.1. Vows
        1.2. Dowries
        1.3. Clothing
        1.4. Ceremonies
    2. **Marriage Rites in the Middle East**
        2.1. Vows
        2.2. Etc.

LITERARY THEMES THESIS APPROACH

If you selected this approach, you must identify the literary themes and then show how they appear in the author's works.

    Thesis Statement: *Romantic themes prevail in two major works of Wordsworth.*

    1. **Romantic Themes**
        1.1. Return to nature
        1.2. Sympathy with humble
        1.3. Escape from convention
    2. **Themes in Wordworth's works**
        2.1. "Tintern Abbey"
            2.1.1. Samples of return to nature
            2.1.2. Samples of sympathy with humble
            2.1.3. Samples of escape from convention
        2.2. "Intimations of Immortality"
            2.2.1. Samples of return to nature
            2.2.2. Etc.

Time for Task 5. 1-3 Hours

TASK 6: CHANGE TOPIC OUTLINE TO A SENTENCE OUTLINE

The next task is to change your **Preliminary Topic Outline** to a **Sentence Outline** in preparation for writing. Each topic should be transformed into a topic sentence around which your paragraphs will be constructed. Remember, a topic sentence is like a little thesis statement. Each sub-topic will contain several paragraphs which "prove" or bear out its topic sentence. The example below shows how the topics are expanded into declarative sentences which can be "proved."

Thesis Statement: *Romantic themes prevail in two major works of Wordsworth*

TOPIC OUTLINE	SENTENCE OUTLINE
1. Romantic Themes	1. Romanticism is associated with several themes which set it apart from neo-Classicism.
1.1. Return to nature	1.1. A return to nature and its beauty characterize the Romantic movement.
1.2. Sympathy with humble.	1.2. The simplicity of the rustic life attracted many Romantic poets.

Time for Task 6: 1-5 Hours

TASK 7: ORGANIZING & USING NOTES

ORGANIZING YOUR SOURCES

This task is to take information from all of your sources and organize it in accordance with your **Sentence Outline**. You must also decide how you want to use each source as you incorporate it into your paper.

Take out your outline and bibliography cards. Get the books, journals, and computer printouts, if any, and locate the pages which contain relevant material. Carefully re-read each page with your sentence outline to guide you. Decide which material fits each outline subtopic. Stick **Post-it Notes** on the top corner of each page with most of the **Post-it Notes** extending beyond the pages so they can be easily seen.

Write the bibliography card code numbers, outline topic numbers, topics, and page number(s) on the part of the Post-it Notes which extend beyond the pages. You might even use different colored **Post-It Notes** for each main topic to make organizing your material easier. Even with your books and magazines closed and piled on your desk, you will be able to locate your sources quickly.

INCORPORATING NOTES INTO YOUR PAPER BY SUMMARIZING, PARAPHRASING, OR QUOTING

There are three basic methods of incorporating reference material into your paper. You can **quote** a source directly, you can **paraphrase** the words of the author in your own words, or you can **summarize** the content. The following instructions illustrate the three techniques.

The passage below is reproduced from a page in Russell Noyes book, *William Wordworth,* published by Twayne Publishers, Inc. in 1971. Assume that you found this passage and intend to use it in your paper to support topic 2.1.1. Samples of theme 'return to nature' in Wordsworth's poem, "Tintern Abbey."

Its repetitive words, phrases, and patterns give to the flowing rhythms a wonderfully resonant and noble beauty. The poetic expression of the impact of the scenic landscape upon the innermost recesses of the poet's mind was as spontaneous as it was powerful. The poem took shape while his feelings were overflowing with excess of joy and while his faith in the power of Nature to dispel "fear or pain or grief" was still at high tide. In after years he qualified and subdued his pronouncements in "Tintern Abbey." But he never lost delight in the simple converse of Nature or his faith that all created things can bring pleasure to the sensitive person impelled by love or praise.

THE RESEARCH PAPER

HOW TO SUMMARIZE, PARAPHRASE, OR QUOTE

SUMMARY: Author's ideas in your words in shortened version.

Directions: Read the passage. Do not look at it again. Rewrite in your own words without your ideas or interpretation. Re-read original to check for accuracy.

The rhythm and phrasing of "Tintern Abbey" reflects the strong feeling developed in Wordworth as he reacted to Nature's landscapes. Later his belief in the power of nature was less fervent, although he always loved the simple joys it brought.

PARAPHRASE: Author's ideas in your words with no attempt to shorten.

Directions: Read passage. Do not look at it again. Rewrite in your own words without your ideas or interpretation, but do not shorten. Make author's ideas simpler. Re-read original to check for accuracy.

"Tintern Abbey" reflects the powerful emotions of near ecstasy Wordsworth felt at the time. The poem's content and form are an outgrowth of the effect of the natural landscape on the poet and his belief that nature could shield humankind from the sadness and pain of life. As he grew older he was less enthusiastic about the ability of Nature to soothe the troubled spirit. Nevertheless, he continued to derive joy from communing with nature.

QUOTATION: Author's words exactly.

Directions: Using quotation marks, copy passage exactly including punctuation, underlining, etc. Even errors shoud be copied and followed with the Latin word, [sic], "thus." in brackets and underlined.

"Its repetitive words, phrases, and patterns give to the flowing rhythms a wonderfully resonant and noble beauty. The poetic expression of the impact of the scenic landscape upon the innermost recesses of the poet's mind was as spontaneous as it was powerful."

PLAGIARISM

Plagiarism is the improper use of another's ideas or language. Paraphrasing closely without giving credit or using original phrases or words without quotation marks are definitely examples of plagiarism. Academic and legal penalties are severe and can include a failing grade, expulsion, and even denial of college degrees. Be scholarly and honest.

ARRANGE NOTES TO MATCH YOUR OUTLINE: PHOTOCOPY or NOTE CARDS or COMPUTER

There are three basic methods to accomplish this task: **photocopying, setting up a new wordprocessing document for notes and outline,** or **writing in longhand.** Read all three methods to see which is better for you.

PHOTOCOPY METHOD OF ORGANIZING NOTES

Most libraries charge only 10 or 15 cents per page for photocopying. At that rate you can copy 100 pages for $10.00 or $15.00 which may well be worth it. Copy all the pages from each book or journal on which you stuck Post-it Notes making sure that you staple them together. Add any printouts you obtained from Internet searches.

Write the **bibliography card code number, outline topic numbers, topics,** and **page numbers** on the top of each photocopied page or paragraph. Add your **bibliography code number** and the **page number** of the material. You will need this information when you prepare the Works Cited or Reference bibliography lists at the end of your paper. Decide whether you will **quote, summarize**, or **paraphrase** the material and make a note of your intention on each page. Continue this process until you have cut and labeled every paragraph. If there are some you cannot use, place these aside in a separate pile.

You may want to staple or paste each labeled paragraph on an 8 x 10 sheet of paper to keep things neater, but **be sure every paragraph is labeled with code number, page number, and topic.**

COMPUTER METHOD OF ORGANIZING NOTES

Open a new document in your word processor and save it as **Outline and Notes.** Type the **first topic number and first topic sentence** of your outline. Scan through the Post-it Notes and locate the source material which you want to use to support the first topic of your outline. Skip a line and type in **bold font** your **bibliography card code number and page number(s)** of the material. You will need this information when you prepare the Works Cited or Reference bibliography at the end of your paper. Add the word, **quote, paraphrase**, or **summary** to indicate how you plan to use the material.

Double space and type the quotation, summary, or paraphrase in the same font as you will use in your paper. Continue the process, typing outline topic sentences and topic numbers followed by the quote, paraphrase, or summary which support each topic. When you have finished, you will have your outline in the computer with the quotes, summaries, and paraphrases you need to support and prove the topic sentences directly under each topic.

LONGHAND METHOD OF ORGANIZING NOTES

You will need a batch of 5 x 8 inch cards for this task. Scan through the Post-it Notes and locate the source material which you want to use to support the first topic of your outline. Write the **bibliography card code number, outline topic number, topic, and page number(s)** of the source on the top of a blank 5 x 8 card. Decide whether you will **quote, summarize** , or **paraphrase** the material and make a note of your intentions on each 5 x 8 card.

Summarize, paraphrase, or quote the information on your first 5 x8 card. Use one side only and a separate card for each idea. Continue this process until you have prepared one of the three types of notes for each paragraph in your source material.

Time for Task 6: 3-8 Hours

TASK 8: WRITE THE FIRST DRAFT

This task is to flesh out your outline. You will write paragraphs based on the topic sentences in the **Sentence Outline.** Write paragraphs by weaving your thoughts around the research notes, but be sure the major thesis and thrust of the paper is your own. Good writers do more than just cut and paste the ideas of others. But before you begin, decide which style of citation you will use.

CITING SOURCES - AUTHOR-DATE OR AUTHOR-PAGE

Most colleges, schools and universities adopt one of several scholarly styles for writing research papers. The most frequently used are the *MLA Handbook for Writers of Research Papers,* Fourth Edition and the *Publication Manual of the American Psychological Association*, Fourth Edition.

As mentioned above, you must tell your reader whose ideas, besides your own, you have used in the paper. By using a citation, you identify the source including the author, title, and publication information enabling your readers to locate the original material. The two manuals suggest different methods of citing sources, but both use parenthetical references in the body of the paper. The **MLA** uses **author and page** while the **APA** uses **author and date.** The two manuals also differ in the formats for presenting bibliographic information provided at the end of the paper.

Decide with your instructor which of the citation styles you will use. Before proceeding, study carefully the specific instructions for each style which you will find in **Chapter 4 MLA Handbook** or **Chapter 9 APA Manual.**

BEGIN WRITING IN EARNEST

Now begin to write in earnest. You can use a typewriter, a wordprocessor, or even old-fashioned yellow legal pads. Double space on the typewriter or wordprocessor and skip lines in longhand to allow for revisions.

Write quickly and forget grammar and style. Your goal is to get your thesis proved by getting your ideas and your research down on paper. Remember to put yourself into the paper. A good research paper is not a collection of quotes and paraphrases of other's ideas. The paper should reflect you. Do not write the introduction or conclusion at this time.

Writing in the third person only, begin with the first topic sentence from your sentence outline and write the paragraphs to "prove" it. Use your paraphrases, summaries, and quotations to support your ideas.

Quotations should comprise no more than one fifth of the paper. Plan to have no more than four citations per page. As you use your quotes, summaries, and paraphrases be sure to write the parenthetical citations for each using the formats in either Chapter 5 or Chapter 9.

Write the transitional sentences and paragraphs which tie the researched material together. Point out disagreements and problems. Work straight through to the end without stopping and put your paper aside for a day when you finish.

WRITING WITH PHOTOCOPY NOTES

If you used the photocopy method of note gathering, you must now transform your photocopied paragraphs into summaries, paraphrases, and quotations and incorporate them into the first draft as you write. Revise the text to insert parenthetical citation in smooth and fluent language. See the sample citations in Chapter 5 or Chapter 9.

Write the **bibliography card code numbers** near each paraphrase, summary, or quote so you will be able to cite the sources accurately in the Works Cited or References list.

WRITING WITH COMPUTER NOTES

If you used the computer method of note gathering, open a new document and save it with the **title of your paper**. Open the document **Outline and Notes.** Both documents will be open. Choose **Tile** from the **Window Menu** of your wordprocessor. The documents will be side by side. Begin writing in your research paper document. When you want to place a paraphrase, quote or summary in your paper, **select the text** in the **Outline and Notes** document and choose **Copy** from the **Edit Menu.** Select your research paper document and move the cursor to the place where you want to insert the material. Choose **Paste** from the **Edit Menu** and the text will be inserted. Revise the text to insert the parenthetical citation in smooth and fluent language.

Type the **bibliography card code numbers** near each paraphrase, summary, or quote so you will be able to cite the sources accurately in the Works Cited or References list.

WRITING WITH LONGHAND NOTE CARDS

If you used the longhand method of note gathering, you now have a collection of note cards containing your summaries, paraphrases, and quotations. Begin writing on the typewriter, in longhand, or on the word processor. You can simply staple the cards directly to the pages of the first draft at the places where you want the summaries, quotes, or paraphrases to appear. On the other hand, you may type them into your paper at the appropriate points as you word process or type your paper. If using longhand, draw lines across the paper above and below the quoted, summarized, or paraphrased material to set it off. Revise the text to insert the parenthetical citation in smooth and fluent language.

Write or type the **bibliography card code numbers and page numbers** near each paraphrase, summary, or quote so you will be able to cite the sources accurately in the Works Cited or References list.

Time for Task 8: 4-8 Hours

TASK 9: REVISE THE FIRST DRAFT

Now re-read your paper for content. Note errors and ideas for changes in the margins. Re-write, cross-out, and add between the lines if using longhand. Delete, cut and paste, and rewrite on the wordprocessor. Use the **Content Checklist** below to be sure your paper is okay. Ask someone else to read your paper to see if it meets all the criteria.

CONTENT CHECKLIST

- Thesis is clearly stated
- Paper is logically developed
- Paper follows outline
- Thesis is proved.
- Sources are cited
- Potential plagiarism checked
- Your ideas are apparent
- Good transitional paragraphs

WRITE THE INTRODUCTION
Tell why you wrote the paper. Describe the positions others have taken on the subject. State your thesis and tell how you approached the topic. Explain the major points in the paper. Discuss the reasons why others should be interested in the subject.

WRITE THE CONCLUSION
Restate the thesis. Summarize the ideas and arguments presented. Explain your conclusions. Discuss leads to further investigation. Tell why you think you paper is interesting and worthwhile.

CHECK FOR GRAMMAR AND STYLE
Re-read the paper for grammar and style. Use your wordprocessor's spell check feature and grammar check if available. Make corrections as needed. Use the Grammar and Style Checklist on the next page to be sure your paper is perfect. See the grammar, usage, and writing review in Chapter 2 for help.

GRAMMAR AND STYLE CHECKLIST

- Clear topic sentences
- Topic sentences proved
- No fragments or run-ons
- Good paragraph transitions
- Consistent tense used
- Subjects and verbs agree
- Pronouns & antecedents agree

- No misplaced modifiers
- Strong verbs and nouns
- Language fluent
- Varied sentence openings
- Spelling correct
- Third person used
- Parallel structure used

Time For Task 9: 3-6 Hours

TASK 10: TYPE THE FINAL DRAFT

Rewrite the paper including all revisions, deletions, and additions. Pay careful attention to the the format of title pages, margins, pagination, citation technique, and especially, the method of preparing the bibliography. Styles vary with regard to handling quotations, too.

Print your paper on good quality, 8 and 1/2 x 11 inch paper on a letter quality printer. After printing your paper, proofread carefully again for omitted words, punctuation, spelling and grammatical errrors. You should now have a paper which you can present to your instructor with pride.

Congratulations! Hope it earns an A+! Your deserve it.

Time For Task 10: 4-8 Hours

PROOFREADING: A WRITING REVIEW

Your paper should contain no spelling, punctuation, or grammatical errors and conform to the standards of usage and style established by the Modern Language Association and American Psychological Association. Language should be non-sexist and free of bias of any kind. This chapter provides a review of these language elements as well as suggestions for improving sentence and writing style.

LANGUAGE MECHANICS

PUNCTUATION

USE COMMAS

- **Before *and, but, for,* and *nor* between independent clauses.**

  The judge approved the verdict, ***but*** the appeals court reversed it.

- **Between *words, phrases,* and *clauses* in series.**

  We assembled ***men, women, girls***, and ***boys***.

- **Between *adjectives* that modify the *same noun*.**

  The flat tax will create ***new, unusual*** hardships.

- **To set off parenthetical comments.**

  Exercising, ***however,*** is not the only way to lose weight.

- **To set off words which, if omitted, would not change the meaning of the sentence.**

  Frank Sinatra, ***one of the most popular singers of the twentieth century,*** will present a concert Tuesday evening.

PUNCTUATION

- To set off clauses beginning with *which, whom, whose, who,* and *that*, which if omitted, would not change the meaning of the sentence.

  The Boeing 747, **which has one of the best safety records,** was responsible for the boom in intercontinental travel.

- After a long introductory clause or phrase.

  If we learn the cause of the expansion, we will be in a position to make better decisions.

USE SEMICOLONS

- Between independent clauses without a conjunction.

  The men in the study were young; **the women were old.**

- To separate items in a series when the items are separated by commas.

  Speakers included **Mr. Jones, the teacher; Ms. Crashet, the principal; and Dr. Rogers, the superintendent.**

USE COLONS

- To introduce a list.

  The following members will attend the convention: **Robertson, Bohannon, and Rabinowitz.**

- To separate a complete, independent clause and a second clause which illustrates or elaborates the first. If the second is a complete sentence it begins with a capital.

  The story is a complete fabrication: **The brothers invented the entire scenario to protect each other.**

USE DASHES

- To show a sharp break in the continuity of a sentence. Use two hyphens, but use sparingly.

  Jim saw himself as handsome--**others saw him as conceited**--and played the role.

USE PARENTHESES

- To show an even sharper break in the continuity of a sentence than the use of dashes.

    The New York art scene (*for some the epitome of hypocrisy*) is alway lively.

USE BRACKETS

- To enclose a parenthesis within a parenthesis.

    (The Lenape tribe [*1710*] was part of the Iroquois group).

USE HYPHENS

Use a good dictionary as a guide, but in general use hyphens:

- In *compound adjectives* beginning with adverbs *ill, better, best, little,* or *well.*

    better-dressed, ill-prepared, little-used, best-known, well-loved

- In *compound adjectives* which *precede a noun* but not in adjectives beginning with an adverb ending in *-ly.*

    slow-moving vehicles, but not *freshly minted money*

- Do not use after prefixes: *after, anti, bi, counter, mid, mini, multi, non, over, pre, pro, semi, socio, sub, super, ultra, under.*

    aftereffects, antifreeze, bipolar, counterattack, miniskirt, multinational, nonjudgemental, overpaid, preschool, profile, semicircular, socioeconomic, subpar, supernova, underclass

USE APOSTROPHES

- To form possessive of a singular noun or a plural noun not ending in *s,* add an apostrophe and an *s.*

    Richard's thesis.   *children's* toys.

- To form possessive of a plural noun ending in *s,* add only an apostrophe.

    motorists' maps

PUNCTUATION

WRITING REVIEW

- **To form the possessive of a singular proper noun, add an apostrophe and an *s.***
  Poe's short stories   **Williams's** latest movie

- **To form the possessive of a plural proper noun, add only an apostrophe.**
  the ***Jeffersons'*** family home

- **To form the possessive of nouns in series when the possession is shared, add an apostrophe and an *s* after the last noun.**
  Jane, Bill, and ***Rose's*** office

- **To form the possessive of nouns in series when possession is separate, add an apostrophe and an s after each noun.**
  Jane's, Bill's, and ***Rose's*** offices

USE PERIODS

- **To end a declarative or imperative sentence.**
  The Russians are coming.   *Face left.*

QUESTION MARKS

- **To end interrogative sentences.**
  How is Bill feeling today?

- **Inside closing quotation marks if the quotation is a question.**
  The teacher asked, *"What time did you finish the test?"*

- **Outside closing quotation marks if the whole sentence is a question.**
  Why is everyone saying, "I know the answer"?

- **Inside closing quotation marks when it replaces a comma or period.**
  "Where has everyone gone?" Mary asked.

SPELLING

PREFERRED AND CONSISTENT SPELLING

Use the latest edition of a good collegiate dictionary as your reference. The **American Psychological Association** accepts the **Merriam-Webster Collegiate Dictionary** as its standard spelling reference. Use the first spelling listed.

WORD-WRAP

Do not hyphenate words at the ends of lines. Use the word-wrap feature of your word processor. If a word does not fit at the end of a line leave the line short.

GRAMMAR AND USAGE

AGREEMENT OF SUBJECT AND VERB

A verb must agree in number and person with its subject even when phrases or clauses separate them.

Wrong:
This *car,* in addition to hundreds of others, *were* selected for export.

Correct:
This *car,* in addition to hundreds of others, *was* selected for export.

***WITH INDEFINITE PRONOUNS: either, neither, everybody, everyone, somebody,* and *everything* are singular and must agree with a singular verb.**

Wrong:
Everyone of the cars *are* on the list.

Correct:
Everyone of the cars *is* on the list.

***WITH COLLECTIVE NOUNS: class, committee, assembly, series,* may be either singular or plural depending on whether the action is on a single group or the individuals within it.**

Action on whole group:
The (whole) *class was selected* to play.

Action on individuals:
The *class* (members) *are* divided on the issue.

WITH PAIRED COORDINATING CONJUNCTIONS: *Neither...nor* and *either...or*

When one noun is singular and one is plural, the verb agrees with the closer noun.

> **Wrong:**
> Neither his brothers nor *Dick were* present.
> **Correct:**
> Neither his brothers nor *Dick was* present.

AGREEMENT OF PRONOUNS AND ANTECEDENTS

A pronoun must agree with its antecedent.

WITH INDEFINITE ANTECEDENT PRONOUNS: *either, neither, everybody, everyone, somebody,* and *everything* are singular and must be followed by singular pronouns.

> **Wrong:**
> *Everyone* is looking for *their* books.
> **Correct:**
> *Everyone* is looking for *his* or *her* books.

WITH PAIRED COORDINATING CONJUNCTIONS: *Neither...nor* and *either...or.* When one noun is singular and one is plural, the pronoun agrees with the closer noun.

> **Wrong:**
> Neither his brothers nor *Dick* has *their* books.
> **Correct:**
> Neither his brothers nor *Dick* has *his* books.

PRONOUNS: *WHO* AND *WHOM*

Who is a subject of a verb and *whom* is an object of a verb or preposition. An easy way to see if the use is correct is to turn the construction around and substitute *he* or *him.* If *he* fits, *who* is correct. If *him* fits, whom is correct. Remember, *whom* and *him* both end in the letter *m.*

> **Wrong:**
> *Who* do you work for?   (You work for *he*.)
> **Correct:**
> *Whom* do you work for?   (You work for *him*.)

RELATIVE PRONOUNS: *THAT* AND *WHICH*

That introduces an element which, if omitted, would change the meaning of the sentence.

> Trees *that are green year round* are called evergreen.

Which introduces an element which, if omitted, would not change the meaning of the sentence.

> Trees, *which are among nature's gifts*, inspire me to write.

SUBORDINATE CONJUNCTIONS: *BECAUSE* AND *SINCE*

Because is used to indicate a causal relationship.

> The device failed *because* preparation was poor.

Since is used to indicate time.

> *Since* the beginning of the test period, several students have reported feeling ill.

MISPLACED MODIFIERS

Be certain modifiers are placed correctly to be sure the meaning is clear.

Bad:

> The dog is for sale. He eats anything and *loves children.*
>
> *(Does he love eating children?)*

Better:

> The dog is for sale. He *loves children* and eats anything.

Bad:

> *Working hard on the term paper, the teacher* told John he was doing well. *(Who is working on the term paper?)*

Better:

> *Working hard on the term paper, John* was praised by his teacher.

GRAMMAR-USAGE

WRITING REVIEW

Be sure that all sentence elements which express parallel ideas are in the same form.

AFTER COORDINATING CONJUNCTIONS: and, but, or, *and* nor
> **Wrong:**
> The author concluded that gross *sales* had improved but the individual *stores* had not. *(comparing sales with stores)*
>
> **Correct:**
> The author concluded that gross *sales* had improved, but that individual store's *sales* had not.

WITH PAIRED COORDINATING CONJUNCTIONS: not only...but also, both...and, either...or, neither...nor, between...and

- **both ...and**
> **Wrong:**
> The courses advertised were **both** *interesting* **and** *of great difficulty.* *(present participle and prepositional phrase)*
>
> **Correct:**
> The courses advertised were **both** *of great interest* **and** *of great difficulty.* *(two prepostional phrases)*

- **not only...but also**
> **Wrong:**
> Members were **not only** *upset* **with the vote, but also** *they resented the officious manner* of the president. *(single adjective and independent clause)*
>
> **Correct:**
> Members were **not only** *upset* with the vote, **but also** *resentful* of the officious manner of the president. *(adjective and adjective)*

- **neither...nor** and **either...or**
> **Wrong:**
> **Neither** the *girls' scores* on the first trial **nor** the *scores of the boys* were correctly recorded. *(adjective modifying noun and prepositional phrase modifying noun)*

Correct:
Neither the *girls' scores* on the first trial **nor** the *boys' scores* were correctly recorded. *(adjective modifying noun and adjective modifying noun)*

- **Between...and**
  Wrong:
  The difference **between** the *ideas* of the world leaders **and** the local *politicians* is apparent. *(noun-ideas and noun-people)*
  Correct:
  The difference **between** the *ideas* of the world leaders **and** the *opinions* of the local politicians is apparent. *(noun-ideas and noun-opinions)*

- **Among elements in series**
  Wrong:
  They were asked *to return* early, *to clean* the site, and *that the group begin* the new work. *(two infinitive phrases and a subordinate clause)*
  Correct:
  They were asked *to return* early, *to clean* the site, and *to begin* work. *(three infinitive phrases)*

IMPROVING WRITING STYLE

VARYING SENTENCE OPENINGS
Avoid the immature style of sentences which always begin with a subject. Use some of the openings suggested below.
   Single Word Modifiers: adjectives or adverbs set off with a comma.
   Phrases: groups of words with neither a subject or predicate.
   Clauses: groups of words with subjects and predicates.
      Subordinate clauses cannot stand alone as a sentence, but usually modify the independent clause.

SINGLE WORD MODIFIERS
Nervously, he walked to the podium.
Disgusted, Mary turned and walked away.

WRITING REVIEW

PREPOSITIONAL PHRASES
After the test, the subjects left.
With brown stains, the coats looked awful.
Down with taxes was the party's war cry.

PRESENT PARTICIPIAL PHRASES
Walking quickly, the group left.
Standing alone, the painting was beautiful.
Writing a term paper is not easy.

PAST PARTICIPIAL PHRASES
Exhausted by his efforts, he died.
Overjoyed with the news, Bob jumped up.
Betrayed by his men, the general resigned.

INFINTIVE PHRASES
To avoid arrest, the immigrants fled.
To make a deal, he will do anything.
To live free is a blessing.

SUBORDINATE CLAUSES
Because the law called for the death penalty, no other verdict was possible.
If the results differ, the careful researcher should examine the procedures.
Although he believed her story, the reporter continued to investigate.
When he attempted to fly the latest model, he lost control of the airplane.
Whether or not he succeeded is not the question.

VARYING SENTENCE LENGTH
Short sentences are excellent to add emphasis or to describe very complicated ideas, but do not overuse them. Add variety by using simple, compound, complex or compound-complex sentences.

SIMPLE SENTENCE: One independent clause

The Republican convention takes place in August.

COMPOUND SENTENCE: Two independent clauses

The project took two months, but the result was worth the wait.

COMPLEX SENTENCE: An independent and a subordinate clause

When he took the witness stand, we knew he would commit perjury.

COMPOUND-COMPLEX SENTENCE: Two or more independent and one or more dependent clauses

He expressed no opinion, and when the others disagreed, he adjourned the meeting.

AVOIDING PASSIVE VOICE

In the passive voice of verbs, the subject of the sentence is the receiver of the action. The use of passive voice gives a dull tone to your writing.

The message was sent by his friends.

Switch to the active voice in which the subject of the sentence does the action.

His friends sent the message.

MAINTAINING VERB TENSE CONSISTENCY

In general, try to maintain the same tense throughout the paper. However, in formal research writing some shifts are acceptable.

PAST TENSE: Action that took place in the past.

Richardson *described*

PRESENT PERFECT TENSE: Action that started in the past and continues to present.

Richardson *has shown*

These tenses are appropriate for review of research literature or discussion of the work of others.

CORRECT VERBS

PAST TENSE
skill development *improved*
Appropriate for describing the results of experiments in APA papers

PRESENT TENSE: Action which takes place in the present.
The results of the investigation *indicate*
Appropriate for discussing results and presenting conclusions in APA papers.

PAST PERFECT TENSE: Action which began in the past and was ended in the past.
The students *had completed* all their work before we arrived.

FUTURE PERFECT TENSE - Action which will begin in the future and end at a specific time in the future.
All of the students *will have received* their grades by this time tomorrow.

TRANSITIONS

WRITING SMOOTH TRANSITIONS

Strive for smoothness in the joining of ideas. Use good transitional words between sentences, and effective transitional sentences between paragraphs or major thoughts. Following are examples of linking words which may be used alone or to introduce transitional phrases, clauses, or sentences.

Contrast:	but, however, although, nevertheless, on the other hand, conversely
Addition:	furthermore, moreover, similarly, for example, along with
Cause-Effect:	as a result, consequently, therefore, because
Time:	next, then, after, since, during, first, afterward, immediately
Location:	among, behind, across, near, beside, down, between, inside
Summary:	consequently, therefore, finally, thus

AVOIDING WORDINESS

Brief, sharp, incisive writing is preferred to longwinded words and phrases which do not enhance understanding. Think of the main idea and state it using a powerful verb. Do not use a thesaurus to find a longer word to impress your teacher or audience.

Bad:
Researchers have been exploring the outer reaches of space in an effort to discover life forms on other planets, but have not been successful at this time.

Better:
Researchers have not found life on other planets.

AVOIDING JARGON

Writers often overuse technical vocabularies which are obstacles to clear understanding.

Bad:
Computer programmers are exploring the infrastructure of cyberspace and prioritizing goals for exploiting business use of the Internet.

Better:
Computer programmers are working to find profitable business uses of the Internet.

AVOIDING SLANG AND COLLOQUIAL LANGUAGE

Avoid slang and colloquial expressions. Use formal English. Do not use contractions.

Bad:
He didn't lose his cool and just blew him off.

Better:
He kept his composure and ignored him.

WORDINESS-JARGON

ELIMINATING BIAS

Careful writers avoid language which may improperly generalize about gender, ethnic groups, socioeconomic class, sexual orientation, religion, and age.

Improper	Proper
mankind, man	people, humankind
stewardess, police woman	flight attendant, police officer
foreman, mailman	supervisor, postal worker
housewife	homemaker
disabled	man with an orthopedic disability.
he will use the machine	he or she will use the machine
his difficulties	his or her difficulties
White, Non-White, Oriental	White, African American, Asian
males, females	men, women, (for high school age or younger - boys, girls)
male nurse	nurse
chairman	chair or chairperson
depressives	people who are depressed

BASIC MACINTOSH INSTRUCTIONS

The following pages will help if you are unfamiliar with basic Macintosh operations. On the other hand, if you know the Macintosh, you can skip this chapter and go directly to the word processing program you are using.

STARTING UP

Press the **triangle power key** or **switch** on the back of the computer. After the smiling Macintosh Icon and Welcome to Macintosh message, the **desktop** or **finder** screen will appear similar to the illustration below. The words desktop and finder are used interchangeably. You may see several windows containing icons for folders or applications.

THE MACINTOSH DESKTOP

The **Main Menu Bar** appears at the top left with the **Apple, File, Edit, View, Label,** and **Special Menu** items. The **Help** and **Application icons** appear at the top right. The **Macintosh Hard Drive Icon** will appear at the top right with the **Trash Icon** at the lower right of the screen. If you do not see a window with the name of your wordprocessor or the **Macintosh HD Window**, double click on the **Macintosh Hard Drive Icon** and the **Macintosh HD Window** will appear similar to the illustration below.

MACINTOSH DESKTOP SCREEN

STARTING UP

THE MACINTOSH DESKTOP OR FINDER

Apple Menu Icon
Click on this icon. A drop-down list of desk accessories such as **Calculator** and **Alarm Clock** appears. Drag to the item you want.

Finder Menu
Click and drag on **File, Edit, View, Label,** or **Special** and drop-down lists appear. Each contains items related to the menu title which accomplish special tasks. Drag to the item you want.

Help Menu Icon
Click and drag to **Show Balloons** in the drop-down list. Whenever you move the pointer over a a menu or icon, the **Balloon** will describe its function.

Application Menu
Click and drag on the **Application Menu** and a drop-down list of applications appears. Drag down to the word processing program you use. Program will be highlighted with a check mark. Release the button. The active program icon replaces the **Application Icon.**

Macintosh Hard Disk Icon
Double click and the **Macintosh HD** active window appears containing icons of the programs on the hard disk.

Trash Can Icon
Drag files or folders to **Trash Can** to temporarily store them. Double click the icon to open the **Trash Window** to see what is in trash. Drag items to be retrieved to another window or click the item. Drag down to **Empty Trash** in the **Special Menu** to delete items in trash. Drag a floppy disk icon to the trash can to eject it.

Title Bar
Drag a **Title Bar** to move a window to a new location.

Active Window
Click anywhere in a window to make it active. **Horizontal lines**, a **Close Box** and **Resize Box** appear in the **Title Bar.**

Close Box
Click to close the window.

Zoom Box
Click to enlarge window to show all files. Click again to reduce.

Resize Box
Drag to lower right corner of window to resize.

Floppy Disk Icon
The **Icon** appears when you insert a floppy disk. Double click to see contents. Click and type the name you want to give your disk.

DESKTOP - FINDER

USING THE MOUSE

Several terms will be used in this book for the mouse:

Pointer: The Pointer may appear as an I-Beam or an arrow.

Click: Move pointer to a place, press the button and release.

Double Click: Click two times.

Drag: Move pointer to a place, hold down button, move mouse to a new place and release.

Choose: Click on a menu and drag down to a choice in the pull down menu.

Select: Drag the pointer across text and release. Text will be highlighted.

Press: Depress a key on the keyboard.

THE ICON HIERARCHY

Macintosh uses **Icons** to represent **Applications, Disks,** and **Folders.** Here is a brief description of the icons you will see in addition to the **Hard Disk, Floppy Disk,** and **Trash Icon**s described on page 3-2.

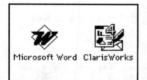

APPLICATION ICONS - Designate software programs like **ClarisWorks, Word,** or **WordPerfect.** Each has a distinctive pattern.

Click to select. Double click to open. A blank page or dialog box will appear.

DOCUMENT ICONS - Appear when you save a document in an application.

Click to select. Double click to open. The application will open and the document appears.

FOLDER ICONS - You create folders to organize your work. Put files and programs in them.

Click to select. Double click to open.

BASIC WORDPROCESSING

SELECTING TEXT

1. Move the **I-beam** to the right of the word or words to be selected.
2. Drag the **I-beam** across the word or words.
3. To select several lines or paragraphs, drag the **I-beam** toward the bottom of the page.

COPYING TEXT

1. Select text.
2. Choose **Copy** from the **Edit Menu** or press **Command C (⌘ C)**.
3. Move the cursor to the spot where you want the text to go.
4. Choose **Paste** from the **Edit Menu** or press **Command V (⌘ V)**.

MOVING TEXT

1. Select text.
2. Choose **Cut** from the **Edit Menu** or press **Command X (⌘ X)**.
3. Move the cursor to the spot where you want the text to go.
4. Choose **Paste** from the **Edit Menu** or press **Command V (⌘ V)**.

DELETING TEXT

1. Select text.
2. Press the **Delete Key**. If you accidentally delete text, immediately choose **Undo** from the **Edit Menu.**
3. Single characters can be deleted by pressing the **Backspace Key** after a character or the **Delete Key** before a character.

OPENING A WORD PROCESSOR THE FIRST TIME

1. Click twice on the **Macintosh HD Icon.** The **Macintosh HD Window** will appear. Choose **by Icon** in the **View Menu.**
2. Click twice on the **Applications Folder** on the **Macintosh HD Window.** The **Applications Window** will appear.
3. Click twice on the **Folder Icon** for your word processor on the **Applications Window. The Word Processing Window** will open. Click on the **Application Icon** for your word processor. The **Icon** will look like one shown on page 3-3. Each word processor will open somewhat differently.
4. Turn to the chapter for your word processor and follow the instructions.
5. When you get to a blank document page, you are ready to begin typing your paper.

PRINTING

If you are working in a lab with several printers follow steps 1-3 first. If you are working with a single printer, begin at step 4.

1. Select **Chooser** from the **Apple Menu.** The **Chooser Dialog Box** will appear. See the **Chooser Dialog Box** illustration below.
2. Click on the **icon** for the **Printer Type** you want to use in the **left hand side** of the dialog box.
3. Select a **specific printer** or **Apple Talk** on the **right hand side** of the dialog box and close the **Chooser** by clicking on its close box.
4. Choose **Page Setup** from the **File Menu.** The **Page Setup Dialog Box** for your printer will appear. See the **Page Setup Dialog Box** illustration below. Be sure the orientation is **Portrait** and the size is **Letter.** Click on **OK.**
5. Choose **Print** from the **File Menu.** The **Printing Dialog Box** will appear. See the **Printing Dialog Box** illustration on page 3-6.
6. Select the **options** you want by clicking on **radio buttons** and **check boxes.** Click on **Print.**

CHOOSER DIALOG BOX

Select the printer type you want to use on the left hand side of the dialog box

Select a specific printer on the right hand side of the dialog box

PAGE SET UP DIALOG BOX

Choose printing options from the Page Setup Dialog Box.

PRINTING

PRINTING DIALOG BOX

LaserWriter "LaserJet 4 Plus"	7.2	Print

Copies: 1   Pages: ● All ○ From: [ ] To: [ ]   Cancel

Paper Source
● All ○ First   From: Cassette ▼   Options
            Remaining From: Cassette ▼

Destination: ● Printer   ○ PostScript® File
Print Pages: ● All ○ Odd Pages Only   ○ Even Pages Only
Section Range: From: 1   To: 1   ☐
☐ Print Hidden Text   ☐   ☐ Print Back To Front

Specify pages or other changes in Printing Dialog Box.

SAVING

1. Choose **Save** from the **File Menu** or press **Command S** (⌘ S).
2. On the first save, the **Save Dialog Box** will appear. See the **Save Dialog Box** illustration on page 3-7.
3. Look at the **Pop-Up List** at the top of the dialog box. It tells where your document will be saved. Probably, it will state the name of your word processing folder. You can click on the **Pop-Up List** and other locations will appear where you can save your work. Perhaps you want to save to your **Floppy Disk** or a **Folder.**
4. Type a name in the **Save as: Box** such as Term Paper.
5. Click on the **Save Button** or **OK.** Your document will be saved.
6. Every five or ten minutes, press **Command S** (⌘ S) to save your work and avert disaster.
7. If you are sharing a computer or if you want to protect yourself against a hard disk failure, you should copy your work from the hard disk to a floppy disk. Drag down to **Quit** in the **File Menu.**
8. The **Word Processing Folder Window** will appear with a **Document Icon** with the name you gave it. The **Application Menu Bar** will be replaced by the **Desktop Main Menu.**
9. Click on the **Resize Box** and drag the **Application Window** toward the upper left corner to expose the right side of the the **Desktop.**
10. Insert a formatted **Floppy Disk** in the disk drive slot. A highlighted, untitled **Floppy Disk Icon** will appear on the right side of the **Desktop.** Type a name for the disk, perhaps using your own name. For example, you might type **Jane's Disk** if your name is Jane, of course.
11. Click on your **Document Icon** and drag it to the **Floppy Disk Icon.** A **Copy Message Box** will appear with a message saying the document is being copied.

SAVING

SAVE AS DIALOG BOX

Location Pop-Up List. Click to see other locations.

List of files or folders in Pop-Up location. You can also click one and save to it.

Click Desktop Button to change location to Desktop.

Save Button

Type the name you want to give your document in the Save as: box.

OPENING YOUR DOCUMENT LATER

1. Follow the steps above to open your **Word Processing Program** from the **Application Window.**
2. Choose **Open** from the **File Menu.** An **Open Dialog Box** will appear like the illustration below. It will appear like the **Save Dialog Box.**
3. Choose the location of your document from the pop-up list. It will be on the **Desktop,** the **Macintosh HD,** or in the **folder** where you saved your document. You may need to click on the pop-up list at the top to see the folders and documents in each location.
4. Use the **scroll bars** to scroll through the files until you locate your document. Double click on your **document name** and **Open.** It will open with its name in the **title bar** and you will be ready to enter text.

OPEN DIALOG BOX

Location Pop-Up List. Click to see other locations.

List of files or folders in Pop-Up location. Scroll to see all in each location.

Click your document name and Open to open document.

OPENING LATER

SHUTTING DOWN

1. Choose **Quit** from the **File Menu** or press **Command Q** (⌘ **Q**) to close the application if you have not already done so. The **Application Window** will appear on the **Desktop.**
2. Click on the **Close Box** of the **Application Window** and it will disappear leaving the **Macintosh HD Window** on the **Desktop.**
3. Click on the **Close Box** of the **Macintosh HD Window** and it will disappear.
4. Now choose **Shut Down** from the **Special Menu** in the **Desktop Menu Bar.** The machine will shut down, the screen will go dark and your floppy disk will eject.

Part Two

Using the *MLA Handbook* to Write Your Paper

Word Processing Applications

Part Two

Using the *MLA Handbook* to Write Your Paper

Word Processing Applications

Author-Page Citation
MLA Handbook for Writers of
Research Papers, 5th Ed., 1999

The **Modern Language Association** is a scholarly organization which traces its roots to 1883. One of its aims has been to standardize and codify practices for researchers and writers. **MLA** style has its widest use among the humanities, but other disciplines have also adopted it.

The latest edition of the *MLA Handbook* contains simplified rules for documenting sources using citations placed in parentheses directly in the text. There is no longer a need for difficult footnoting or endnoting.

The *MLA Handbook* also includes documentation guidelines for new electronic sources such as CD-ROMs, electronic journals and e-mail.

PARENTHETICAL AUTHOR-PAGE CITATION

The author's name and the specific page number(s) where the material is located in the work are placed in parenthesis in the text. When the author's name appears in the text only the page number(s) need to be placed in the parenthesis. A little practice may be necessary to insert the references and keep the writing fluent. Author-page citation samples are on pages 4-2 through 4-4.

Every source cited in the text must be documented in a Works Cited list at the end of the paper. It is important that references be cited accurately. Works cited samples are on pages 4-5 through 4-14.

PUNCTUATION OF AUTHOR-PAGE CITATIONS

It is preferable to place the parenthetical reference at the end of the sentence. End the sentence without punctuation. Leave one space and add the parenthetical reference followed by the appropriate punctuation mark. Exception: When long quotations are set off from the text, leave one space after the end punctuation and add the parenthetical reference without any punctuation.

M L A   H A N D B O O K

PARENTHETICAL AUTHOR-PAGE CITATION SAMPLES

BOOK - SINGLE AUTHOR
Insert the last name(s) of the author(s) and page number(s) in the parentheses.

> This concept has been reported earlier (Jones 148).

or

If author's name appears in the text, insert only the page number(s) in the parenthesis.

> Jones reported this concept (148).

BOOK - MULTIPLE AUTHORS
Insert all authors' last names and the page number(s) in the parenthesis.

> An opposing idea has been explored (Brown, Smith, and Rogers 179-81).

or

If authors' names appear in the text, insert only the page number(s) in the parenthesis.

> Brown, Smith, and Rogers explored an opposing idea (179-81).

MULTIPLE WORKS BY THE SAME AUTHOR(S)
If two or more works by the same author(s) will be cited, insert author(s) name(s) followed by a comma, the title, if short, or a short version, and the page number(s) in the parenthesis.

> Most humans experience depression, often for reasons unknown to them (Rogers, <u>Psychology</u> 171-73).

or

If author(s) name(s) and title appear in the text, insert only the page number(s) in the parenthesis.

> In <u>Psychology and Modern Man,</u> Rogers explains that most humans experience depression, often for reasons unknown to them (171-73).

PARENTHETICAL AUTHOR-PAGE CITATION SAMPLES

or
If two or more works by same author will be cited and author's name appears in text, insert the title and page number in the parentheses.

> Rogers explains that most humans experience depression, often for reasons unknown to them (<u>Psychology and Modern Man</u> 171-173).

WHOLE WORK
Author's name and title of whole work may appear in text without parentheses.

> Shakespeare's <u>Hamlet</u> has been called his most enigmatic tragedy.

MULTI-VOLUME WORK
Insert author's name and volume number followed by a colon, space and page number(s) in parentheses.

> Economic policy should provide for maintenance of full employment (Johnson 2: 273).

or
If author's name and volume appear in the text, place only the page number(s) in parentheses.

> In volume 2, Johnson suggests that economic policy should provide for maintenance of full employment (273).

or
If the whole volume is cited without reference to pages, insert the author's name and abbreviation for volume in the parentheses.

> Economic policy should provide for maintenance of full employment (Johnson, vol. 2).

CORPORATE OR GOVERNMENT PUBLICATIONS
Insert corporate author in text and place page number(s) in parentheses.

> In 1984 the United States Department of Defense issued a report denying activity in Paraguay (31).

or
Insert corporate author and page number(s) in parentheses.

> A recent report denies any United States activity in Paraguay (United States Department of Defense 31).

PARENTHETICAL AUTHOR-PAGE CITATION SAMPLES

MAGAZINE OR JOURNAL ARTICLES
Use same techniques as for books

NOVELS
Insert the page number followed by a semicolon and the chapter number preceded by the abbreviation for the part or chapter.

> The opening words of <u>Moby Dick</u>, "Call me Ishmael," quickly identify the narrator (1; ch.1).

PLAYS
Insert division: act, scene, canto, book, or part and line(s) separated by periods in the parentheses but omit page numbers. In general, use arabic numerals rather than roman unless otherwise directed.

> The queen finds relief in believing her son, Hamlet mad (3.4.105).

POETRY
Cite by division and line: canto, book, or part separated by periods in the parenthesis (similar to plays), but omit page numbers. If only lines are cited, spell out the word, line or lines, and type the number(s).

> Shelley's "Ozymandias" ironically describes the ephemeral nature of fame and power in the statement, "Look on my works, ye Mighty, and despair! / Nothing beside remains (lines 10-13).

WORK LISTED BY TITLE
Insert title or abbreviation and page number(s) in parentheses

> The <u>New Yorker</u> reprinted a story on country dining ("Country Inns and Byways" 213).

or
Insert title of whole unsigned work in parentheses

> The spectrum is visible when white light is sent through a prism ("Color and Light").

ONLINE SOURCES
If no page numbers are given, omit page numbers and use appropriate sample from above.

> Braking reaction time varied widely (Rabine).

MLA WORKS CITED SAMPLES

WORKS CITED

A bibliography called **Works Cited,** printed on a separate page at the end of the paper, provides complete publication information for all of the sources cited in your paper. The citations in the text must lead the reader to the source in the **Works Cited** bibliography.

Start the list on a new page. Center the words, Works Cited, in upper and lower case on the top line. Double space and type the first entry. Type the first line flush left and indent following lines, if any, one half inch. Double space between and within entries.

Samples shown below are single spaced to save space.

BOOK - NO NAMED AUTHOR
Handbook of Pre-Columbian Art. New York:
   Johnson, 1988.

BOOK - ONE AUTHOR
Gershman, Herbert S. The Surrealist Revolution
   in France. Ann Arbor: U of Michigan P,
   1994.

BOOK - MULTIPLE AUTHORS
Raffer, Bernard C., Richard Friedman, and Robert
   A. Baron. New York in Crisis. New York:
   Harper, 1986.

BOOK - SAME AUTHOR(S) - USE 3 HYPHENS AFTER FIRST ENTRY
---. A Study of Life. New York: Norton, 1993.

BOOK - EDITED
Melville, Herman. Moby Dick. Ed. J.P. Small.
   Boston: Houghton, 1973.

BOOK - TRANSLATION
Maurois, Andre. Lelia. Trans. Gerard Hopkins.
   New York: Harper, 1954.

BOOK - CORPORATE AUTHOR
National Policy Association. Welfare Reform.
   New York: McGraw, 1992.

MULTIVOLUME WORK - CITING ONE VOLUME ONLY
Smith, Richard K. A History of Religion in the
   United States. Vol. 3. Chicago: U of
   Chicago, 1993.

MLA WORKS CITED SAMPLES

MULTIVOLUME WORK - CITING MORE THAN ONE VOLUME
Smith, Richard K. <u>A History of Religion in the United States</u>. 4 vols. Chicago: U of Chicago, 1993.

GOVERNMENT PUBLICATION
United States. Dept. of Labor. <u>Labor Relations in the Steel Industry</u>. Washington: GPO, 1994.

DISSERTATION - UNPUBLISHED
Samson, Robert. "The Influence of Economic Deprivation on Academic Achievement." Diss. New York U, 1985.

DISSERTATION - PUBLISHED BY UNIVERSITY MICROFILMS
Garon, Lois. <u>Socialist Ideas in the Works of Emile Zola</u>. Diss. Brown U, 1992. Ann Arbor: UMI, 1993. 921437.

POEMS, ESSAYS, SHORT STORIES, PLAYS IN ANTHOLOGIES
Poe, Edgar Allan. "The Raven." <u>Great American Poetry</u>. Ed. Richard Johnson. New York: McGraw, 1978. 38-40.

ARTICLE IN REFERENCE BOOK - UNSIGNED
"DNA." <u>Encylopedia Americana</u>. 1994 ed.

ARTICLE IN REFERENCE BOOK - SIGNED
Smith, Richard. "Color and Light." <u>Encyclopedia Brittanica</u>. 1994 ed.

PERIODICALS

NEWSPAPER ARTICLE - SIGNED
May, Clifford. "Religious Frictions Heat Up in Rwanda." <u>New York Times</u> 12 Aug. 1994, late ed.: A1.

MAGAZINE ARTICLE - UNSIGNED
"Making of a Candidate for President." <u>Time</u> 20 Jul. 1984: 40-42.

MAGAZINE ARTICLE - SIGNED
Kuhn, Susan. "A New Stock Play in Saving and Loans." <u>Fortune</u> 15 May 1995: 67-72.

MLA WORKS CITED SAMPLES

EDITORIAL - UNSIGNED
"China's Conscience." Editorial. <u>New York Times</u>
19 May 1995, late ed.: A22.

EDITORIAL - SIGNED
Brownhurst, Marshall S. "Rush to Judgement."
Editorial. <u>Wall Street Journal</u> 5 Jun. 1995:
A15.

ABSTRACT IN ABSTRACTS JOURNAL
Frischman, Josephine K. "Analysis of Bias in
Selecting Test Times." <u>Journal of
Experimental Psychology</u> 98 (1992): 325-31.
<u>Psychological Abstracts</u> 80 (1993): item
7321.

ARTICLE IN LOOSELEAF COLLECTION - SOCIAL ISSUES RESOURCES SERIES - SIRS
Cruver, Philip C. "Lighting the 21st Century."
<u>Futurist</u> Mar. 1990: 29-34. <u>Energy</u>. Ed.
Eleanor Goldstein. Vol. 4. Boca Raton:
SIRS, 1991. Art. 84.

ARTICLE IN MICROFICHE COLLECTION - NEWSBANK
Chieper, Randy. "Welfare Reform Debates." <u>New
York Times</u> 20 Apr. 1994, late ed.: A12.
<u>Newsbank: Welfare and Social Problems</u> 17
(1994): fiche 2, grids A9-13.

REVIEW OF BOOK, FILM, OR PERFORMANCE
INCLUDE AUTHORS, DIRECTORS, CONDUCTORS, PERFORMERS, OTHERS AS PERTINENT
Maslin, Janet. "New Challenges for the Caped
Crusader." Rev. of <u>Batman Forever</u>, dir.
Joel Schumacher. <u>New York Times</u> 16 Jun.
1995, late ed.: C1.

ARTICLE - SIGNED IN JOURNAL WHICH USES ISSUE NUMBERS
Brogdan, Robert. "Religious Freedom and School
Holidays." <u>Phi Delta Kappan</u> 68 (1984):
700-02.

ARTICLE - SIGNED IN JOURNAL WHICH PAGES ISSUES SEPARATELY
Jones, Mary. "Urban Poetry." <u>American Review</u>
13.2 (1987): 66-73.

MLA WORKS CITED SAMPLES

NON-PRINT SOURCES

TELEVISION OR RADIO PROGRAM
Include if appropriate "EpisodeTitle." Program Title. Series Title.
Actors. Directors. Producers. Network. Call Letters, City. Date.

"Pollution in the Desert." Narr. Mike Wallace.
Prod. Jock Fenway. Dir. John Brett. Sixty
Minutes. CBS WCBS, New York. 6 Mar. 1994.

SOUND RECORDING
Cite first whichever is emphasized: Composer. Performer.
Conductor. Title. Artists. Audiocasssette or LP if not a CD.
Manufacturer, Date or N.D. if unknown.

Webber, Andrew Lloyd. Phantom of the Opera.
Perf. Michael Crawford, Sarah Brightman, and
Steve Barton. Audiocassette. EMI, 1987.

FILM
Include Title. Director. Also, if pertinent, Writers. Performers.
Producers. Distributor, Year.

Raiders of the Lost Ark. Dir. Steven Spielberg.
Paramount, 1982.

INTERVIEW - BROADCAST

Gramm, Phil. Interview with Charlie Rose.
Charlie Rose. WNET, New York. 6 May 1994.

INTERVIEW - PERSONAL

Kennedy, Robert. Personal Interview. 11 January
1971.

ELECTRONIC PUBLICATIONS

The citation of print publications has long been standardized, but with the coming of electronic publishing, scholars have only begun to lay down the basic rules for citing this new material. Because electronic publications are not as permanent as bound paper volumes, more bibliographic information is required for these works. For example, if the work was originally in print, the print bibliographical data should be included.

The sample citations which follow conform to those recommended in the *MLA Style Manual and Guide to Scholarly Publishing,* 2nd ed. 1998 and the *MLA Handbook for Writers of Research Papers,* 5th ed. 1999.

MLA WORKS CITED SAMPLES

CD-ROM - DISKETTE - MAGNETIC TAPE

NON-PERIODICAL DOCUMENT ON CD-ROM, DISKETTE, OR MAGNETIC TAPE
Include Author (or if only editor or translator instead of author follow with a comma and abbreviation). <u>Title</u>. Editor or Translator (if relevant). Publication Medium. Edition or Version (if relevant). Place of Publication: Publisher, Electronic Publication Date.

Conrad, Joseph. <u>Victory</u>. CD-ROM. Cambridge, Eng.:
    Chadwyck-Healey, 1994.

Braunstein, Roger, ed. <u>Hamlet</u>. By William
    Shakespeare. CD-ROM. New York: Hastings,
    1996.

United States. Dept. Of Commerce. "Railroad
    Tonnage Reports." 1993. <u>National Trade
    Data Bank</u>. Magnetic Tape. US Dept. of
    Commerce. Apr. 1994.

NON-PERIODICAL DOCUMENT ON CD-ROM, DISKETTE, OR MAGNETIC TAPE PREVIOUSLY IN PRINT
Author. Print Publication Information. <u>Title</u>. Publication Medium, Place of Publication: Publisher, Electronic Publication Date.

Hemingway. <u>Complete Works of Hemingway</u>. Ed.
    Richard Jomes. Columbus: Ohio UP, 1993.
    CD-ROM. New York: Gale, 1996.

PERIODICAL DOCUMENT ON CD-ROM, DISKETTE, OR MAGNETIC TAPE ALSO PUBLISHED IN PRINT
Author. "Title." Print Publication Information. <u>Database Title</u> (if available). Publication Medium. Vendor. Electronic Publication Date.

Barron, James. "New York Welfare Programs in
    Jeopardy." <u>New York Times</u> 8 May 1995, late
    ed.: C1. <u>New York Times Ondisc</u>. CD-ROM.
    UMI-Proquest. Nov. 1995.

TELEVISION OR RADIO PROGRAM ON CD-ROM, DISKETTE, OR MAGNETIC TAPE

Sills, Beverly. "Opera Today." Interview. <u>Charlie
    Rose</u>. PBS. 15 August 1995. Transcript.
    <u>Broadcast News</u>. CD-ROM. Primary Source
    Media. January 1996. 19 screens.

MLA WORKS CITED SAMPLES

FILM OR FILM CLIP ON CD-ROM, DISKETTE, OR MAGNETIC TAPE
```
Binder, Mike, dir. Crossing the Bridge. 1995.
      CD-ROM. New York: Touchstone, 1997.
```

WORK OF ART ON CD-ROM
```
Van Gogh, Vincent. Trees in the Asylum Garden.
      1889. Microsoft Art Gallery, London. CD-ROM.
      Redmond: Microsoft, 1996.
```

ONLINE SOURCES

Because there is yet no agreed upon standard for citing electronic works and because electronic media often "disappear" or are modified, great care must be used in citing these works. The version you access may differ from the original so it is important to include the access date as well as the original date if available.

For material which appeared first in print, the dates of print and electronic publication as well as the access date should be provided. The Uniform Resource Locator (URL) is the best way to identify an online source. However, great care should be used in transcribing URLs because of the possibility of error. If you need to divide a URL between two lines, do so only after a slash. Use no hyphen at the break. Enclose the URL in angle brackets.

ONLINE SCHOLARLY PROJECT
Title. Project Editor (if available). Electronic Publication Information including Version Number (if relevant). Date of Electronic Publication. Sponsoring Institution. Date of Access Electronic Address.
```
Voice of the Shuttle: English Literature
      Restoration and Eighteenth Century. Ed. Alan
      Liu. Apr. 1998. U of California, Santa
      Barbara. 20 Jun. 1998 <http://
      humanitas.ucsb.edu/shuttle/eng-18th.html>.
```

POEM OR OTHER MATERIAL IN AN ONLINE SCHOLARLY PROJECT
Author's Name. "Title." Project Title. Project Editor (if available). Electronic Publication Information including Version Number (if relevant). Date of Electronic Publication. Sponsoring Institution. Date of Access Electronic Address
```
Butler, Josephine E. "Native Races and the War."
      Victorian Women Writers Project. Ed. Perry
      Willet. 1998. Indiana U. 15 May 1998
      <http://www.indiana.edu/~letrs/vwwp/butler/
      native.html>.
```

MLA WORKS CITED SAMPLES

PROFESSIONAL OR PERSONAL SITE

Name of Site Creator (if given). <u>Site Title</u> (if there is one or the words Home Page not underlined. Institution or Organization (if associated with site). Access Date Electronic Address.

<u>Chartered Institute of Marketing Page</u>. 22 Jan.
  1998 <http://www.cim.co.uk/>.

ONLINE BOOK

Author (if given). or Editor or Translator with appropriate abbreviation (ed., trans.). <u>Title</u>. Editor or Compiler or Translator (if relevant). Print Publication Information (if relevant). Access Date Electronic Address.

Conrad, Joseph. <u>Heart of Darkness</u>. New York:
  Harper Brothers, 1910. 15 Jan. 1998
  <http://sunsite.berkeley.edu/Literature/
  Conrad/Heart of Darkness/01.html>.

Paine, Thomas. <u>The Rights of Man</u>. 1792. 12 April
  1998 <gopher://gopher.vt.edu:10010/02/
  129/4>.

ONLINE PERIODICALS

Author (if given). "Title." <u>Periodical Name</u>. Volume and or Issue Number(if given) Publication Date. Number of Pages or Paragraphs (if numbered). Access Date Electronic Address.

ONLINE NEWSPAPER

Bradley, Ann. "Educated Consumers." <u>Education Week
  on the Web</u>. 26 Mar. 1997. 4 Apr. 1998
  <http://www.edweek.org/ew/vol-16/
  26consum.h16>.

ONLINE SCHOLARLY JOURNAL

Curley, Thomas. "Johnson and America." <u>The Age of
  Johnson</u> 6 (1994) 22 Apr. 1998 <http://
  www.english.upenn.edu/~Jlynch/AJ/>.

Schneider, Joe. "A Cautionary Word About
  Charters." <u>The School Administrator</u> 54.7
  (1997). 22 Jan. 1998 <http://www.aasa.org/
  SchoolAdmin/aug9703.htm>.

MLA WORKS CITED SAMPLES

ONLINE SCHOLARLY JOURNAL

"Events in Congress: March 20-April 2, 1998."
    Chronicle of Higher Education. 20 Mar.
    1998. 15 Apr. 1998 <http://
    chronicle.merit.edu/.events/.ewash.html>.

ONLINE REVIEW (May be Untitled)

Brailsford, William. Rev. of The Laurel and the
    Ivy: The Story of Charles Stewart Parnell
    and Irish Nationalism, by Robert Kee.
    Crisis Magazine (1996). 12 Jun 1998 <http://
    www.eppc.org/library/articles/brailsford/
    brev_feb96.html>.

ONLINE MAGAZINE ARTICLE

Thompson, Dick. "Rendezvous for Old Rivals." Time
    27 Mar. 1995. 20 Apr. 1998 <http://www.
    pathfinder.com/time/magazine/archive/1995/
    950327/950327.space.html>.

Gobel, Dave. "Distance Learning - Educating in
    Cyberspace." Online Magazine 12 Apr. 1998.
    9 May 1998 <http://www.online-magazine.com/
    lgu.html>.

ONLINE EDITORIAL (May be Untitled)

"Small Schools as an Investment." Editorial. New
    York Times on the Web 1 May 1988. 20 May
    1998 <http://www.nytimes.com/yr/mo/day/
    editorial/01fri3.html>.

ONLINE ABSTRACT

Green, R.J. "Intelligent Robotic Systems: A
    Research Perspective." Abstracts of MJCS
    6.11 12 Feb. 1996. Abstract. 13 May 1998
    <http://mjcs.fsktm.um.edu.my/MJCS/Volume_6/
    VOL_6_No1.1>.

ONLINE LETTER TO THE EDITOR (May be Untitled)

Harrison, Lawrence E. Letter. New York Times on
    the Web 4 May 1998. 18 Jun. 1998 <http://
    www.nytimes.com/yr/mo/day/letters/
    lharri.html>.

MLA WORKS CITED SAMPLES

OTHER ELECTRONIC SOURCES

ONLINE TELEVISION OR RADIO PROGRAM

Baron-Faust, Rita. "Night Vision Loss>:" Report
    on Medicine. CBS Radio. WCBS, New York. 4
    May 1998. Transcript. 10 Jun. 1998 <http://
    newsradio88.com/medicine/history/may_1998/
    may_4.html>.

ONLINE MAP

"Maps of Liberia." Map. Geography and Map
    Division. Library of Congress. 15 Mar. 1998
    <http://memory.loc.gov/ammem/gmdhtml/
    libhtml/libhome.html>.

ONLINE WORK OF ART

Wores, Theodore. A Garden Shrine, Sugita.
    Spanierman Gallery, New York. 12 Jun. 1998
    <http://spanierman.com/wores.htm>.

ONLINE CARTOON

Trudeau, G.B. "Doonesbury." Cartoon. New York
    Times on the Web. 5 May 1998. 6 Aug. 1998
    <http://www2.uclick.com/client/nyt/db/>.

ONLINE POSTING

Author. "Title." (from subject line) Online posting. Date of Posting.
Forum Name. Access Date List Address or E-mail Address of List
Moderator

Glavac, Maria S. "Busy Educator's Guide." Online
    posting. 5 May 1988. NETTRAIN Digest. 26
    May 1988 <listserv@listserv.acsu.buffalo.edu>.

ONLINE SOUND CLIP OR SOUND RECORDING

Pershing, John J. "From the Battlefields of
    France." 1918. American Leaders Speak:
    Recordings from World War I and the 1920
    Election. 1996. American Memory. Lib. of
    Congress, Washington. 20 Jun. 1998
    <http://lcweb2.loc.gov/ammem/nfexper.html>.

MLA WORKS CITED SAMPLES

ONLINE POEM

Coleridge, Samuel T. "Kubla Khan." 1798. Jan.
    1998 <http://english-www.hss.cmu.edu/
    poetry/kubla-khan.html>.

ONLINE GOVERNMENT DOCUMENT

U. S. Dept. of State. (1998). Counter Terrorism
    Rewards Program. 21 Feb. 1998 <http://www.
    heroes.net/pub/heroes/content2.html>.

FILE TRANSFER PROTOCOL (FTP)

"In the Courts." National Newsletter of the ACLU.
    Spring 1994. 14 Nov. 1997 <ftp://ftp.psi.
    net/aclu/newsletter/380courts>.

E-MAIL

Include "Title." (if any) taken from the subject line in quotation
marks

Richardson, Robert. E-mail to the author. 14 Jul.
    1997.

Casserly, James. "Aviation News." E-mail to
    Robert A. Baron. 27 Jun. 1998.

MLA QUOTATIONS

Prose

Quotations of four lines or less are not set off from the text but are placed within double quotation marks. Quotations may be placed at the beginning, middle, or end of sentences.

> Thomas Paine, in his pamphlet, The Crisis,
>
> wrote the stirring line, "These are the times
>
> that try men's souls."

If the quotation ends the sentence and a parenthetical citation is required, omit the period in the sentence and place the period after the reference.

> Thomas Paine, in his pamphlet, The Crisis,
>
> wrote the stirring line, "These are the times
>
> that try men's souls" (14).

For longer quotations, use a comma or colon after the last word of text, double space and type the quotation with no quotation marks. Indent ten spaces or one inch from the left margin and double space quote. Parenthetical citations following longer quotations follow the punctuation at the end of the last sentence.

> Writing to bolster the country after the
>
> discouraging first days of the war, Paine
>
> wrote:
>
> > These are the times that try men's
> >
> > souls. The summer soldier and the
> >
> > sunshine patriot will, in this crisis,
> >
> > shrink from the service of their
> >
> > country; but he that stands it *now*,
> >
> > deserves the love and thanks of man and
> >
> > woman. (18)

If two or more paragraphs are quoted one after another, indent the first line of each paragraph three more spaces or an additional quarter of an inch. If the first paragraph quoted does not begin a paragraph in the original, do not indent it.

Use double quotation marks for quotations within a long quotation.

Poetry

Poetry of three lines or less is placed in double quotation marks within the text. Separate lines of poetry which appear in a single line of text by a slash (/) with a space before and after the slash.

> Robert Frost's short poem describing how
>
> fate plays a role in human lives, ends
>
> with the lines, "Two roads diverged in a
>
> wood, and I-- / I took the one less
>
> traveled by, / And that has made all the
>
> difference (11).

For longer poems, use same procedure as for prose. Lines which do not fit on one line should be continued on the next line and indented three spaces or an additional quarter of an inch. To improve appearance, it is OK to indent fewer than one inch or ten spaces if that will allow the longer lines to fit on one text line. Unusual spacing of poetry should be followed as closely as possible.

Drama

Use a comma or colon after the last word of text, double space and indent ten spaces or one inch from the left margin. Capitalize the character's name, punctuate with a period and type the quotation. Indent following lines by the same character three spaces or an additional one quarter inch. Begin following character's lines by indenting ten spaces or one inch. Parenthetical citations follow the punctuation at the end of the last quoted line.

> The opening lines of Shakespeare's Hamlet
>
> create a mood of foreboding with this

exchange between the guards:

> BERNARDO. Who's there?
>
> FRANCISCO. Nay, answer me. Stand
>
>   and unfold yourself! (1.1.1-2)

Punctuation of Quotations

Periods and commas are placed inside quotation marks. Question marks and exclamation marks not originally in the quotation go outside the quotation marks. If a parenthetical reference ends a quoted line, place the period after the reference.

Quotation Within a Quotation

Use single quotation marks to set off a quotation within a quotation.

Ellipsis

When omitting words, phrases or sentences from quoted material, enclose three spaced periods within square brackets. Do not space after the first bracket or after the last period.

Ellipsis in the Middle of a Quoted Sentence

Leave a space before the first bracket and after the last bracket.

> Describing the differences between the views of Western and non-Western nations about ethnic cleansing, Michael Wines states, "But to many other nations, the Kosovo atrocities [...] were just the broken eggs of yet another national omelet, and the West was a self-righteous, ever-more meddlesome cook."

Ellipsis at the End of a Quoted Sentence
Leave a space before the first bracket, place the closing period after the last bracket with no space and end with a quotation mark

Describing the differences between the

views of Western and non-Western nations of ethnic

cleansing, Michael Wines writes, "But to many

other nations, the Kosovo atrocities that Germany

equated with its own past and President Clinton

labeled `vicious' and `terrifying' were just the

broken eggs of yet another national omelet [...]."

MLA NUMBERS
In general use arabic numerals for all numbers not spelled out, except for the occasional use of roman numerals.

- **Spell numbers of one or two words.**
    three   one thousand   five million

- **Use numerals for numbers of more than two words.**
    3.56   2,456   1,489, 602

- **Use numerals for numbers which precede units of measurement.**
    24 volts   121.5 megahertz, 6 centimeters

- **Use numerals for numbers in comparisons of data.**
    The July temperature ranged from 67 to 90.

- **Use numerals with abbreviations, addresses, dates, and page numbers.**
    12 lbs. $10.00   316 5th Avenue   page 3
    April 21, 1929

- **Use a combination of numerals and words for large numbers.**
    14.7 billion dollars

- **Use capital roman numerals in outlines and after names of individuals**
    Henry VIII   Richard III   Topic III

- **Use lowercase roman numerals for pages of a book which are numbered in roman numerals.** page iv

SAMPLE MLA FIRST TEXT PAGE (TITLE PAGE)

1"

½"

Quarles   1

3 spaces

Roger P. Quarles

Double space

Professor Onklaw

Sociology 112

9 September 1995

Center title

➤ Workfare Programs in Three States

Double space

      President Clinton pledged an "end to welfare as we know it" as part of the 1992 election campaign. However, the administration has been unable to get the Congress to act on the suggested reforms and, as a result, the states have proposed a wide range of experimental initiatives (Kellam 795). Several are

1" ➤ based on the concept of workfare, a popular idea with both ◄—1"— Republicans and Democrats.

      When Congress passed the Jobs Opportunities and Basic Skills Program (JOBS) in 1988, it gave states matching funds to develop programs. Wisconsin, Delaware, and California are among the states which have begun workfare programs (796).

Author-page citation

However, the picture is not altogether sanguine. Some critics of the workfare concept including Gilbert claim that workfare will increase welfare costs and simultaneously increase the numbers of homeless persons (795). There are arguments that despite the faults of the old AFDC program fifty percent of recipients are off welfare within two years (Gilbert 47). Others state that a lack of funds for job training and child care will make workfare programs impossible to maintain (Kaus 23).

      Wisconsin's workfare program, often cited as a model, has not worked well for the clients or the employers its critics say. The goal, simple as it sounds, to reduce dependence on welfare by putting people back on their feet, is obviously not as easy as

1"

MLA TEXT PAGE

SAMPLE MLA TEXT PAGE
WITH AUTHOR-PAGE CITATION

it seems. Still there are some successes and the lessons learned
from the experimentation of the states has been invaluable. The
problem is a major one for America as seen by the statistics.
Ten years ago fewer than four million families received welfare.
Currently, five million families with about 14 million people
receive benefits under the welfare system (Kellam 795).

Delaware's Department of Health and Social Services
implemented its First Step Employment and Training Program in
1986, even before Federal legislation under the JOBS program.
Under the current system, applicants eligible for Aid to Families
with Dependent Children must enroll in an educational program,
which frequently leads to a general equivalency diploma (GED).
Candidates may be referred to the Delaware Technical and
Community College for eight weeks of training in "life skills."
With intitiative, some qualify for degrees from the college with
support from regular monthly benefit payments, child care and
Medicaid (Kaus 23).

Author-page citation

About 1.1 billion dollars in federal aid was available under
the JOBS program to states capable of putting up matching funds.
The federal government provided 1.8 million dollars to Delaware
and the state matched with $978,558. The state now operates 12
multi-service centers that serve as one stop facilities for
individuals and families seeking federal aid (Kellam 796).

As late as August, 1994 President Clinton and Senator Dole
presented different visions of welfare reform to state governors.
Clinton took administrative action to approve state programs
which put welfare recipients to work and which denied increases
in food stamps to those who will not take jobs (795).

1″

SAMPLE MLA TABLE

MLA TABLE

As can be seen in Table 1, the percentage of welfare recipients
in workfare programs has increased over the years.

Quarles   12

3 spaces

Table 1

Percentage of Welfare Recipients in Workfare Programs in Four
States

Year	California	Delaware	New York	Wisconsin
1988	20	31	21	19
1989	21	33	27	22
1990	24	36	29	26
1991	31	39	34	29
1992	37	41	37	33
1993	45	44	39	34
1994	47	49	41	35
1995	53	49	46	39

Because costs of workfare programs have been underestimated
by reformers, most states are working with haste to develop
programs which will utilize federal block grants effectively
without materially increasing costs. Such costs would have to be
borne by local taxation, a politically difficult challenge.

Several problems need to be solved. First, the majority of
welfare recipients are single mothers receiving Aid to Dependent
Children funds. If these mothers are sent to work, expensive
child care arrangements will have to be made. New programs and
new bureaucracies will be born. Second, most welfare clients are
in dire need of job training. Many suffer from various mental and
social pathologies as well as other personal and other problems.

MLA HANDBOOK

SAMPLE MLA WORKS CITED PAGE

MLA WORKS CITED PAGE

1"

Works Cited

Bernstein, Phillip R., Charles D. Delanson, and Paul Connelson.
"Attitudinal Changes in Mothers Engaged in Job Training."
Journal of Applied Psychology 78 (1993): 452-457.

Carlson, Roberta J.   The Dream and the Dilemma: Welfare in
America.   New York: Macmillan, 1994.

Conniff, Ruth.   "Cutting the Lifeline: The Real Welfare Fraud."
The Progressive Feb. 1992: 25-28

Cowan, Noah.   "The Big Lie About Workfare."   Utne Reader May-
June 1992: 28-29.

Gilbert, Neil.   "Why the New Workfare Won't Work."   Commentary
May 1994: 47.

Kaus, Mickey.   "Tough Enough: A Promising Start on Welfare
Reform."   The New Republic 25 Apr. 1994: 22-23.

Kellam, Susan.   "Welfare Experiments: Are States Leading the Way
Toward National Reform?"   Congressional Quarterly Researcher
16 Sept.1994: 795-796.

Robinson, Karl, and Bernard R. Politcheck.   The Politics of
Welfare Reform.   New York: McGraw Hill, 1994.

Schwartz, Miriam.   "The Role of the Mother in AFDC Families."
Consulting Psychology Journal: Practice and Research 45.4
(1993): 27-29.

United States.   Dept. of Health and Human Services.   Survey of
Jobs Training Programs.   Washington: GPO, 1992.

"Workfare Debate Heats Up in Legislatures."   Washington Post   21
Aug. 1993: A3.

1"   1"

1"

Modern Language Association
Author-Page Citation
With ClarisWorks 4

OPENING CLARISWORKS THE FIRST TIME

1. Click twice on the **Macintosh HD Icon.** The **Macintosh HD Window** will appear. Choose **by Icon** in the **View Menu.**
2. Click twice on the **Applications Folder** on the **Macintosh HD Window.** The **Applications Window** will appear.
3. Click twice on the **ClarisWorks Folder Icon** on the **Applications Window.** The **ClarisWorks Window** will appear. Click on the **ClarisWorks Application Icon.** The **Main Menu** will change to the **ClarisWorks Menu.**
4. Click twice on **Word Processing.** A **Blank Document Page** will appear under the **ClarisWorks Menu Bar**, a **Ruler** and a **Button Bar.** It will be labeled, **Untitled 1 (WP).**
5. The cursor I-Beam will be flashing at the left margin.
6. You are ready to begin typing your paper.

CLARISWORKS DOCUMENT PAGE WINDOW

OPENING YOUR DOCUMENT LATER

1. Follow the steps above to open **ClarisWorks** from the **Application Window.**
2. Choose **Open** from the **File Menu.** An **Open Dialog Box** will appear. See the **Open Dialog Box** illustration on **page 3-7** in **Chapter 3 Basic Macintosh.**
3. Choose the location of your document from the pop-up list. It will be on the **Desktop,** the **Macintosh HD,** or in the **folder** where you saved your document. You may need to click on the pop-up list at the top to see the folders and documents in each location.
4. Use the **scroll bars** to scroll through the files until you locate your document. Click on your document name. It will open with its name in the **title bar** and you will be ready to enter text.

MARGINS

The setting for **MLA** papers is one inch on top, bottom, and sides which is the default setting for **ClarisWorks.** You can change the margins if required by your instructor, but do not right justify or hyphenate words.

1. Choose **Document** in the **Format Menu.** The **Document Dialog Box** will open. Type the modified margins in inches in each of the **Margins Boxes.** Do not click on **Mirror Facing Pages** or **Facing Pages Side-By-Side** because research papers are printed on only one side of each page.
2. Click on **OK.** If the **OK** button has a double line around it you can press the **Return Key** instead.

LINE SPACING

MLA papers are double spaced throughout. The default setting for **ClarisWorks** is single spacing. Change the setting before you begin typing.

1. Click twice on the **Increase Spacing Button** with two horizontal bars in the **Button Bar.** It is between the **Tabs** and **Justification Buttons.** The setting in the window will shift to **2 li.**

FONT

Font is the term used to describe the shape of the type used in typing. The **MLA** suggests using a standard typeface in

10 or 12 point size similar to that found in typewriters. **Courier** and **Times Roman** are good examples. Although **ClarisWorks** enables you to change the font, the size, and a whole range of styles such as bold, condensed, and shadow, select one simple typeface and keep it in the plain text style.

`This is 12 point Courier font.`

1. Choose **Courier** in the **Font Menu**. **Courier** will be underlined.
2. Choose **12 Point** in the **Size Menu**.

ITALICS AND UNDERLINING

Prior to the invention of computers and wordprocessing programs, writers used underlining to designate words which were to be italicized by the printer. Many colleges and universities still require such underlining and frown on the use of italics in formal papers. You should discuss this matter with your instructor if you wish to use italics.

Foreign words and the titles of books, magazines, and newspapers are underlined to indicate italics.

1. Select the text you want to underline or italicize.
2. Drag down to **Underline** in the **Style Menu** or press **Command U** (⌘ **U).**
3. Drag down to **Italic** in the **Style Menu** or press **Command I (⌘ I).**

CENTERING AND JUSTIFYING

Justification describes how words are placed on the page: flush left, flush right, or centered. **ClarisWorks** allows you to spread the words on each line across the page so the right margin is straight or right justified. Although **MLA** papers should not be justified, you will need to center or move some text at times.

1. Select the text you want to center or move.
2. Find the four **Justification Buttons** with several horizontal lines symbolizing lines of text under the ruler in the **Button Bar.**
3. Click on the **Center Justification Button** to center text.
4. Click on the appropriate **Justification Button** to move text left or right.

INDENTION

MLA papers are indented one half inch. The **ClarisWorks** default setting is one half inch, but you may want to change indents for quotations or other purposes.

1. Click anywhere in the paragraph.
2. Choose **Paragraph** from the **Format Menu**. The **Paragraph Dialog Box** will appear.
3. Press **Tab** to move the highlight to the **First Line Indent Box**.
4. Type the correct value in tenths of an inch. Click **OK** to set the first line indent.
5. Press **Enter** or click on **OK** and the first line will be indented the proper space.
6. When quotations require both left and right indents, use this procedure, but change both **Left** and **Right Indent Boxes** after clicking in the passage to be quoted.

PAGINATION

Beginning with the first page, **MLA** papers carry a right justified heading one half inch from the top of the page with your last name in upper and lower case followed by the page number in arabic numerals. **See sample pages on pages 4-19 through 4-22.**

1. Choose **Insert Header** from the **Format Menu**. A blinking cursor will appear at the left margin in a **Header box**.
2. Choose **Insert Page #** from the **Edit Menu**. The **Insert Page Number Dialog Box** will appear with the **Page Number Radio Button** selected and **arabic numerals** selected in the **Representation Pull Down Menu**. Click on **OK**.
3. The cursor will appear just to the right of the number 1 at the left margin. Press the **Left Arrow Key** to move the cursor to left of number 1.
4. Press the **Space Bar** three times to move the number 1 three spaces to the right.
5. Press the **Left Arrow Key** three times to move the cursor to the left margin.
6. Type your last name. The cursor will be at the last letter of your name.
7. Press the **Left Arrow Key** to move the cursor to the beginning of your name.

8. Click the **Right Justification Button** in the **Button Bar.** Your name and page number 1 will shift to the right margin.
9. Click at the left margin of the first line of the text space under the header box to move the cursor there.

TITLE PAGE

MLA papers do not have a formal title page. **Your name**, **instructor's name**, **course number,** and **date** are grouped at the upper left corner of the first page. **See sample Title Page on page 4-19.**

1. Move the cursor to the top line of the first page.
2. Type in upper and lower case, **your full name,** first name first, on the top line, the **instructors's name** on the second line, the **course number** on the third line, and the **date** on the fourth line, double spaced at the left margin.
3. Double space and center the **title** in upper and lower case.
4. Double space an begin your paper.

AUTHOR-PAGE CITATIONS

MLA papers use a simple system of citing sources by stating the author's name and page number(s) of the work in parentheses. Citations are placed directly in the text. No special keystrokes are necessary. The citations lead readers to the alphabetical list of sources in the **Works Cited** list at the end of the paper. Follow the **explanation** and **examples of parenthetical citations** on **pages 4-2 through 4-4.** See the **sample Text Page** with author-page citations on **page 4-20.**

1. Citations are placed directly in the text. No special keystrokes are necessary.

WORKS CITED LIST

The **Works Cited** list is printed at the end of the paper and presents the full bibliographic information for every source cited in the body of your paper. Do not include sources you may have consulted, but did not use.

It is a good idea to prepare the **Works Cited** list before you actually start the paper so you will know how to cite the references in the text. **See the sample formats for Works Cited entries on pages 4-5 through 4-14 and the sample Works Cited page on page 4-21.**

1. Move the cursor to the end of the last line of text. Press **Enter** to place the cursor on a new blank line.
2. Choose **Insert Page Break** from the **Format Menu.** The cursor will move to a new page.
3. Center the words, **Works Cited,** in upper and lower case on the top line. Double space.
4. Type entries in alphabetical order using the appropriate format for the type of reference you are citing. The first line of each entry begins at the left margin with following lines double spaced and indented a half inch.
5. Double space within and between entries.

TABLES

Tables should be used sparingly. Use them only when data will be better presented in tabular form. Avoid confusing the reader by breaking up text with too many tables. Do not duplicate information in the text which appears in a table. A table should supplement material in the text, but it should also be understandable alone.

Tables are assigned arabic numerals and brief titles and are located as close as possible to their mention in the text. Every column must have a short heading. The data in the left column usually describes the major independent variable.

Use horizontal rules only and use vertical spacing to make the table easily readable. Double space within tables. **See the sample Table on page 4-22.**

1. Move the cursor to the place in the text where the table will be inserted. Leave three blank lines.
2. Type the words, **Table 1**, flush left without a period.
3. Double space and type the **title** flush left in upper and lower case. Extra lines of title are centered and double spaced.
4. Double space and type a **line of hyphens** across the page.

5. You must now set up the rows and columns which make up the table. Each column must have a header and these should be spaced evenly across the top of the table. The first column of the table is at the left margin. The last column should be near the right margin.

6. Find the **four Tab Triangles** on the left side of the **Button Bar.** One is **shaded** on the **left**, one on the **bottom,** one on the **right,** and one on the **top.** The one shaded on the left aligns columns on the left side of the tab, the one shaded on the bottom centers columns on the tab, the one shaded on the right aligns columns on the right side of the tab, and the one shaded at the top aligns columns of numbers along a decimal point.

7. Drag the **Center Triangle Tab Icon** to the approximate location on the ruler where the second header should be. Follow the same procedure for the remaining header locations.

8. Type the **first header** flush with the left margin. Capitalize the first letters of major words in each heading.

9. Press the **Tab Key** and type the second header under its **Tab Icon.** Press the **Tab Key** again and type the third header. Continue the procedure until all headers are typed.

9. Select any header and drag its **Triangle Tab Icon** left or right. The header will move with the icon to a new location. Use this method to adjust the locations of the headers until they are properly spaced.

10. Press **Enter** to double space and type a line of hyphens under the headers.

11. Enter data under each header by pressing tab to reach the next column. When you type the numbers to enter data, they will be centered under the **Tab Icons.** Be sure to align decimal points using the **Decimal Point Tab Icon.**

12. Press **Enter** to double space and type a line of hyphens across the page.

SPELL CHECK

1. Choose **Check Document Spelling** in the **Writing Tools Submenu** of the **Edit Menu** or press **Command = (⌘ =).** The **Spelling Dialog Box** will appear over the document window with misspelled words highlighted.

2. Click on one of the word options offered to correct it.

3. Click on **Replace** to replace the misspelled word with the correct one. Click on **Ignore** if the word is a special use word not in the **Spell Check** dictionary.

4. Continue the process until the entire document been checked.

5. Click on **Done.**

CLARISWORKS
Spell Check

PRINTING

See page 3-5 in Chapter 3. Basic Macintosh for instructions.

SAVING

See page 3-6 in Chapter 3. Basic Macintosh for instructions.

Modern Language Association
Author-Page Citation With WordPerfect

OPENING WORDPERFECT THE FIRST TIME

1. Click twice on the **Macintosh HD Icon.** The **Macintosh HD Window** will appear. Choose **by Icon** in the **View Menu.**
2. Click twice on the **Applications Folder** on the **Macintosh HD Window.** The **Applications Window** will appear.
3. Click twice on the **WordPerfect Folder Icon** on the **Applications Window.** Click on the **WordPerfect Application Icon.** A **Blank Document Page** will appear labeled **untitled.** The **Main Menu** will change to the **WordPerfect Menu.**
4. Click on **Ruler, Layout,** and **Font** in the **Button Bar.** A **ruler** and **Layout** and **Font Button Bars** will appear on the **Blank Document Page.**
5. The cursor I-Beam will be flashing at the left margin.
6. You are ready to begin typing your paper.

WORDPERFECT DOCUMENT PAGE WINDOW

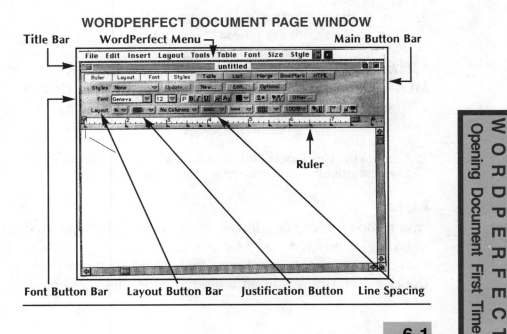

Title Bar   WordPerfect Menu   Main Button Bar

Ruler

Font Button Bar   Layout Button Bar   Justification Button   Line Spacing

OPENING YOUR DOCUMENT LATER

1. Follow the steps above to open **WordPerfect** from the **Application Window.**
2. Choose **Open** from the **File Menu.** An **Open Dialog Box** will appear. See the **Open Dialog Box** illustration on **page 3-7** in **Chapter 3 Basic Macintosh.**
3. Choose the location of your document from the pop-up list. It will be on the **Desktop,** the **Macintosh HD,** or in the **folder** where you saved your document. You may need to click on the menu at the top to see the folders and documents in each location.
4. Use the **scroll bars** to scroll through the files until you locate your document. Click on your document and it will open with its name in the **title bar** and you will be ready to enter text.

MARGINS

The setting for **MLA** papers is one inch on top, bottom, and sides which is the default setting for **WordPerfect.** You can change the margins if required by your instructor, but do not right justify or hyphenate words.

1. Choose **Margins** in the **Layout Menu.** The **Margins Dialog Box** will open. Type the modified margins in inches in each of the **Margins Boxes.**
2. Click on **OK.** If the **OK** button has a double line around it you can press the **Return Key** instead.

LINE SPACING

MLA papers are double spaced throughout. The default setting for **WordPerfect** is single spacing. Change the setting before you begin typing.

1. Click on the **Line Spacing Button** with three horizontal lines in the **Layout Button Bar** above the ruler. Drag down to **2.**

FONT

Font is the term used to describe the shape of the type used in typing. The **MLA** suggests using a standard typeface in 10 or 12 point size similar to that found in typewriters. **Courier** and **Times Roman** are good examples. Although

WordPerfect enables you to change the font, the size, and a whole range of styles such as bold, condensed, and shadow, select one simple typeface and keep it in the plain text style.

> This is 12 point Courier font.

1. Drag down to **Courier** in the **Font Menu** or the **Font Button Bar. Courier** will appear in the window.
2. Choose **12** in the **Size Menu** or pull down the **Size Pop-up Menu** in the **Font Bar** to **12.**

ITALICS AND UNDERLINING

Prior to the invention of computers and wordprocessing programs, writers used underlining to designate words which were to be italicized by the printer. Many colleges and universities still require such underlining and frown on the use of italics in formal papers. You should discuss this matter with your instructor if you wish to use italics.

Foreign words and the titles of books, magazines, and newspapers are underlined to indicate italics.

1. Select the text you want to underline or italicize.
2. Drag down to **Underline** in the **Style Menu** or press **Command U** (⌘ U) or press the **U Button** in the **Font Button Bar.**
3. Drag down to **Italicize** in the **Style Menu** or press **Command I** (⌘ I) or press the **I Button in the Button Bar.**

CENTERING AND JUSTIFYING

Justification describes how words are placed on the page: flush left, flush right, or centered. **WordPerfect** allows you to spread the words on each line across the page so the right margin is ragged or right justified. Although **MLA** papers should not be justified, you will need to center or move some text at times.

1. Select the text you want to center or move.
2. Find the **Justification Button** under the ruler in the **Layout Button Bar** and drag down to **Left, Center,** or **Right** as needed.

INDENTION

MLA papers are indented one half inch. The **WordPerfect** default setting is one half inch, but you may want to change indents for quotations or other purposes.

1. Select the text for which you want to change indents.
2. Change the left and right margins using the instructions in **MARGINS** above.
3. Click on the first paragraph in which you want to indent the first line. Find the **First-Line Indent Marker** on the left side of the ruler. It looks like a V-shaped tab. Drag it to the ruler setting you want.
4. When finished with quoted or other material, change the margins and indents to the regular settings.

PAGINATION

Beginning with the first page, **MLA** papers carry a right justified heading one half inch from the top of the page with your last name in upper and lower case followed by the page number in arabic numerals. **See sample pages on pages 4-19 through 4-22.**

1. Choose **New** in the **submenu** in **Header/Footer** in the **Layout Menu**.   The **New Header/Footer Dialog Box** will appear with the **Header A Radio Button** selected. Click on **OK**.
2. The **Title Header A** window will open with **Button Bars** similar to those in the regular document window.
3. Click on the **Page Icon** in the **Header Button Bar** which looks like a page with the upper right corner turned down and a **+1** on the page. The number 1 will appear at the left margin.
4. Press the **Left Arrow Key** to move the cursor to left of number 1.
5. Type your last name in upper and lower case.
6. Press **Spacebar** three times to move the number 1 three spaces to the right.
7. Press the **Left Arrow Key** to move the cursor to the left of your name.
8. Click on the **Justication Button** and drag down to **Right Justification** to bring your name and the number 1 to the right margin.
9. Click the **Close Box** of the **Header Window**.
10. Choose **Print Preview** from the **File Menu** to check your settings.

WORDPERFECT
Indention and Pagination

TITLE PAGE

MLA papers do not have a formal title page. **Your name, instructor's name, course number,** and **date** are grouped at the upper left corner of the first page. **See sample Title Page on page 4-19.**

1. Move the cursor to the top line of the first page.
2. Type in upper and lower case, **your full name,** first name first, on the top line, the **instructors's name** on the second line, the **course number** on the third line, and the **date** on the fourth line, double spaced at the left margin.
3. Double space and center the **title** in upper and lower case.
4. Double space an begin your paper.

AUTHOR-PAGE CITATIONS

MLA papers use a simple system of citing sources by stating the author's name and page number(s) of the work in parentheses. Citations are placed directly in the text. No special keystrokes are necessary. The citations lead readers to the alphabetical list of sources in the **Works Cited** list at the end of the paper. Follow the **explanation** and **examples of parenthetical citations** on **pages 4-2 through 4-4.** See the **sample Text Page** with author-page citations on **page 4-20.**

1. Citations are placed directly in the text. No special keystrokes are necessary.

WORKS CITED LIST

The **Works Cited** list is printed at the end of the paper and presents the full bibliographic information for every source cited in the body of your paper. Do not include sources you may have consulted, but did not use. It is a good idea to prepare the **Works Cited** list before you actually start the paper so you will know how to cite the references in the text. **See the sample formats for Works Cited entries on pages 4-5 through 4-14 and the sample Works Cited page on page 4-21.**

1. Move the cursor to the end of the last line of text. Press **Enter** to place the cursor on a new blank line.
2. Choose **Insert Page Break** from the **Insert Menu**. The cursor will move to a new page.
3. Center the words, **Works Cited**, in upper and lower case on the top line. Double space.
4. Type entries in alphabetical order using the appropriate format for the type of reference you are citing. The first line of each entry begins at the left margin with following lines double spaced and indented a half inch. Double space between entries.

TABLES

Tables should be used sparingly. Use them only when data will be better presented in tabular form. Avoid confusing the reader by breaking up text with too many tables. Do not duplicate information in the text which appears in a table. A table should supplement material in the text, but it should also be understandable alone.

Tables are assigned arabic numerals and brief titles and are located as close as possible to their mention in the text. Every column must have a short heading. The data in the left column usually describes the major independent variable.

Use horizontal rules only and use vertical spacing to make the table easily readable. Double space within tables. See the **sample Table** on **page 4-22**.

You can set up tables in two ways: by using the **Table Menu** or by **Setting Tabs** on the **Ruler.**

1. Move the cursor to the place in the text where the table will be inserted. Leave three blank lines.
2. Type the words, **Table 1**, flush left without a period.
3. Double space and type the **title** flush left in upper and lower case. Extra lines of title are centered and double spaced.
4. Double space and type a **line of hyphens** across the page.
5. You must now set up the rows and columns which make up the table. Each column must have a header and these should be spaced evenly across the top of the table. The first column of the table is at the left margin. The last column should be near the right margin. Decide which method of setting up the rows and columns is best for you.

USING THE TABLE MENU METHOD

1. Select **New** from the **Table Menu.** The **New Table Dialog Box** will appear. Enter the number of columns and rows you need and press **OK.** A blank table containing the correct number of cells will appear with a double ruled border and single ruling between the rows and columns. The rules will be removed later.

2. Type the header titles in the top cells. Capitalize the first letters of major words of each header. Press **Tab** or the **Right Arrow Key** to move to the next cell. Press **Enter** at the end of a word in a cell to move the cursor to the next line within that cell or select **Row Height** from the **Table Menu.** The **Row Height Dialog Box** will appear. Click **Multi-Line** and **OK** if you want the text to word-wrap in that cell.

3. Type the data into the cells under the headers. You may find that some cells need to made wider, narrower, taller, or shorter. Select the column whose width you want to change. Select **Column Width** from the **Table Menu.** The **Column Width Dialog Box** will appear. Type in the correct width you need and click **OK.** Select the row whose height you want to change. Select **Row Height** from the **Table Menu.** The **Row Height Dialog Box** will appear. Click the **Fixed Radio Button** and type in the correct height you need and click **OK.**

4. You can also change height and width by moving the cursor to the edge of a column or row. The cursor will change to a double arrow and you can drag the rule to make the cell the required size.

5. Center headers and data in each cell using the **Justification Button.**

6. Select **Table Border** in the **Table Menu.** Pull down to **None.** Type a line of hyphens across the bottom of the table. You also need to type a line of hyphens double spaced between the headers and the data.

or

USING THE SETTING TABS ON THE RULER METHOD

1. Find the **Tab Button** in the **Layout Button Bar.** It is the first button on the left and has two triangles in it.

2. Drag down to **Clear Tabs.** All of the **Default Tab Triangles** set 1/2 inch apart will disappear.

3. Drag down to the **Center Triangle.** Move the cursor to the top line of the page just below the ruler. As it crosses the line it becomes an **arrow.**

4. Move the arrow to the approximate location of the second header and release. A **small black triangle** will appear under the numbers

in the ruler. Continue placing the triangles in the approximate locations you want the headers.

5. Type the first header at the left margin. Press **Tab** and type the second header. Repeat the process until all the headers are typed.

6. Select any header. Click on the **Tab Triangle** above it. A vertical line will extend down through the header. Now drag the **triangle** left or right and the header will move with it adjusting the spacing of the header Move the other headers, if necessary, until they are properly spaced.

7. Double space and type a line of hyphens across the page under the headers.

8. Double space and center data in each of the columns using tabs. Double space between lines. If a column contains decimal points, use the **Decimal Tab Triangle** in the pop-up menu under the **Tab Button** in the **Layout Bar.**

9. Double space and type a line of hyphens across the page under the data.

SPELL CHECK

1. Choose **Speller** in the **Tools Menu** or press **Command E** (⌘ **E**). The **Spelling Dialog Box** will appear on top of the document window.

2. Click on **Check** and drag down to **Document.**

3. Press **Start.** The **misspelled word** will appear with **alternative words** suggested.

4. Scroll through the list until you find the correct word. Press **Replace.**

5. Continue until you have checked the entire document.

PRINTING

See page 3-5 in Chapter 3 Basic Macintosh for instructions.

SAVING

See page 3-6 in Chapter 3 Basic Macintosh for instructions.

Modern Language Association
Author-Page Citation
With Microsoft Word

OPENING MICROSOFT WORD FIRST TIME

1. Click twice on the **Macintosh HD Icon.** The **Macintosh HD Window** will appear. Choose **by Icon** in the **View Menu.**
2. Click twice on the **Applications Folder** on the **Macintosh HD Window.** The **Applications Window** will appear.
3. Click twice on the **Microsoft Word Folder Icon** on the **Applications Window.** The **Microsoft Word Window** will open. Click on the **Microsoft Word Icon. A Blank Document Window** will appear. The **Main Menu** will change to the **Microsoft Word Menu.**
4. A **Standard Toolbar,** a **Formatting Toolbar, and** a **Ruler** will appear under the **Menu Bar.**
5. The cursor I-Beam will be flashing at the left margin.
6. You are ready to begin typing your paper.

MICROSOFT WORD DOCUMENT PAGE WINDOW

Close box   Document title bar   Menu bar   Zoom box

Standard toolbar   Formatting toolbar   Horizontal Ruler

OPENING YOUR DOCUMENT LATER

1. Follow the steps above to open **Microsoft Word** from the **Application Window.**
2. Choose **Open** from the **File Menu.** An **Open Dialog Box** will appear. See the **Open Dialog Box** illustration on **page 3-7** in **Chapter 3 Basic Macintosh**.
3. Choose the location of your document from the pop-up list. It will be on the **Desktop,** the **Macintosh HD,** or in the **folder** where you saved your document. You may need to click on the pop-up list at the top to see the folders and documents in each location.
4. Use the **scroll bars** to scroll through the files until you locate your document. Click on your document and it will open with its name in the **title bar** and you will be ready to enter text.

MARGINS

The setting for **MLA** papers is one inch on top, bottom, and sides which is the default setting for **Microsoft Word.** You can change the margins if required by your instructor, but do not right justify or hyphenate words.

1. Choose **Document Layout** in the **File Menu.** The **Document Layout Dialog Box** will appear.
2. Click the **Margins Tab** and type the modified margins in inches in each of the margins boxes or click the arrow buttons to increase or decrease the settings. Do not click on **Mirror Margins** because research papers are printed on only one side of each page.
3. Click on **OK.**

LINE SPACING

MLA papers are double spaced throughout. The default setting for **Microsoft Word** is single spacing. Change the setting before you begin typing.

1. Choose **Paragraph** in the **Format Menu.** The **Paragraph Dialog Box** will open.
2. Choose **Double** from the **Line Spacing drop down list.**
3. Click **OK.**

FONT

Font is the term used to describe the shape of the type used in typing. The **MLA** suggests using a standard typeface in 10 or 12 point size similar to that found in typewriters. **Courier** and **Times Roman** are good examples. Although **Microsoft Word** enables you to change the font, the size, and a whole range of styles such as bold, condensed, and shadow, select one simple typeface and keep it in the plain text style.

```
This is 12 point Courier font.
```

1. Choose **Font** from the **Format Menu**. The **Font Dialog Box** will appear.
2. Choose **Courier** from the **Font Scrollable List** and **12** from the **Size Scrollable List.**
3. Click on **OK.**

or

1. Click on the **Font** and **Size Buttons** in the **Formatting Toolbar**. Drop down lists will appear.
2. Click on **Courier** and **12.**

ITALICS AND UNDERLINING

Prior to the invention of computers and wordprocessing programs, writers used underlining to designate words which were to be italicized by the printer. Many colleges and universities still require such underlining and frown on the use of italics in formal papers. You should discuss this matter with your instructor if you wish to use italics.

Foreign words and the titles of books, magazines, and newspapers are underlined to indicate italics.

1. Select the text you want to underline or italicize.
2. Choose **Font** from the **Format Menu**. The **Font Dialog Box** will appear.
3. Choose **Italic** or **Underline** from the **Font Style scrollable list.**
4. Click on **OK.**

or

1. Select text and click on the *I* or U buttons in the **Formatting Tool Bar.**

CENTERING AND JUSTIFYING

Justification describes how words are placed on the page: flush left, flush right, or centered. **Microsoft Word** allows you to spread the words on each line across the page so the right margin is straight or right justified. Although **MLA** papers should not be justified, you will need to center or move some text at times.

1. Select the text you want to center or move.
2. Click on the appropriate **Justification Button** just to the right of the **B, *I*, U Buttons** in the **Formatting Toolbar** to center or move text.

INDENTION

MLA papers are indented one half inch. The **Microsoft Word** default setting is one half inch, but you may want to change indents for quotations or other purposes.

1. Select the text for which you want to change indents.
2. Choose **Paragraph** from the **Format Menu.** The **Paragraph Dialog Box** will appear.
3. Change the **Left** and **Right Indentation** settings by typing in new settings or clicking on the **increase** or **decrease arrows.**
4. Click on **OK.**

PAGINATION

Beginning with the first page, **MLA** papers carry a right justified heading one half inch from the top of the page with your last name in upper and lower case followed by the page number in arabic numerals. **See sample pages on pages 4-19 through 4-22.**

1. Choose **Header** and **Footer** from the **View Menu.** The text will dim and the cursor will appear in the header space. The **Header and Footer Toolbar** will also appear.
2. Click the **Switch Between Header and Footer Button** which is the first button on the left to be sure you are in the header space.
3. Click the **Page Number Button** which has a number sign on an icon page with a folded corner in the **Header and Footer Toolbar** The number 1 will appear at the left margin.

4. The cursor will appear just to the right of the number 1 at the left margin. Press the **Left Arrow Key** to move the cursor to the left of the number 1.
5. Press the **Space Bar** three times to move the number 1 three spaces to the right.
6. Press the **Left Arrow Key** to move the cursor to the left margin.
7. Type your last name. The cursor will be at the last letter of your name.
8. Press the **Left Arrow Key** to move the cursor to the beginning of your name.
9. Click the **Right Justification Button** in the **Formatting Toolbar.** Your name and page number 1 will shift to the right margin.

TITLE PAGE

MLA papers do not have a formal title page. **Your name, instructor's name, course number,** and **date** are grouped at the upper left corner of the first page. **See sample Title Page on page 4-19.**

1. Move the cursor to the top line of the first page.
2. Type in upper and lower case, **your full name,** first name first, on the top line, the **instructor's name** on the second line, the **course number** on the third line, and the **date** on the fourth line, double spaced at the left margin.
3. Double space and center the **title** in upper and lower case. Double space and begin your paper.

AUTHOR-PAGE CITATIONS

MLA papers use a simple system of citing sources by stating the author's name and page number(s) of the work in parentheses. Citations are placed directly in the text. No special keystrokes are necessary. The citations lead readers to the alphabetical list of sources in the Works Cited list at the end of the paper. Follow the **explanation** and **examples** of **parenthetical citations** on **pages 4-2 through 4-4.** See the **sample Text Page** with author-page citations on **page 4-20.**

1. Citations are placed directly in the text. No special keystrokes are necessary.

WORKS CITED LIST

The **Works Cited** list is printed at the end of the paper and presents the full bibliographic information for every source cited in the body of your paper. Do not include sources you may have consulted, but did not use. It is a good idea to prepare the **Works Cited** list before you actually start the paper so you will know how to cite the references in the text. **See the sample formats for Works Cited entries on pages 4-5 through 4-14 and the sample Works Cited page on page 4-21.**

1. Move the cursor to the end of the last line of text. Press **Enter** to place the cursor on a new blank line.
2. Choose **Break** from the **Insert Menu.** The **Break Dialog Box** will appear.
3. Click on the **Page Break Button** and **OK.**
4. Center the words, **Works Cited,** in upper and lower case on the top line. Double space.
5. Type entries in alphabetical order using the appropriate format for the type of reference you are citing. The first line of each entry begins at the left margin with following lines double spaced and indented a half inch.
6. Double space within and between entries.

TABLES

Tables should be used sparingly. Use them only when data will be better presented in tabular form. Avoid confusing the reader by breaking up text with too many tables. Do not duplicate information in the text which appears in a table. A table should supplement material in the text, but it should also be understandable alone.

Tables are assigned arabic numerals and brief titles and are located as close as possible to their mention in the text. Every column must have a short heading. The data in the left column usually describes the major independent variable.

Use horizontal rules only and use vertical spacing to make the table easily readable. Double space within tables. **See the sample Table on page 4-22.**

You can set up tables in two ways: by using the **Table Menu** or by **Setting Tabs** on the **Ruler.**

1. Move the cursor to the place in the text where the table will be inserted. Leave three blank lines.
2. Type the words, **Table 1**, flush left without a period.
3. Double space and type the **title** flush left in upper and lower case. Extra lines of title are centered and double spaced.
4. Double space and type a **line of hyphens** across the page.
5. You must now set up the rows and columns which make up the table. Each column must have a header and these should be spaced evenly across the top of the table. The first column of the table is at the left margin. The last column should be near the right margin. Decide which method of setting up the rows and columns is best for you.

USING THE TABLE MENU METHOD
1. Double space and move the cursor under the title.
2. Choose **Insert Table** from the **Table Menu.** The **Insert Table Dialog Box** will appear.
3. Click **Table Wizard** and the first of six **Table Wizard Dialog Boxes** will appear.
4. Select **Style 1**, the simplest style in the first dialog box. Click **Next** to go to the next dialog box. Enter the **Number of Columns** in the second, the **Column Headings** in the third, the **Number of Rows** and **Row Headings** in the fourth, the **Alignment of Data and Headings** in the fifth, and the **Table Orientation** in the sixth dialog box.
5. Type the first header in the first cell on the left. Click on the **Left Justification Button** in the **Button Bar** to move the header to the left margin of the cell. Capitalize the first letters of major words in the headers. Center the remaining headers in their respective cells by clicking on the **Center Justification Button** in the **Button Bar.**
6. Enter data by clicking in each cell and typing. Cells will become taller if more than one line is entered.
7. Press **Tab** to move to the next cell to the right. Press **Shift Tab** to move back one cell. Press **Down Arrow Key** to move down by row. Press **Up Arrow Key** to move up by row.
8. To delete cells, select cells by dragging across them. Choose

Delete Cells from the **Table Menu.** The **Delete Cells Dialog Box** will appear. Choose the selection and click **OK.**

9. After all data is entered, you will have to eliminate the borders including all the vertical rules. Click on the **Borders Button** in the **Formatting Toolbar.** It is the last button on the right and is a square divided into quarters with bold outside borders. The **Borders Toolbar** will appear.

10. Select the entire table and click on the **No Border Button** which is the last button on the right. All rules should disappear.

11. Drag down to a **dashed line** in the **Line Style Drop Down List** and click on the **Bottom Border Button** to draw a dashed line across the bottom. You will have to ink in a dashed line between the headers and the data in the table.

USING THE TAB - RULER METHOD

1. Type the **first header** flush with the left margin. Capitalize important words in the header as in a title.

2. Look at the extreme left end of the ruler. You will see a **Tab Alignment Button** with an **L-shaped marker.** Each time you click on it the marker will change to an **upside down T**, a **backwards L**, or an **upside down T with a dot** . The **L-shape** is the **Tab Alignment Button** for **aligning text at the left letter**, the **upside down T** is for **centering text at the tab**, the **backwards L** is for **aligning text at the right letter**, and the **upside down T with a dot** is for **aligning numbers at a decimal point.**

3. Click on the **Tab Alignment Button** until it changes to the **upside down T.**

4. Click in the ruler to set a tab at the approximate location where the second header should be. Continue the process by clicking in the ruler at the approximate locations where each header should be.

5. Press the **Tab Key** and type the second header. It will be centered at the tab location. Follow the same procedure with the remaining headers.

6. Double space and type a line of hyphens under the headers.

7. Double space and enter data in each column by pressing the **Tab Key** to move the cursor to the next column. Double space between rows.

8. After entering data, double space and type a line of hyphens under the data.

SPELL CHECK

1. Choose **Spelling** from the **Tools Menu**. The **Spelling Dialog Box** will open.
2. Misspelled words will appear in the **Not in Dictionary Box** with the correctly spelled word in the **Change to Box**. Other variations of the word will appear in the **Suggestions Scroll Box**.
3. If the correct word is in the **Change to Box**, click **Change** or **Change All** to correct the word wherever it appears in the paper.
4. If the word you want is in the **Suggestions Scroll List**, click on it and then click **Change**.
5. If the word is correctly spelled as is, and **Word's Spell Check** does not recognize it, click **Ignore**.

PRINTING

See page 3-5 in Chapter 3. Basic Macintosh for instructions.

SAVING

See page 3-6 in Chapter 3. Basic Macintosh for instructions.

Modern Language Association
Author-Page Citation
With Microsoft Works

OPENING MICROSOFT WORKS FIRST TIME

1. Click twice on the **Macintosh HD Icon.** The **Macintosh HD Window** will appear. Choose **by Icon** in the **View Menu.**
2. Click twice on the **Applications Folder** on the **Macintosh HD Window.** The **Applications Window** will appear.
3. Click twice on the **Microsoft Works Folder Icon** on the **Applications Window. The Startup Screen** will appear. Click on **Word Processor** to select it. Click on **New** in the **File Menu** and a blank **Document Window** will appear labeled **Untitled1 (WP).** The **Main Menu** will change to the **Microsoft Works Menu.**
4. Choose **Toolbar** and **Ruler** from the **View Menu.** The **Toolbar and Ruler** will appear under the **Menu Bar.**
5. The cursor I-Beam will be flashing at the left margin.
6. You are ready to begin typing your paper.

MICROSOFT WORKS DOCUMENT PAGE WINDOW

Ruler   Works Menu   Font   Font Size   Toolbar   Title Bar

Tabs   Justification Buttons   Line spacing

OPENING YOUR DOCUMENT LATER

1. Follow the steps above to open **Microsoft Works** from the **Application Window.**
2. Choose **Open** from the **File Menu.** An **Open Dialog Box** will appear. See the **Open Dialog Box** illustration on **page 3-7** in **Chapter 3 Basic Macintosh.**
3. Choose the location of your document from the pop-up list. It will be on the **Desktop,** the **Macintosh HD,** or in the **folder** where you saved your document. You may need to click on the pop-up list at the top to see the folders and documents in each location.
4. Use the **scroll bars** to scroll through the files until you locate your document. Click on your document and it will open with its name in the **title bar** and you will be ready to enter text.

MARGINS

The setting for **MLA** papers is one inch on top, bottom, and sides which is the default setting for **Microsoft Word.** You can change the margins if required by your instructor, but do not right justify or hyphenate words.

1. Choose **Page Setup** from the **File Menu.** The **Page Setup Dialog Box** will appear.
2. Click on the **Document Button.** The **Document Dialog Box** will appear. Type the modified margins in inches in each of the margins boxes.
3. Click on **OK.**

LINE SPACING

MLA papers are double spaced throughout. The default setting for **Microsoft Works** is single spacing. Change the setting before you begin typing.

1. Click anywhere in the first paragraph of your paper.
2. Click on the **2.0 Line Spacing Button** in the **ruler.** It is the third button on the left with the widest spacing.

FONT

Font is the term used to describe the shape of the type used in typing. The **MLA** suggests using a standard typeface in 10 or 12 point size similar to that found in typewriters. **Courier** and **Times Roman** are good examples. Although

MICROSOFT WORKS
Margins - Line Spacing - Font

Microsoft Works enables you to change the font, the size, and a whole range of styles such as bold, condensed, and shadow, select one simple typeface and keep it in the plain text style.

```
This is 12 point Courier font.
```

1. Click on the **Font Pop-up Menu** in the **Tool Bar**. Drag down to **Courier**.
2. Click on the **Type Size Pop-up Menu** in the **Tool Bar.** Drag down to **12.**

ITALICS AND UNDERLINING

Prior to the invention of computers and wordprocessing programs, writers used underlining to designate words which were to be italicized by the printer. Many colleges and universities still require such underlining and frown on the use of italics in formal papers. You should discuss this matter with your instructor if you wish to use italics.

Foreign words and the titles of books, magazines, and newspapers are underlined to indicate italics.

1. Select the text you want to underline or italicize.
2. Click on the *I* or U buttons in the **Tool Bar.**

CENTERING AND JUSTIFYING

Justification describes how words are placed on the page: flush left, flush right, or centered. **Microsoft Works** allows you to spread the words on each line across the page so the right margin is straight or right justified. Although **MLA** papers should not be justified, you will need to center or move some text at times.

1. Select the text you want to center or move.
2. Click on the appropriate **Justification Button** just to the left of the **Line Spacing Buttons** in the **Ruler** to center or move text.

MICROSFT WORKS
Italics and Justifying

INDENTION

MLA papers are indented one half inch. The **Microsoft Works** default setting is one half inch, but you may want to change indents for quotations or other purposes.

1. To change the position of the first line in a paragraph, click on the **First Line Indent Mark** just under the number 1 on the ruler and drag it to the appropriate tick on the ruler. There are two **Indent Marks** on the ruler, the top mark is the **First Line Indent Mark** and the bottom mark is the **Left Indent Mark** which controls the rest of the paragraph. In **Works 4.0,** you must hold down the shift key to move the **Left Indent Mark** to the right without moving the **First Line Indent Mark.**

2. To change the right hand indent of a paragraph, click on the **Right Indent Mark** which is just under the 7.5 inch mark on the ruler and drag it to the appropriate tick on the ruler.

PAGINATION

Beginning with the first page, **MLA** papers carry a right justified heading one half inch from the top of the page with your last name in upper and lower case followed by the page number in arabic numerals. **See sample pages on pages 4-19 through 4-22.**

Microsoft Works 3.0
1. Open your term paper document at the first page of text.
2. Choose **Show Header** from the **Windows Menu**. The **Header Window** will appear with its own ruler and buttons.
3. Be sure the cursor is at the left margin. If it is not, click on the **Left Justification Button** in the ruler.
4. Type your last name, move the cursor three spaces to the right by pressing the **Space Bar** three times.
5. Click on the **Page Number Button**. It is just to the right of the **Clock Button.** The number 1 will appear.
6. Select the entire header and click on the **Right Justification Button.** The header will move to the right side of the page and will appear on every page.

Microsoft Works 4.0
1. Open your term paper document at the first page of text. There is a box at the top of the document page which is the **Header Box.**

MICROSOFT WORKS
Indention and Pagination

2. Move the cursor inside the **Header Box** by clicking inside the **Box.** The **Page Number Button** appears in the ruler next to the **Date, Time,** and **Bulleted List Buttons. Special Center** and **Right Tab Stops** also appear in the ruler.
3. Press the **Tab Key** to move the cursor to the **Right Tab Stop.**
4. Type your name and move the cursor three spaces to the right by pressing the **Space Bar** three times.
5. Click on the **Page Number Button** in the **Ruler.** The **Page Icon** will appear three spaces to the right of your name. The actual page numbers will appear when you print your paper or when you select **Print Preview** in the **Print Dialog Box.**

TITLE PAGE

MLA papers do not have a formal title page. **Your name, instructor's name, course number,** and **date** are grouped at the upper left corner of the first page. **See sample Title Page on page 4-19.**

1. Move the cursor to the top line of the first page.
2. Type in upper and lower case, **your full name,** first name first, on the top line, the **instructors's name** on the second line, the **course number** on the third line, and the **date** on the fourth line, double spaced at the left margin.
3. Double space and center the **title** in upper and lower case.
4. Double space an begin your paper.

AUTHOR-PAGE CITATIONS

MLA papers use a simple system of citing sources by stating the author's name and page number(s) of the work in parentheses. Citations are placed directly in the text. No special keystrokes are necessary. The citations lead readers to the alphabetical list of sources in the Works Cited list at the end of the paper. Follow the **explanation** and **examples** of **parenthetical citations** on **pages 4-2 through 4-4**. See the **sample Text Page** with author-page citations on **page 4-20.**

1. Citations are placed directly in the text. No special keystrokes are necessary.

WORKS CITED LIST

The **Works Cited** list is printed at the end of the paper and presents the full bibliographic information for every source cited in the body of your paper. Do not include sources you may have consulted, but did not use. It is a good idea to prepare the **Works Cited** list before you actually start the paper so you will know how to cite the references in the text. **See the sample formats for Works Cited entries on pages 4-5 through 4-14 and the sample Works Cited page on page 4-21.**

1. Move the cursor to the end of the last line of text. Press **Enter** to place the cursor on a new blank line.

Microsoft Works 3.0
2. Choose **Insert Page Break** from the **Document Menu.** A **Manual Page Break Marker** of small dashes will appear across the page.

Microsoft Works 4.0
2. Choose **Page Break** from the **Insert Menu.**

3. Center the words, **Works Cited**, in upper and lower case on the top line. Double space.
4. Type entries in alphabetical order using the appropriate format for the type of reference you are citing. The first line of each entry begins at the left margin with following lines double spaced and indented a half inch. Double space between entries.

MICROSOFT WORKS
Works Cited and Tables

TABLES

Tables should be used sparingly. Use them only when data will be better presented in tabular form. Avoid confusing the reader by breaking up text with too many tables. Do not duplicate information in the text which appears in a table. A table should supplement material in the text, but it should also be understandable alone.

Tables are assigned arabic numerals and brief titles and are located as close as possible to their mention in the text. Every column must have a short heading. The data in the left column usually describes the major independent variable.

Use horizontal rules only and use horizontal spacing to make the table easily readable. Double space within tables. **See the sample Table on page 4-22.**

1. Move the cursor to the place in the text where the table will be inserted. Leave three blank lines.
3. Type **Table 1** flush left in upper and lower case without a period on the top line.
4. Double space and type the **title** flush left and underlined. Capitalize only the first letters of major words. Extra lines of title are flush left and double spaced.
5. Double space and type a **solid line** across the page by pressing **Shift** and **Underline Keys.**
6. You must now set up the rows and columns which make up the table. Each column must have a header and these should be spaced evenly across the top of the table.
7. When you press the **Tab Key,** the cursor moves one half inch to the right and the first character of text will be aligned on the tab stop. This is the **Microsoft Works** default setting. To set up the table you will have to change the **Tab** settings.
8. Find the four upward pointing arrows on the ruler which are the **Tab Stops.** The one on the left is the **Left Align Stop** and has a right pointing tail, the one in the center is the **Center Align Stop** has no tail, the next on the right is the **Right Align Stop** and has a left pointing tail, and the last has no tail but has a decimal point on its right and is the **Decimal Align Stop.** When you tab to the **Right Align Tab Stop,** the last character will be aligned on the stop. When you tab to the **Center Align Tab Stop,** the characters will be centered on either side of the stop. When you tab on the **Decimal Align Stop,** decimal points will be aligned under the stop.
9. Click on the **Center Tab Stop** in the **Ruler** to select it and click in the ruler to set a tab at the approximate location where the second header should be. Continue the process by clicking in the ruler at the approximate locations where the remaining headers should be.
10. Type the first header at the left margin. Press the **Tab Key** and type the second header. It will be centered at the tab location. Follow the same procedure with the remaining headers. Capitalize the first word of each header.
11. Double space and type a line of hyphens.

MICROSFT WORKS
Tables

12. Double space and enter data in each column by pressing the **Tab Key** to move the cursor to the next column. Double space. Click on the **Decimal Align Stop** and move it on the ruler to any column containing decimal data.
13. After entering data, double space and type a line of hyphens.

SPELL CHECK

1. Place the cursor at the point in the document you want to begin checking.

Microsoft Works 3.0

2. Choose **Spelling** from the **Document Menu.**

Microsoft Works 4.0

2. Choose **Spelling** from the **Tools Menu.**

3. The **Spelling Dialog Box** will appear with any misspelled words on the **Not in Dictionary Line** with the correctly spelled word in the **Change to Box.** Other variations for the word will appear in the **Suggestions Scroll Box.**
4. If the correct word is in the **Change to Box**, click **Change** or **Change All** to correct the word wherever it appears in the paper.
5. If the word you want is in the **Suggestions Scroll List**, click on it and then click **Change.**
6. If the word is correctly spelled as is, and **Word's Spell Check** does not recognize it, click **Ignore.**

PRINTING

See page 3-5 in Chapter 3. Basic Macintosh for instructions.

SAVING

See page 3-6 in Chapter 3. Basic Macintosh for instructions.

MICROSOFT WORKS
Spell Check - Printing - Saving

Part 3

Using the *Publication Manual of the APA* to Write Your Paper

Word Processing Applications

Part Three

Using the *Publication Manual of the APA* to Write Your Paper

Word Processing Applications

Chapter Nine

Author-Date Citation

Publication Manual of the American Psychological Association, 4th Ed.

The **American Psychological Association** has been publishing the *Publication Manual* since 1952. As the name of the organization implies, the *Manual* is primarily intended to guide writers and researchers in the field of psychology. However, writers in other disciplines have adopted the author-date citation method.

The fourth edition of the *Publication Manual* contains updated information on the preparation of papers as well as formats for citing electronic media such as CD-ROMs and electronic data bases. Particular attention has been given to the elimination of gender, racial, and socioeconomic bias in scientific writing.

PARENTHETICAL AUTHOR-DATE CITATION

The author's name and the date of the work are placed in parenthesis in the text. When the author's name appears in the text only the date needs to be placed in the parenthesis. A little practice may be necessary to insert the citation and keep the writing fluent. Author-date citation samples are on pages 9-2 and 9-3.

Every source cited in the text must be documented in a Reference List at the end of the paper. It is important that references be cited accurately to permit readers to find and use the sources. Reference samples are on pages 9-4 through 9-9.

Parenthetical citations may be placed anywhere in the sentence, but be sure to maintain a smooth writing style, inserting the citation at natural pause in thought. When both the author's name and date appear in the parenthesis, separate them with a comma.

PARENTHETICAL AUTHOR-DATE CITATION SAMPLES

WORK - SINGLE AUTHOR

Insert last name of author and year of publication in parentheses in the text.

> A study of reactive inhibition (Smith, 1979) indicated

or

If author's name appears in text, insert only the year of the work in parentheses.

> Smith's (1979) study of reactive inhibition indicated

In a second or later mention of same work within a paragraph, the year may be omitted if there will be no confusion.

> In his study of reactive inhibition, Smith also found

WORK - TWO AUTHORS

Mention of a work by two authors should always include both names separated by an *ampersand (&)* in the parentheses and the word, *and*, in the text.

> In an explanation of mental disorder, (Rogers & Phillips, 1978) described

> Rogers and Phillips (1978) studied mental disorder

WORK - MULTIPLE AUTHORS

First mention of a work by three or more authors should include all the authors separated by an *ampersand (&)* in the parenthesis and the word, *and*, in the text.

> Published studies which illustrate the P technique (Cattel, Cattel & Rhymer, 1947) stress the relationship

> Published studies by Cattel, Cattel and Rhymer which illustrate the P technique

PARENTHETICAL AUTHOR-DATE CITATION SAMPLES

Later mention of a work by three or more authors. Cite only the last name of first author and the Latin abbreviation, et al., (not underlined and no period after et) and the year only if there is no confusion.

> In a study of P technique, Cattel et al.
> (1947) discovered

In a second or later mention of same work within a paragraph, the year may be omitted if there will be no confusion.

> Cattell et al. discovered

For a work with six or more authors, cite only the last name of the first author followed by et al. and the year for the first and subsequent citations. Use an *ampersand (&)* in the reference list.

> Smith, et al. (1996) investigated

Include initials of authors with the same last name

CORPORATE AUTHOR

The name of associations, government agencies, and organizations, should usually be spelled out in text at least at the first mention.

> Statistical reports on mental illness in
> the armed forces (National Institute of
> Mental Health [NIMH], 1989) indicated

Subsequent mention may be abbreviated if not confusing and if the reader can readily identify the source in the reference list.

> The study of mental illness (NIMH, 1989)
> indicated

WORK - NO NAMED AUTHOR

Use the first few words of the reference list entry which will probably be the title and date for the citation in the text.

> Latest study of the brain reveals new
> understandings of brain waves ("New Brain
> Study," 1995).

REFERENCES - BIBLIOGRAPHY

A bibliography called, References, printed on a separate page at the end of the paper, provides complete publication information for all of the sources cited in your paper. The citations in the text must lead the reader to the source in the Reference list. Entries are alphabetized letter by letter by author's last names, an association, or title if author is not known. Following are samples of reference citations.

APA REFERENCE SAMPLES

BOOK - NO AUTHOR
Psychology and you (1990). New York: Macmillan.

BOOK - ONE AUTHOR
Helmstadter, G. C. (1991). Research concepts in human behavior. New York: Houghton.

BOOK - MULTIPLE AUTHORS
Mathews, T. R., & Lawser, P. Q. (1993). Theories of management. New York: McGraw-Hill.

BOOK - CORPORATE AUTHOR
American Psychological Association. (1994). Publication manual of the American Psychological Association (4th ed.). Washington, DC: Author.
(When publisher and author are the same, use the word, Author, as name of publisher)

BOOK - MULTIVOLUME
Brosnia, R. (Ed.). (1989). Personality: Theory and practice (Vols. 1-4). New York: Macmillan.

BOOK - EDITOR INSTEAD OF AUTHOR
Feigenbaum, E., & Feldman, J. (Eds.). (1991). Computers and thought. New York: McGraw-Hill.

BOOK - REVISED EDITION
Robertson, J. (1989). Contemporary issues in psychology (Rev. ed.). New York: Praeger.

ARTICLE OR CHAPTER IN EDITED BOOK
Schwartz, R. P. (1990). Learning styles. In F.S. Keenan & L.F. Bird (Eds.), Education for the nineties (pp. 312-322). New York: Avon.

APA REFERENCE SAMPLES

DIAGNOSTIC AND STATISTICAL MANUAL OF MENTAL DISORDERS

American Psychiatric Association. (1994). Diagnostic and statistical manual of mental disorders (4th ed.). Washington, DC: Author.

ENCYCLOPEDIA ARTICLE - SIGNED

Johnson, R. S. (1994). Radioactivity. In The new encyclopedia Britannica (Vol. 25, pp. 453-455). Chicago: Encyclopedia Britannica.

ENCYCLOPEDIA ARTICLE - UNSIGNED

Somalia. (1993). In The new encyclopedia Britannica (Vol. 25, pp. 550-556). Chicago: Encyclopedia Britannica.

PERIODICALS

JOURNAL ARTICLE - ONE AUTHOR

Braverman, D. (1962). Normative and ipsative measurement in psychology. Psychological Review, 69, 295-305.

JOURNAL ARTICLE -TWO AUTHORS
JOURNAL PAGINATED BY ISSUE AND NUMBER

Roberts, J. R., & Smithson, B. (1975). Family orientations of Chinese college students. Journal of Marriage and the Family, 34(4), 29-37.

JOURNAL ARTICLE - THREE TO FIVE AUTHORS

Bronkowski, L. P., Johnson, R. J., Oppenheimer, K. S., & Pushkin, B. J. (1994). Age as a factor in flight training. Journal of Applied Psychology, 79, 421-427.

MAGAZINE ARTICLE

Horowitz, C. H. (1994, October 10). Is Rikers about to explode? New York, 27, 29-37.

NEWSPAPER ARTICLE - SIGNED

Barron, J. (1995, June 30). Brain studies give clues on depression. New York Times, pp. A1, A3.

NEWSPAPER ARTICLE - UNSIGNED

Gene seen as possible link to AIDS. (1996, August 10). The New York Times, p. A1.

APA REFERENCE SAMPLES

MONONOGRAPH WITH ISSUE NUMBER AND SERIAL OR WHOLE NUMBER

Coswell, R., & Klingenstein, P. R. (1965). A computer model of personality. <u>Psychological Monographs, 79</u>(1, Whole No. 540).

MONOGRAPH BOUND SEPARATELY AS JOURNAL SUPPLEMENT

Johnson, P. Q., & Pritchard, K. (1969). Creativity. <u>Journal of Experimental Psychology Monographs, 80,</u>(1, Pt. 2).

MONOGRAPH BOUND IN JOURNAL WITH CONTINUOUS PAGES

Hirsch, J., & Brown, R. W. (1974). Analysis of bias in selecting test times [Monograph]. <u>Journal of Experimental Psychology, 98,</u> 325-331.

REPORTS

GOVERNMENT PRINTING OFFICE REPORT

United States Public Health Service. (1990). <u>Statistical tables for medical research</u> (USPHS Publication No. 37). Washington, DC: U.S. Government Printing Office.

REPORT DIRECT FROM GOVERNMENT AGENCY

U.S. Department of Health and Human Services. (1994). <u>Breast cancer: geographic studies</u> (AHCPR Publication No. 94-0313). Rockville, MD: Author.

NATIONAL TECHNICAL INFORMATION SERVICE (NTIS) REPORT

Braveson, R. B., & Rogers, E. S. (1992). <u>Authentic assessment and teacher variables.</u> Ann Arbor: University of Michigan. (NTIS No. RS 93-721 215/KR)

EDUCATIONAL RESOURCES INFORMATION CENTER (ERIC) REPORT

Cook, J. V. (1992). <u>Teaching styles</u> (Report No. NCRTL-RJ-46-3). New York, NY: Center for Research on Teaching. (ERIC Document Reproduction Service No. ED 241 079)

APA REFERENCE SAMPLES

DOCTORAL DISSERTATIONS

DOCTORAL DISSERTATION IN DISSERTATION ABSTRACTS INTERNATIONAL OBTAINED FROM A UNIVERSITY

Baron, A. (1990). The use of personality factors as criteria for grouping pupils for computer instruction (Doctoral dissertation, New York University, 1990). Dissertation Abstracts International, 49, 4379A

DOCTORAL DISSERTATION IN DISSERTATION ABSTRACTS INTERNATIONAL OBTAINED ON UNIVERSITY MICROFILM

Baron, A. (1990). The use of personality factors as criteria for grouping pupils for computer instruction. Dissertation Abstracts International, 49, 4379A. (University Microfilms No. ABD72-13497)

UNPUBLISHED DOCTORAL DISSERTATION

Smeterna, C. K. (1993). Stuttering and its effects on academic achievement. Unpublished doctoral dissertation, University of Michigan, Ann Arbor.

REVIEWS

REVIEW OF BOOK, FILM, OR VIDEO

Shanahan, P. M. (1994). Challenging the giants [Review of the book Freud and Jung]. Contemporary Psychology, 39, 321-322.

AUDIOVISUAL SOURCES

TELEVISION - EPISODE FROM A SERIES

Place the name of the writer in author location. Place the name of the director in parentheses after the title. Place the name of the producer in the editor location.

Moyers, B. (1995). The field of time (D. Grubin, Director). In R. Rogers (Producer), The language of life with Bill Moyers. New York: WNET.

APA REFERENCE SAMPLES

FILM-VIDEOTAPE-AUDIOTAPE-SLIDES-WORKS OF ART
Place the name of major contributors first, followed by their functions in parentheses. Place the medium in brackets after the title. Give the location and name of distributor.

Markson, J. (Producer), & Cohen, K. (Director). (1995). <u>The golden touch</u> [Film]. New York: MCA.

SOUND RECORDING
Place the name of major contributors first, followed by their function in parentheses. Place the medium in brackets after the title. Give the location and name of distributor.

Browning, R. Z. (Speaker). (1991). <u>Treatment of phobia</u> [Cassette Recording No. 419-212-79A-B]. Washington, DC: American Psychological Association.

CD-ROM - ELECTRONIC DATA TAPE - CARTRIDGE TAPE
Use the same formats for author, date, and title elements as print material. After title and before the period, insert in brackets the type of medium. Add location and name of producer..

Branson, T.J. (1996). <u>Astronomy Today</u> (2nd ed.) [CD-ROM]. New York: World Publishing.

ABSTRACT ON CD-ROM
Author. (Year). Title [CD-ROM]. Journal Title Volume (issue). Abstract from: Source and retrieval number

King, A. J. (1992). Longitudinal study of stuttering [CD-ROM]. <u>Journal of Applied Psychology, 77,</u> 410-417. Abstract from: SilverPlatter File: PsycLIT Item: 79-18421.

JOURNAL ARTICLE ON CD-ROM
Author. (Year). Title [CD-ROM]. <u>Journal Title Volume</u> (issue), paging or indicator of length. Supplier/Database name Identifier or number (if available).

Rogers, R.R. (1994, June). Perseveration in driving habits [CD-ROM]. <u>Journal of Applied Psychology 4</u>, 5-6. 1994 SIRS/SIRS 1994 Psychology/Volume 4/Article 12A

APA REFERENCE SAMPLES

INTERNET SOURCES

With the rapid expansion of electronic publishing, conventions for citing Internet references are revised periodically. The examples given here reflect the standards established by the APA in 1998. Any citation should let the reader know as much bibliographic information as possible and enable him or her to find the source. If both electronic and print versions are identical, the print form of citation is preferred.

Therefore, references should begin with all the data that would be provided for a print document. Place the Internet data at the end of the citation beginning with the words, Retrieved from, the date of access, and the Internet address (URL). The access date is important because electronic material may change, disappear, or move to a different site. If you need to divide a URL between two lines, do so only after a slash. Use no hyphen at the break.

E-MAIL
E-mail and information obtained in discussion groups or bulletin boards is not permanently available and should be cited as personal communication in the body of your paper, but not cited in the reference list.

R. King, (personal communication, March 26, 1998)

ON-LINE JOURNAL ARTICLE
Author. (Year). Title [Paging or indicator of length]. Journal Title [Type of medium], volume(issue). Retrieved Date from the World Wide Web: URL

Braverman, D. (1962). Normative and ipsative measurement in psychology [13 paragraphs]. Psychological Review 69. Retrieved January 26, 1998 from the World Wide Web: gopher://panda1.uottowa.ca

ON-LINE JOURNAL ARTICLE - FILE TRANSFER PROTOCOL (FTP)
Rogers, R. R. (1993, June). Perseveration in driving habits [4 paragraphs]. Psycholoquy [On-line serial], 4(13). Retrieved January 15, 1995 from the World Wide Web: ftp://duke.edu/pub/harnad/Psycholoquy/1993.Volume.3.volume.4.psycoloquy.93.4.13.base-rate.11.rogers

APA MANUAL

APA REFERENCE SAMPLES

ON-LINE MAGAZINE ARTICLE

Author. (Year, month day for weeklies - month for monthlies). Title. Magazine Title, volume (if given), paging or indicator of length. Retrieved Date from the World Wide Web: URL

Jones, M. (1996, October 16). Mid East peace? Time 41 paragraphs. Retrieved September 15, 1997 from the World Wide Web: http://www.time.com/jones.html

Gobel, Dave. (1998, April 1998). Distance Learning - Educating in Cyberspace. Online Magazine 22 paragraphs. Retrieved May 9, 1998 from the World Wide Web: http://www.online-magazine.com/lgu.html

ON-LINE NEWSPAPER ARTICLE

Author. (Year, month day). Title. Newspaper Title, paging or indicator of length. Retrieved Date from the World Wide Web: URL

Bradley, Ann. (1997, Mar 26). Educated Consumers. Education Week on the Web, 15 paragraphs. Retrieved April 4, 1998 from the World Wide Web: http://www.edweek.org/ew/vol-16/26consum.h16

ON-LINE EDITORIAL

Title [Editorial]. (Year, Month Day). Newspaper Title. Retrieved Date from the World Wide Web: URL

Small Schools as an Investment [Editorial]. (1998, May 1). New York Times on the Web. Retrieved May 20, 1998 from the World Wide Web: http://www.nytimes.com/yr/mo/day/editorial/01fri3.html

ON-LINE LETTER TO THE EDITOR (May be Untitled)

Author. (Year, Month Day). [Letter to the editor]. Newspaper title. Retrieved Date from the World Wide Web: URL

Harrison, Lawrence E. (1998, May 4). [Letter to the editor]. New York Times on the Web. Retrieved June 18 1998 from the World Wide Web: http://www.nytimes.com/yr/mo/day/letters/lharri.html

APA REFERENCE SAMPLES

PROFESSIONAL OR INSTITUTIONAL HOME PAGE

American Psychological Association Home Page. Retrieved May 7, 1998 from the World Wide Web: http://www.apa.org

ON-LINE BOOK

Author, (Year). Title. Publication Location: Publisher. Retrieved Date from the World Wide Web: URL

Conrad, Joseph, (1910). Heart of Darkness. New York: Harpers. Retrieved January 15, 1998 from the World Wide Web ftp://wiretap.area.com/Library/Classic/darkness.txt

ON-LINE GOVERNMENT DOCUMENT

United States Department of State. (1998). Counter Terrorism Rewards Program. Retrieved February 21 1998 from the World Wide Web: http://www.heroes.net/pub/heroes/content2.html

ON-LINE ENCYCLOPEDIA

Author. (Date). Title. In Title of Encyclopedia. Publisher's location: Publisher. Retrieved Date from the World Wide Web: URL

James, William. (1897). The will to believe. In The internet encyclopedia of philosophy. New York: Longmans, Green and Company. Retrieved May 15, 1998 from the World Wide Web: http://www.utm.edu/research/iep/text/james/will/will.htm

ONLINE REVIEW (May be Untitled)

Author. (Date). Title [Review of the book Title] Name of On-line Program. Retrieved Date from the World Wide Web: URL

Bowen, Wayne H. (1988). [Review of the book Fascism: A history]. History Reviews On-Line 4. Retrieved September 5, 1988 from the World Wide Web:http://www.depauw.edu/dtrinkle/hrol/eatwell.html

APA QUOTATIONS

Quotations of 40 words or less:
Run into text and set off with double quotation marks. Place periods and commas within closing quotation marks. Place other punctuation inside quotation marks when they appear in the original material. Use single quotation marks for quotations within a quotation.

> Richardson (1996) found that "younger
> subjects learned three of the skills more
> rapidly than older subjects" (p. 29).

Quotations of more than 40 words:
Introduce the quotation by ending the preceding line with a colon. Double space and indent one half inch or five spaces from the left margin. Double space and type the quotation double spaced without quotation marks. If more than one paragraph is quoted, indent the first line of each an additional half inch or five more spaces. Do not use punctuation after the parenthetical reference.

> Richardson (1996) found the following:
>
> > The younger subjects learned color
> > selection, timing, and manipulation at
> > a much faster rate than the older
> > subjects. The largest difference in
> > learning rate occurred in the timing
> > skill. (p. 29)

QUOTATION WITHIN A QUOTATION
Use single quotation marks to set off a quotation within a quotation.

ELLIPSIS
When omitting words, phrases or sentences from quoted material, use three periods with a space before the first and a space after the last. Type four periods to indicate an ellipsis between two sentences. One period will end the sentence and be followed by three periods.

Among soldiers, some . . . succeed in

recording in prose or poetry the thrill and

horror of their experience, and their

personal reflections about war.

APA NUMBERS

- **Use words for numbers below 10, and use numerals for numbers 10 and above.**

    Three subjects   *Seven* experimental trials

- **Use numerals in numbers below 10 when comparing with numbers 10 and above.**

    5 of the *26* groups   *2* subjects in Group A
    failed compared with *16* subjects in Group B

- **Use numerals for numbers preceding measurement units.**

    frequency *121.5* megahertz   *6* cm

- **Use numerals in numbers representing mathematical functions.**

    the *3*rd decile   *3%*   *6* times as often

- **Use numerals in dates, ages, sums of money, subjects in experiments, page numbers, and chapter numbers.**

    June *2, 1996*   *5* year olds,   *$30.00*
    2 hrs   page *7*

- **Use words for *zero* and *one* when words are more understandable, and when not used with numbers 10 and above.**

    one-time usage   *zero* sum game

APA CAPITALIZATION

Capitalize the following:

First word in a complete sentence

    The members of the family met.

Capitalize only the first word of titles in reference lists.

    Rogers, B. Q., (1995).   Effects of aircraft
    noise on residents.

Proper nouns

    African-American

Nouns followed by numerals or letters

    Experiment 6
    Table 6

But not parts of books or tables

    chapter 6
    column 3

Test titles

    Scholastic Aptitude Test

Derived factors within a factor analysis

    Stress Factor 9

Variables and effects with multiplication signs

    the Speed x Time equation

But

    variables of speed and time

APA ABBREVIATIONS

Use abbreviations with care, understanding that overuse can cause confusion and uneven writing.

Abbreviate the following:
Common terms not listed as abbreviations in *Webster's Collegiate*
> HIV, FBI, NASA, FDA

Terms frequently used in *APA Journals*
> (MMPI) Minnesota Multiphasic Personality
>   Inventory
> (CR) conditioned response
> (CS) conditioned stimulus

But do not abbreviate O, E, or S for observer, experimenter, or subject.

Measurement units with numeric values
> 44 cm, 121 Hz, 1300 ppm

Latin Abbreviations
Use Latin abbreviations in parenthetical copy and English translation in nonparenthetical copy.

e.g.,	for example	i.e.,	that is
vs.	versus	cf.	compare

Punctuation of abbreviations
Use periods with initials of names, U. S. as an adjective, Latin abbreviations, reference abbreviations.
> A. J. Andrews   U. S. Army   i.e.   Vol. 2

Do not use periods with state names, capital letter and measurement abbreviations.
> CA   PA   NIMH   APA   cm   hr

Plurals of abbreviations
Add an *s* without an apostrophe.
> IRAs   Eds.   vols.

But form plural of page by writing pp.

SAMPLE APA TITLE PAGE

2–3 word brief title → Workfare Effectiveness   1

← 1" → Running Head: EFFECTIVENESS OF WORKFARE IN THREE STATES

5 spaces

Abbreviated title—all caps
Not more than 50 characters
including punctuation and spaces

½"

Center full title on page → Effectiveness of Workfare Programs in

Double space   Wisconsin, Delaware, and California from 1992 to 1994

Roger P. Quarles ← Your name

Double space   Michigan State University ← Your school

SAMPLE APA ABSTRACT PAGE

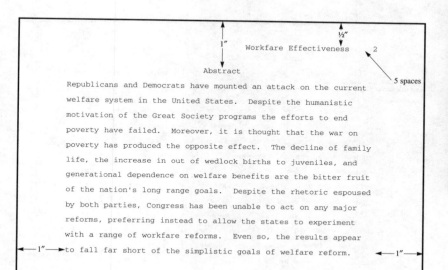

½″

1″   Workfare Effectiveness   2

5 spaces

Abstract

Republicans and Democrats have mounted an attack on the current welfare system in the United States. Despite the humanistic motivation of the Great Society programs the efforts to end poverty have failed. Moreover, it is thought that the war on poverty has produced the opposite effect. The decline of family life, the increase in out of wedlock births to juveniles, and generational dependence on welfare benefits are the bitter fruit of the nation's long range goals. Despite the rhetoric espoused by both parties, Congress has been unable to act on any major reforms, preferring instead to allow the states to experiment with a range of workfare reforms. Even so, the results appear to fall far short of the simplistic goals of welfare reform.

1″   1″

Type in single paragraph
No indention
Do not exceed 960 characters
including punctuation and spaces

APA MANUAL

SAMPLE APA FIRST TEXT PAGE

Workfare Effectiveness 3

Effectiveness of Workfare Programs in Wisconsin, Delaware, and
California from 1992 to 1994

Full title centered

President Clinton pledged an "end to welfare as we know it"
as part of the 1992 election campaign. However, the
administration has been unable to get the Congress to act on the
suggested reforms and, as a result, the states have proposed a
wide range of experimental initiatives (Kellam, 1994). Several
are based on the concept of workfare, a popular idea with both
Republicans and Democrats.

When Congress passed the Jobs Opportunities and Basic Skills
Program (JOBS) in 1988, it gave states matching funds to develop
programs. Wisconsin, Delaware, and California are among the
states which have begun workfare programs (Kellam, 1994).

Author-date citation

However, the picture is not altogether sanguine. Some critics of
the workfare concept including Gilbert claim that workfare will
increase welfare costs and simultaneously increase the numbers of
homeless persons (1994). There are arguments that despite the
faults of the old AFDC program fifty percent of recipients are
off welfare within two years (Gilbert, 1994). Others state that
a lack of funds for job training and child care will make
workfare programs impossible to maintain. (Kaus, 1994).

Wisconsin's workfare program, often cited as a model, has
not worked well for the clients or the employers say its critics
(Conniff, 1992). The goal, simple as it sounds, to reduce
dependence on welfare by putting people back on their feet, is
obviously not as easy as it seems. Nevertheless, there have been

1"

SAMPLE *APA* TABLE

½″
1″ Workfare Effectiveness   12

5 spaces

Table 1

Percentage of Welfare Recipients in Workfare Programs in Four
States

Year	California	Delaware	New York	Wisconsin
1988	20	31	21	19
1989	21	33	27	22
1990	24	36	29	26
1991	31	39	34	29
1992	37	41	37	33
1993	45	44	39	34
1994	47	49	41	35
1995	53	49	46	39

1″ ————→ 1993   ←———— 1″

APA MANUAL

SAMPLE APA REFERENCE PAGE

Double space → References

Bernstein, P. R., Delanson, C. D., & Connelson, P. (1993). Attitudinal changes in mothers engaged in job training. _Journal of Applied Psychology, 78,_ 452-457.

Carlson, R. J. (1994). _The dream and the dilemma: Welfare_ ←—1″—→_in America._ New York: Macmillan.

Conniff, R. (1992, February). Cutting the lifeline: The real welfare fraud. _The Progressive,_ 25-28.

←—½″ indent —→Cowan, N. (1992, May-June). The big lie about workfare. _Utne Reader,_ 28-29.

Gilbert, N. (1994, May) Why the new workfare won't work. _Commentary,_ 47.

Kaus, M. (1994, April 25).s Tough enough: A promising start on welfare reform. _The New Republic,_ 22-23.

Kellam, S. (1994, September 16). Welfare experiments: Are states leading the way toward national reform? _Congressional Quarterly Researcher,_ 795-796.

Robinson, K., & Politcheck, B. R. (1994). _The politics of welfare reform._ New York: McGraw Hill

Schwartz, M. (1993). The role of the mother in AFDC families. _Consulting Psychology Journal: Practice and Research._ _45_(4), 27-29.

U.S. Department of Health and Human Services. (1992). _Survey of Jobs Training Programs_ (AHCPR Publication No. 92-0451). Rockville, MD: Author.

Workfare debate heats up in legislatures. (1993, August 21). _The Washington Post,_ p. A3.

APA REFERENCE PAGE

American Psychological Association
Author-Date Citation
With ClarisWorks 4

OPENING CLARISWORKS THE FIRST TIME

1. Click twice on the **Macintosh HD Icon.** The **Macintosh HD Window** will appear. Choose **by Icon** in the **View Menu.**
2. Click twice on the **Applications Folder** on the **Macintosh HD Window.** The **Applications Window** will appear.
3. Click twice on the **ClarisWorks Folder Icon** on the **Applications Window.** The **ClarisWorks Window** will appear. Click on the **ClarisWorks Application Icon.** The **Main Menu** will change to the **ClarisWorks Menu.**
4. Click twice on **Word Processing.** A **Blank Document Page** will appear under the **ClarisWorks Menu Bar**, a **Ruler** and a **Button Bar.** It will be labeled, **Untitled 1 (WP).**
5. The cursor I-Beam will be flashing at the left margin.
6. You are ready to begin typing your paper.

CLARISWORKS DOCUMENT PAGE WINDOW

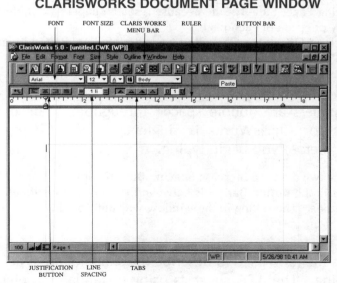

OPENING YOUR DOCUMENT LATER

1. Follow the steps above to open **ClarisWorks** from the **Application Window.**
2. Choose **Open** from the **File Menu.** An **Open Dialog Box** will appear. See the **Open Dialog Box** illustration on **page 3-7** in **Chapter 3 Basic Macintosh.**
3. Choose the location of your document from the pop-up list. It will be on the **Desktop,** the **Macintosh HD,** or in the **folder** where you saved your document. You may need to click on the pop-up list at the top to see the folders and documents in each location.
4. Use the **scroll bars** to scroll through the files until you locate your document. Click on your document name. It will open with its name in the **title bar** and you will be ready to enter text.

MARGINS

The setting for **APA** papers is one inch on top, bottom, and sides which is the default setting for **ClarisWorks.** You can change the margins if required by your instructor, but do not right justify or hyphenate words.

1. Choose **Document** in the **Format Menu.** The **Document Dialog Box** will open. Type the modified margins in inches in each of the **Margins Boxes.** Do not click on **Mirror Facing Pages** or **Facing Pages Side-By-Side** because research papers are printed on only one side of each page.
2. Click on **OK.** If the **OK** button has a double line around it you can press the **Return Key** instead.

LINE SPACING

APA papers are double spaced throughout. The default setting for **ClarisWorks** is single spacing. Change the setting before you begin typing.

1. Click twice on the **Increase Spacing Button** with two horizontal bars in the **Button Bar.** It is between the **Tabs** and **Justification Buttons.** The setting in the window will shift to **2 li.**

FONT

Font is the term used to describe the shape of the type used in typing. The **APA** suggests using a standard typeface in

12 point size similar to that found in typewriters. **Courier** and **Times Roman** are good examples. Although **ClarisWorks** enables you to change the font, the size, and a whole range of styles such as bold, condensed, and shadow, select one simple typeface and keep it in the plain text style.

> `This is 12 point Courier font.`

1. Choose **Courier** in the **Font Menu**. **Courier** will be underlined.
2. Choose **12 Point** in the **Size Menu**.

ITALICS AND UNDERLINING

Underlining is used to indicate words which are to be italicized in a printed version. Writers following **APA** style should not use italics unless approved by the instructor. The titles of books, periodicals, volume numbers in reference lists, some test scores, and Latin scientific terms are underlined to indicate italics.

1. Select the text you want to underline or italicize.
2. Drag down to **Underline** in the **Style Menu** or press **Command U** (⌘ **U**).
3. Drag down to **Italic** in the **Style Menu** or press **Command I** (⌘ **I**).

CENTERING AND JUSTIFYING

Justification describes how words are placed on the page: flush left, flush right, or centered. **ClarisWorks** allows you to spread the words on each line across the page so the right margin is ragged or right justified. Although **APA** papers should not be justified, you will need to center or move some text at times.

1. Select the text you want to center or move
2. Find the four **Justification Buttons** with several horizontal lines symbolizing lines of text under the ruler in the **Button Bar.**
3. Click on the **Center Justification Button** to center text.
4. Click on the appropriate **Justification Button** to move text left or right.

INDENTION

APA papers are indented one half inch. The **ClarisWorks** default setting is one half inch, but you may want to change settings for quotations or other purposes.

1. Click anywhere in the paragraph.
2. Choose **Paragraph** from the **Format Menu**. The **Paragraph Dialog Box** will appear.
3. Press **Tab** to move the highlight to the **First Line Indent Box**.
4. Type the correct value in tenths of an inch. Click **OK** to set the first line indent.
5. Press **Enter** or click on **OK** and the first line will be indented the proper space.
6. When quotations require both left and right indents, use this procedure, but change both **Left** and **Right Indent Boxes** after clicking in the passage to be quoted.

PAGINATION

Beginning with the first page, **APA** papers carry a right justified heading one half inch from the top of the page with the first two or three words of the title of your paper in upper and lower case followed by the page number in arabic numerals. **See the sample pages on pages 9-16 through 9-20.**

1. Choose **Insert Header** from the **Format Menu**. A blinking cursor will appear at the left margin in a **Header box**.
2. Choose **Insert Page #** from the **Edit Menu**. The **Insert Page Number Dialog Box** will appear with the **Page Number Radio Button** selected and **arabic numerals** selected in the **Representation Pull Down Menu**. Click on **OK**.
3. The cursor will appear just to the right of the number 1 at the left margin. Press the **Left Arrow Key** to move the cursor to left of number 1.
4. Press the **Space Bar** five times to move the number 1 five spaces to the right.
5. Press the **Left Arrow Key** five times to move the cursor to the left margin.
6. Type the first two or three words of the title. The cursor will be at

the last letter of the title.

7. Press the **Left Arrow Key** to move the cursor to the beginning of the title.
8. Click the **Right Justification Button** in the **Button Bar.** The title and page number 1 will shift to the right margin.
9. Click at the left margin of the first line of the text space under the header box to move the cursor there.

TITLE PAGE

APA papers have a specific format for the title page which contains a **running head**, the **title,** the **author's name,** and **affiliation. See sample title page on page 9-16.**

1. Move the cursor to the top line of the first page.
2. Type at the left margin the words, **Running Head:** in upper and lower case followed by a colon, leave one space and type, all in upper case, an **abbreviated title** of fewer than 50 characters including punctuation and spaces.
3. Center the **full title** in upper and lower case on the page. Double space if two or more lines.
4. Center **your name** in upper and lower case one double space below the title.
5. Center **your school name** in upper and lower case one double space below your name.

ABSTRACT PAGE

Formal **APA** papers include an **abstract page** which summarizes the paper. It is always numbered page 2. **See the sample Abstract Page on page 9-17.**

1. Move the cursor to the end of the last word in the **title page.**
2. Choose **Insert Page Break** from the **Format Menu.** The cursor will move to a new page which will be page 2.
3. Center the word, **Abstract**, in upper and lower case on the top line and double space.
4. Type the **abstract,** a summary of your paper, in a single paragraph without paragraph indention in fewer than 960 characters including punctuation and spacing.

TEXT

APA papers begin text on the third page. **See the sample Text Page on Page 9-18.**

1. Move the cursor to the last line in the abstract page. Press **Enter** to place the cursor on a new blank line.
2. Choose **Insert Page Break** from the **Format Menu.** The cursor will move to a new page which will be page 3.
3. Center the title of your paper in upper and lower case double spaced at the top of the page.
4. Double space and begin typing text.

AUTHOR-DATE CITATION

APA papers use a simple system of citing sources by stating the author's name and date of publication of the work in parentheses. Citations are placed directly in the text. No special keystrokes are necessary. The citations lead readers to the alphabetical list of sources in the **References** list at the end of the paper. Follow the **explanation** and **examples** on **pages 9-2 and 9-3.**

1. Citations are placed directly in the text. No special keystrokes are necessary.

REFERENCES LIST

The **References** list is printed at the end of the paper and presents full bibliographic information for every source cited in the body of your paper. Do not include sources you may have consulted, but did not use. It is a good idea to prepare the **References** list before you actually start writing the paper so you will know how to cite the references in the text. **See sample formats for References entries on pages 9-4 through 9-11 and the sample References Page on page 9-20.**

1. Move the cursor to the end of the last line of text. Press **Enter** to place the cursor on a new blank line.
2. Choose **Insert Page Break** from the **Format Menu.** The cursor will move to a new page.

3. Center the word, **References,** in upper and lower case on the top line. Double space.
4. Type entries in alphabetical order using the appropriate format for the type of reference you are citing.
5. Indent the first line of each entry one half inch. Double space within and between entries.

TABLES

Tables should be used sparingly. Use them only when data will be better presented in tabular form. Avoid confusing the reader by breaking up text with too many tables. Do not duplicate information in the text which appears in a table. A table should supplement material in the text, but it should also be understandable alone.

Tables are assigned arabic numerals and brief titles and are located as close as possible to their mention in the text on a separate page. Every column must have a short heading. The data in the left column usually describes the major independent variable.

Use horizontal rules only and use horizontal spacing to make the table easily readable. Double space within tables. **See the sample Table Page on page 9-19.**

1. Move the cursor to the end of the last line of text before the table to be inserted. Press **Enter** to move the cursor to a new blank line.
2. Choose **Insert Page Break** from the **Format Menu.** The cursor will move to a new page.
3. Type **Table 1** flush left in upper and lower case without a period on the top line.
4. Double space and type the **title** flush left and underlined. Capitalize only the first letters of major words. Extra lines of title are flush left and double spaced.
5. Double space and type a **solid line** across the page by pressing **Shift** and **Hyphen Keys.**
6. You must now set up the rows and columns which make up the table. Each column must have a header and these should be spaced evenly across the top of the table. Leave at least three spaces between columns.

7. Find the **four Tab Triangles** on the left side of the **Button Bar.** One is **shaded** on the **left,** one on the **bottom,** one on the **right,** and one on the **top.** The one shaded on the left aligns columns on the left side of the tab, the one shaded on the bottom centers columns on the tab, the one shaded on the right aligns columns on the right side of the tab, and the one shaded at the top aligns columns of numbers along a decimal point.

8. Drag the **Center Triangle Tab Icon** to the approximate location on the ruler where the first header should be. Follow the same procedure for the remaining header locations.

9. Press the **Tab Key** to move the cursor to the first header location and type the header. Press the **Tab Key** and type the next header. Continue until all headers are typed. Capitalize only the first letter of the first word of each header.

10. Select any header and drag its **Triangle Tab Icon** left or right. The header will move with the icon to a new location. Use this method to adjust the locations of the headers until they are properly spaced.

11. Press **Enter** to double space and type a solid line under the headers.

12. Enter data under each header by pressing tab to reach the next column. When you type the numbers to enter data, they will be centered under the **Tab Icons.** Be sure to align decimal points using the **Decimal Point Tab Icon.**

13. Press **Enter** after the last entry to double space and type a solid line across the page.

SPELL CHECK

1. Choose **Check Document Spelling** in the **Writing Tools Submenu** of the **Edit Menu** or press **Command = (⌘ =).** The **Spelling Dialog Box** will appear over the document window with misspelled words highlighted.

2. Click on one of the word options offered to correct it.

3. Click on **Replace** to replace the misspelled word with the correct one. Click on **Ignore** if the word is a special use word not in the **Spell Check** dictionary.

4. Continue the process until the entire document is done. The **Replace Button** will say **Done** when the entire document has been checked.

5. Click on **Done.**

PRINTING

See page 3-5 in Chapter 3. Basic Macintosh for instructions.

SAVING

See page 3-6 in Chapter 3. Basic Macintosh for instructions.

American Psychological Association
Author-Date Citation
With WordPerfect

OPENING WORDPERFECT THE FIRST TIME

1. Click twice on the **Macintosh HD Icon.** The **Macintosh HD Window** will appear. Choose **by Icon** in the **View Menu.**
2. Click twice on the **Applications Folder** on the **Macintosh HD Window.** The **Applications Window** will appear.
3. Click twice on the **WordPerfect Folder Icon** on the **Applications Window.** Click on the **WordPerfect Application Icon.** A **Blank Document Page** will appear labeled **untitled.** The **Main Menu** will change to the **WordPerfect Menu.**
4. Click on **Ruler, Layout,** and **Font** in the **Button Bar.** A **ruler** and **Layout** and **Font Button Bars** will appear on the **Blank Document Page.**
5. The cursor I-Beam will be flashing at the left margin.
6. You are ready to begin typing your paper.

WORDPERFECT DOCUMENT PAGE WINDOW

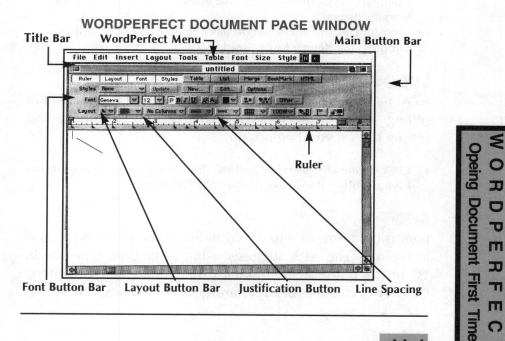

Title Bar   WordPerfect Menu   Main Button Bar

Ruler

Font Button Bar   Layout Button Bar   Justification Button   Line Spacing

OPENING YOUR DOCUMENT LATER

1. Follow the steps above to open **WordPerfect** from the **Application Window.**
2. Choose **Open** from the **File Menu.** An **Open Dialog Box** will appear. See the **Open Dialog Box** illustration on **page 3-7** in **Chapter 3 Basic Macintosh.**
3. Choose the location of your document from the pop-up list. It will be on the **Desktop,** the **Macintosh HD,** or in the **folder** where you saved your document. You may need to click on the menu at the top to see the folders and documents in each location.
4. Use the **scroll bars** to scroll through the files until you locate your document. Click on your document and it will open with its name in the **title bar** and you will be ready to enter text.

MARGINS

The setting for **APA** papers is one inch on top, bottom, and sides which is the default setting for **WordPerfect.** You can change the margins if required by your instructor, but do not right justify or hyphenate words.

1. Choose **Margins** in the **Layout Menu.** The **Margins Dialog Box** will open. Type the modified margins in inches in each of the **Margins Boxes.**
2. Click on **OK.** If the **OK** button has a double line around it you can press the **Return Key** instead.

LINE SPACING

APA papers are double spaced throughout. The default setting for **WordPerfect** is single spacing. Change the setting before you begin typing.

1. Click on the **Line Spacing Button** with three horizontal lines in the **Layout Button Bar** above the ruler. Drag down to **2.**

FONT

Font is the term used to describe the shape of the type used in typing. The **APA** suggests using a standard typeface in 10 or 12 point size similar to that found in typewriters. **Courier** and **Times Roman** are good examples. Although

WordPerfect enables you to change the font, the size, and a whole range of styles such as bold, condensed, and shadow, select one simple typeface and keep it in the plain text style.

```
This is 12 point Courier font.
```

1. Drag down to **Courier** in the **Font Menu** or the **Font Button Bar.** **Courier** will appear in the window.
2. Choose **12** in the **Size Menu** or pull down the **Size Pop-up Menu** in the **Font Bar** to **12.**

ITALICS AND UNDERLINING

Underlining is used to indicate words which are to be italicized in a printed version. Writers following **APA** style should not use italics unless approved by the instructor. The titles of books, periodicals, volume numbers in reference lists, some test scores, and Latin scientific terms are underlined to indicate italics.

1. Select the text you want to underline or italicize.
2. Drag down to **Underline** in the **Style Menu** or press **Command U** (⌘ **U**) or click the U **Button** in the **Font Button Bar.**
3. Drag down to **Italicize** in the **Style Menu** or press **Command I** (⌘ **I**) or press the **I Button** in the **Font Button Bar.**

CENTERING AND JUSTIFYING

Justification describes how words are placed on the page: flush left, flush right, or centered. **WordPerfect** allows you to spread the words on each line across the page so the right margin is ragged or right justified. Although **APA** papers should not be justified, you will need to center or move some text at times.

1. Select the text you want to center or move.
2. Find the **Justification Button** under the ruler in the **Layout Button Bar** and drag down to **Left, Center,** or **Right** as needed.

WORDPERFECT
Italics and Justifying

INDENTION

APA papers are indented one half inch. The **WordPerfect** default setting is one half inch, but you may want to change settings for quotations or other purposes.

1. Select the text for which you want to change indents.
2. Change the left and right margins using the instructions in **MARGINS** above.
3. Click on the first paragraph in which you want to indent the first line. Find the **First-Line Indent Marker** on the left side of the ruler. It looks like a V-shaped tab. Drag it to the ruler setting you want.
4. When finished with quoted or other material, change the margins and indents to the regular settings.

PAGINATION

Beginning with the first page, **APA** papers carry a right justified heading one half inch from the top of the page with the first two or three words of the title of your paper in upper and lower case followed by the page number in arabic numerals. **See the sample pages on pages 9-16 through 9-20**

1. Choose **New** in the **submenu** in **Header/Footer** in the **Layout Menu.** The **New Header/Footer Dialog Box** will appear with the **Header A Radio Button** selected. Click on **OK.**
2. The **Title Header A** window will open with **Button Bars** similar to those in the regular document window.
3. Click on the **Page Icon** in the **Header Button Bar** which looks like a page with the upper right corner turned down and a **+1** on the page. The number 1 will appear at the left margin.
4. Press the **Left Arrow Key** to move the cursor to left of number 1.
5. Type the first two or three words of the title in upper and lower case.
6. Press **Spacebar** five times to move the number 1 five spaces to the right.
7. Press the **Left Arrow Key** to move the cursor to the left of the title.
8. Click on the **Justification Button** and drag down to **Right Justification** to bring the short title and the number 1 to the right margin.
9. Click the **Close Box** of the **Header Window.**
10. Choose **Print Preview** from the **File Menu** to check your settings.

TITLE PAGE

APA papers have a specific format for the title page which contains a **running head**, the **title,** the **author's name,** and **affiliation. See sample title page on page 9-16.**

1. Move the cursor to the top line of the first page.
2. Type at the left margin the words, **Running Head:** in upper and lower case followed by a colon, leave one space and type, all in upper case, an **abbreviated title** of fewer than 50 characters including punctuation and spaces.
3. Center the **full title** in upper and lower case on the page. Double space if two or more lines.
4. Center **your name** in upper and lower case one double space below the title.
5. Center your **school name** in upper and lower case one double space below your name.

ABSTRACT PAGE

Formal **APA** papers include an **abstract page** which summarizes the paper. It is always numbered page 2. **See the sample Abstract Page on page 9-17.**

1. Move the cursor to the end of the last word in the **title page.**
2. Choose **Insert Page Break** from the **Format Menu.** The cursor will move to a new page which will be page 2.
3. Center the word, **Abstract**, in upper and lower case on the top line and double space.
4. Type the abstract, a summary of your paper, in a single paragraph without paragraph indention in fewer than 960 characters including punctuation and spacing.

TEXT

APA papers begin text on the third page. **See the sample Text Page on Page 9-18**

1. Move the cursor to the last line in the **abstract page.** Press **Enter** to place the cursor on a new blank line.
2. Choose **Insert Page Break** from the **Format Menu.** The cursor will move to a new page which will be page 3.
3. Center the **title** of your paper in upper and lower case double spaced at the top of the page.
4. Double space and begin typing text.

WORDPERFECT
Title Page - Abstract Page - Text

AUTHOR-DATE CITATION

APA papers use a simple system of citing sources by stating the author's name and date of publication of the work in parentheses. Citations are placed directly in the text. No special keystrokes are necessary. The citations lead readers to the alphabetical list of sources in the **References** list at the end of the paper. Follow the **explanation** and **examples** of parenthetical citations on **pages 9-2 and 9-3.**

1. Citations are placed directly in the text. No special keystrokes are necessary.

REFERENCES LIST

The **References** list is printed at the end of the paper and presents full bibliographic information for every source cited in the body of your paper. Do not include sources you may have consulted, but did not use. It is a good idea to prepare the **References** list before you actually start writing the paper so you will know how to cite the references in the text. **See sample formats for References entries on pages 9-4 through 9-11 and the sample References Page on page 9-20.**

1. Move the cursor to the end of the last line of text. Press **Enter** to place the cursor on a new blank line.
2. Choose **Insert Page Break** from the **Insert Menu.** The cursor will move to a new page.
3. Center the word, **References,** in upper and lower case on the top line. Double space.
4. Type entries in alphabetical order using the appropriate format for the type of reference you are citing. Indent the first line of each entry one half inch with following lines double spaced. Double space within and between entries.

TABLES

Tables should be used sparingly. Use them only when data will be better presented in tabular form. Avoid confusing the reader by breaking up text with too many tables. Do not duplicate information in the text which appears in a table. A table should supplement material in the text, but it should also be understandable alone.

Tables are assigned arabic numerals and brief titles and are located as close as possible to their mention in the text on a separate page. Every column must have a short heading. The data in the left column usually describes the major independent variable.

Use horizontal rules only and use horizontal spacing to make the table easily readable. Double space within tables. **See the sample Table Page on page 9-19.**

You can set up tables in two ways: by using the **Table Menu** or by **Setting Tabs** on the **Ruler.**

1. Begin each table on a separate page. Move the cursor to the end of the last line of text. Press **Enter** to place the cursor on a new blank line.
2. Choose **Insert Page Break** from the **Insert Menu.** The cursor will move to a new page.
3. Type **Table 1** flush left in upper and lower case without a period on the top line.
4. Double space and type the **title** flush left and underlined. Capitalize only the first letters of major words. Extra lines of title are flush left and double spaced.
5. Double space and type a **solid line** across the page by pressing **Shift** and **Underline Keys.**
6. You must now set up the rows and columns which make up the table. Each column must have a header and these should be spaced evenly across the top of the table. Leave at least three spaces between columns. Decide which method of setting up the rows and columns is best for you.

USING THE TABLE MENU METHOD
1. Select **New** from the **Table Menu.** The **New Table Dialog Box** will appear. Enter the number of columns and rows you need and press **OK.** A blank table containing the correct number of cells will appear with a double ruled border and single ruling between the rows and columns. The rules will be removed later.
2. Type the header titles in the top cells. Capitalize only the first letter of the first word of each header. Press **Tab** or the **Right**

WORDPERFECT Tables

Arrow Key to move to the next cell. Press **Enter** at the end of a word in a cell to move the cursor to the next line within that cell or select **Row Height** from the **Table Menu.** The **Row Height Dialog Box** will appear. Click **Multi-Line** and **OK** if you want the text to word-wrap in that cell.

3. Type the data into the cells under the headers. You may find that some cells need to made wider, narrower, taller, or shorter. Select the column whose width you want to change. Select **Column Width** from the **Table Menu.** The **Column Width Dialog Box** will appear. Type in the correct width you need and click **OK.** Select the row whose height you want to change. Select **Row Height** from the **Table Menu.** The **Row Height Dialog Box** will appear. Click the **Fixed Radio Button** and type in the correct height you need and click **OK.**

4. You can also change height and width by moving the cursor to the edge of a column or row. The cursor will change to a double arrow and you can drag the rule to make the cell the required size.

5. Center headers and data in each cell using the **Justification Button.**

6. Select **Table Border** in the **Table Menu.** Pull down to **None.** Type a solid line across the bottom of the table. You also need to rule a single line double spaced between the headers and the data.

or

USING THE SETTING TABS ON THE RULER METHOD

1. Find the **Tab Button** in the **Layout Button Bar.** It is the first button on the left and has two triangles in it.

2. Drag down to **Clear Tabs.** All of the **Default Tab Triangles** set 1/2 inch apart will disappear.

3. Drag down to the **Center Triangle.** Move the cursor to the top line of the page just below the ruler. As it crosses the line it becomes an **arrow.**

4. Move the arrow to the approximate location of the first header and release. A **small black triangle** will appear under the numbers in the ruler. Continue placing the triangles in the approximate locations you want the headers.

5. Press **Tab** and type the first header. Press **Tab** and type the second header. Repeat the process until all the headers are typed.

6. Select any header. Click on the **Tab Triangle** above it. A vertical line will extend down through the header. Now drag the **triangle** left or right and the header will move with it adjusting the spacing of the header. Move the other headers, if necessary, until they are

properly spaced.

7. Double space and type a solid line across the page under the headers.

8. Double space and center data in each of the columns using tabs. Double space between lines. If a column contains decimal points, use the **Decimal Tab Triangle** in the pop-up menu under the **Tab Button** in the **Layout Bar.**

9. Double space and type a solid line across the page under the data.

SPELL CHECK

1. Choose **Speller** in the **Tools Menu** or press **Command E** (⌘ **E**). **Spelling Dialog Box** will appear on top of the document window.

2. Click on **Check** and drag down to **Document.**

3. Press **Start.** The **misspelled word** will appear with **alternative words** suggested.

4. Scroll through the list until you find the correct word. Press **Replace.**

5. Continue until you have checked the entire document.

PRINTING

See page 3-5 in **Chapter 3. Basic Macintosh for instructions.**

SAVING

See page 3-6 in **Chapter 3. Basic Macintosh for instructions.**

American Psychological Association
Author-Date Citation With Microsoft Word

OPENING MICROSOFT WORD FIRST TIME

1. Click twice on the **Macintosh HD Icon.** The **Macintosh HD Window** will appear. Choose **by Icon** in the **View Menu.**
2. Click twice on the **Applications Folder** on the **Macintosh HD Window.** The **Applications Window** will appear.
3. Click twice on the **Microsoft Word Folder Icon** on the **Applications Window.** The **Microsoft Word Window** will open. Click on the **Microsoft Word Icon. A Blank Document Window** will appear. The **Main Menu** will change to the **Microsoft Word Menu.**
4. A **Standard Toolbar,** a **Formatting Toolbar, and** a **Ruler** will appear under the **Menu Bar.**
5. The cursor I-Beam will be flashing at the left margin.
6. You are ready to begin typing your paper.

MICROSOFT WORD DOCUMENT PAGE WINDOW

Close box   Document title bar   Menu bar   Zoom box

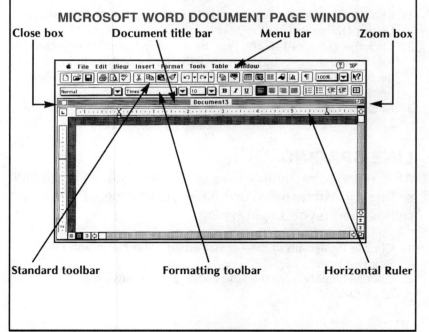

Standard toolbar   Formatting toolbar   Horizontal Ruler

OPENING YOUR DOCUMENT LATER

1. Follow the steps above to open **Microsoft Word** from the **Application Window.**
2. Choose **Open** from the **File Menu.** An **Open Dialog Box** will appear. **See the Open Dialog Box illustration on page 3-7 in Chapter 3 Basic Macintosh.**
3. Choose the location of your document from the pop-up list. It will be on the **Desktop,** the **Macintosh HD,** or in the **folder** where you saved your document. You may need to click on the pop-up list at the top to see the folders and documents in each location.
4. Use the **scroll bars** to scroll through the files until you locate your document. Click on your document and it will open with its name in the **title bar** and you will be ready to enter text.

MARGINS

The setting for **APA** papers is one inch on top, bottom, and sides which is the default setting for **Microsoft Word.** You can change the margins if required by your instructor, but do not right justify or hyphenate words.

1. Choose **Document Layout** in the **File Menu.** The **Document Layout Dialog Box** will appear.
2. Click the **Margins Tab** and type the modified margins in inches in each of the margins boxes or click the arrow buttons to increase or decrease the settings. Do not click on **Mirror Margins** because research papers are printed on only one side of each page.
3. Click on **OK.**

LINE SPACING

APA papers are double spaced throughout. The default setting for **Microsoft Word** is single spacing. Change the setting before you begin typing.

1. Choose **Paragraph** in the **Format Menu.** The **Paragraph Dialog Box** will open.
2. Choose **Double** from the **Line Spacing drop down list.**
3. Click **OK.**

FONT

Font is the term used to describe the shape of the type used in typing. The **APA** suggests using a standard typeface in 10 or 12 point size similar to that found in typewriters. **Courier** and **Times Roman** are good examples. Although **Microsoft Word** enables you to change the font, the size, and a whole range of styles such as bold, condensed, and shadow, select one simple typeface and keep it in the plain text style.

This is 12 point Courier font.

1. Choose **Font** from the **Format Menu**. The **Font Dialog Box** will appear.
2. Choose **Courier** from the **Font Scrollable List** and **12** from the **Size Scrollable List**.
3. Click on **OK**.

or

1. Click on the **Font** and **Size Buttons** in the **Formatting Toolbar**. Drop down lists will appear.
2. Click on **Courier** and **12**.

ITALICS AND UNDERLINING

Underlining is used to indicate words which are to be italicized in a printed version. Writers following **APA** style should not use italics unless approved by the instructor. The titles of books, periodicals, volume numbers in reference lists, some test scores, and Latin scientific terms are underlined to indicate italics.

1. Select the text you want to underline or italicize.
2. Choose **Font** from the **Format Menu**. The **Font Dialog Box** will appear.
3. Choose **Italic** or **Underline** from the **Font Style scrollable list**.
4. Click on **OK**.

or

1. Select text and click on the *I* or U buttons in the **Formatting Tool Bar**.

MICROSOFT WORD
Fonts and Italics

CENTERING AND JUSTIFYING

Justification describes how words are placed on the page: flush left, flush right, or centered. **Microsoft Word** allows you to spread the words on each line across the page so the right margin is ragged or right justified. Although **APA** papers should not be justified, you will need to center or move some text at times.

1. Select the text you want to center or move.
2. Click on the appropriate **Justification Button** just to the right of the **B, *I*, U Buttons** in the **Formatting Toolbar** to center or move text.

INDENTION

APA papers are indented one half inch. The **Microsoft Word** default setting is one half inch, but you may want to change indents for quotations or other purposes.

1. Select the text for which you want to change indents.
2. Choose **Paragraph** from the **Format Menu.** The **Paragraph Dialog Box** will appear.
3. Change the **Left** and **Right Indentation** settings by typing in new settings or clicking on the **increase** or **decrease arrows.**
4. Click on **OK.**

PAGINATION

Beginning with the first page, **APA** papers carry a right justified heading one half inch from the top of the page with the first two or three words of the title of your paper in upper and lower case followed by the page number in arabic numerals. **See the sample pages on pages 9-16 through 9-20.**

1. Choose **Header** and **Footer** from the **View Menu.** The text will dim and the cursor will appear in the header space. The **Header and Footer Toolbar** will also appear.
2. Click the **Switch Between Header and Footer Button** which is the first button on the left to be sure you are in the header space.
3. Click the **Page Number Button** which has a number sign on an icon page with a folded corner in the **Header and Footer Toolbar** The number 1 will appear at the left margin.

4. The cursor will appear just to the right of the number 1 at the left margin. Press the **Left Arrow Key** to move the cursor to the left of the number 1.
5. Press the **Space Bar** five times to move the number 1 five spaces to the right.
6. Press the **Left Arrow Key** to move the cursor to the left margin.
7. Type the first three words of the title of the paper. The cursor will be at the last letter of the title.
8. Press the **Left Arrow Key** to move the cursor to the beginning of the title.
9. Click the **Right Justification Button** in the **Formatting Toolbar**. The title and page number 1 will shift to the right margin.

TITLE PAGE

APA papers have a specific format for the title page which contains a **running head**, the **title**, the **author's name**, and **affiliation. See sample title page on page 9-16.**

1. Move the cursor to the top line of the first page.
2. Type at the left margin the words, **Running Head:** in upper and lower case followed by a colon, leave one space and type, all in upper case, an **abbreviated title** of fewer than 50 characters including punctuation and spaces.
3. Center the **full title** in upper and lower case on the page. Double space if two or more lines.
4. Center **your name** in upper and lower case one double space below the title.
5. Center **your school name** in upper and lower case one double space below your name.

ABSTRACT PAGE

Formal **APA** papers include an **abstract page** which summarizes the paper. It is always numbered page 2. **See sample Abstract Page on page 9-17.**

1. Move the cursor to the end of the last word in the **title page.** Press **Enter** to place the cursor on a new blank line.
2. Choose **Break** from the **Insert Menu.** The **Break Dialog Box** will appear.
3. Click on the **Page Break Button** and **OK.**
4. Center the word, **Abstract**, in upper and lower case on the top line and double space.

5. Type the abstract, a summary of your paper, in a single paragraph without paragraph indention in fewer than 960 characters including punctuation and spacing.

TEXT

APA papers begin text on the third page. **See the sample Text Page on page 9-18.**

1. Move the cursor to the end of the last line of text on the Abstract Page. Press **Enter** to place the cursor on a new blank line.
2. Choose **Break** from the **Insert Menu.** The **Break Dialog Box** will appear.
3. Click on the **Page Break Button** and **OK.**
4. Center the **title** of your paper in upper and lower case double spaced at the top of the page.
5. Double space and begin typing text.

AUTHOR-DATE CITATION

APA papers use a simple system of citing sources by stating the author's name and date of publication of the work in parentheses. Citations are placed directly in the text. No special keystrokes are necessary. The citations lead readers to the alphabetical list of sources in the **References** list at the end of the paper. Follow the **explanation** and **examples** on **pages 9-2 and 9-3.**

1. Citations are placed directly in the text. No special keystrokes are necessary.

REFERENCES LIST

The **References** list is printed at the end of the paper and presents full bibliographic information for every source cited in the body of your paper. Do not include sources you may have consulted, but did not use. It is a good idea to prepare the **References** list before you actually start writing the paper so you will know how to cite the references in the text. **See sample formats for References**

entries on pages 9-4 through 9-11 and the sample References Page on page 9-20.

1. Move the cursor to the end of the last line of text. Press **Enter** to place the cursor on a new blank line.
2. Choose **Break** from the **Insert Menu.** The **Break Dialog Box** will appear.
3. Click on the **Page Break Button** and **OK.**
4. Center the word, **References,** in upper and lower case on the top line. Double space.
5. Type the entries using the appropriate format for the type of reference you are citing.
6. Indent the first line of each entry one half inch. Double space within and between entries.

TABLES

Tables should be used sparingly. Use them only when data will be better presented in tabular form. Avoid confusing the reader by breaking up text with too many tables. Do not duplicate information in the text which appears in a table. Tables should supplement material in the text, but it should also be understandable alone.

Tables are assigned arabic numerals and brief titles.and are located as close as possible to their mention in the text on a separate page. Every column must have a short heading. The data in the left column usually describes the major independent variable.

Use horizontal rules only and use horizontal spacing to make the table easily readable. Double space within tables. **See the sample Table Page on page 9-19.**

You can set up tables in two ways: by using the **Table Menu** or by **Setting Tabs** on the **Ruler.**

1. Begin each table on a separate page. Move the cursor to the end of the last line of text. Press **Enter** to place the cursor on a new blank line.
2. Choose **Break** from the **Insert Menu.** The **Break Dialog Box** will

appear.

3. Click on the **Page Break Button** and **OK.**
4. Type **Table 1** flush left in upper and lower case without a period on the top line.
5. Double space and type the **title** flush left and underlined. Capitalize only the first letters of major words. Extra lines of title are flush left and double spaced.
6. Double space and type a **solid line** across the page by pressing **Shift** and **Underline Keys.**
7. You must now set up the rows and columns which make up the table. Each column must have a header and these should be spaced evenly across the top of the table. Leave at least three spaces between columns. Decide which method of setting up the rows and columns is best for you.

USING THE TABLE MENU METHOD

1. Double space and move the cursor under the title.
2. Choose **Insert Table** from the **Table Menu.** The **Insert Table Dialog Box** will appear.
3. Click **Table Wizard** and the first of six **Table Wizard Dialog Boxes** will appear.
4. Select **Style 1**, the simplest style in the first dialog box. Click **Next** to go to the next dialog box. Enter the **Number of Columns** in the second, the **Column Headings** in the third, the **Number of Rows** and **Row Headings** in the fourth, the **Alignment of Data and Headings** in the fifth, and the **Table Orientation** in the sixth dialog box.
5. Enter the headers in each cell along the top of the table. Click on the **Center Justification Button** in the **Button Bar** to center headers in their respective cells. Capitalize the first word of each header.
6. Enter data by clicking in each cell and typing. Cells will become taller if more than one line is entered.
7. Press **Tab** to move to the next cell to the right. Press **Shift Tab** to move back one cell. Press **Down Arrow Key** to move down by row. Press **Up Arrow Key** to move up by row.
8. To delete cells, select cells by dragging across them. Choose **Delete Cells** from the **Table Menu.** The **Delete Cells Dialog Box** will appear. Choose the selection and click **OK.**
9. After all data is entered, you will have to eliminate the borders including all the vertical rules. Click on the **Borders Button** in the **Formatting Toolbar.** It is the last button on the right and is a square divided into quarters with bold outside borders. The

Borders Toolbar will appear.

10. Select the entire table and click on the **No Border Button** which is the last button on the right. All rules should disappear.

11. Drag down to a **1 point line** in the **Line Style Drop Down List** and click on the **Bottom Border Button** to draw a line across the bottom. You will have to ink in a line between the headers and the data in the table.

USING THE TAB - RULER METHOD

1. Look at the extreme left end of the ruler. You will see a **Tab Alignment Button** with an **L-shaped marker.** Each time you click on it the marker will change to an **upside down T**, a **backwards L**, or an **upside down T with a dot** . The L-shape is the **Tab Alignment Button** for **aligning text at the left letter**, the **upside down T** is for **centering text at the tab**, the **backwards L** is for **aligning text at the right letter**, and the **upside down T with a dot** is for **aligning numbers at a decimal point.**

2. Click on the **Tab Alignment Button** until it changes to the **upside down T.**

3. Click in the ruler to set a tab at the approximate location where the first header should be. Continue the process by clicking in the ruler at the approximate locations where each header should be.

4. Press the **Tab Key** and type the first header. It will be centered at the tab location. Capitalize the first word of each header. Follow the same procedure with the remaining headers.

5. Double space and underline by pressing **Shift Hyphen Keys.**

6. Double space and enter data in each column by pressing the **Tab Key** to move the cursor to the next column. Double space between rows.

7. After entering data, double space and underline by pressing **Shift Hyphen Keys.**

SPELL CHECK

1. Choose **Spelling** from the **Tools Menu**. The **Spelling Dialog Box** will open.

2. Misspelled words will appear in the **Not in Dictionary Box** with the correctly spelled word in the **Change to Box**. Other variations of the word will appear in the **Suggestions Scroll Box.**

3. If the correct word is in the **Change to Box**, click **Change** or **Change All** to correct the word wherever it appears in the paper.

4. If the word you want is in the **Suggestions Scroll List**, click on it and then click **Change.**

5. If the word is correctly spelled as is, and **Word's Spell Check** does not recognize it, click **Ignore.**

MICROSOFT WORD
Tables - Spell Check

MICROSOFT WORD
Printing and Saving

PRINTING

See page 3-5 in Chapter 3. Basic Macintosh for instructions.

SAVING

See page 3-6 in Chapter 3. Basic Macintosh for instructions.

Author-Date Citation With Microsoft Works

OPENING MICROSOFT WORKS FIRST TIME

1. Click twice on the **Macintosh HD Icon.** The **Macintosh HD Window** will appear. Choose **by Icon** in the **View Menu.**
2. Click twice on the **Applications Folder** on the **Macintosh HD Window.** The **Applications Window** will appear.
3. Click twice on the **Microsoft Works Folder Icon** on the **Applications Window. The Startup Screen** will appear. Click on **Word Processor** to select it. Click on **New** in the **File Menu** and a blank **Document Window** will appear labeled **Untitled1 (WP).** The **Main Menu** will change to the **Microsoft Works Menu.**
4. Choose **Toolbar** and **Ruler** from the **View Menu.** The **Toolbar and Ruler** will appear under the **Menu Bar.**
5. The cursor I-Beam will be flashing at the left margin.
6. You are ready to begin typing your paper.

MICROSOFT WORKS DOCUMENT PAGE WINDOW

Ruler   Works Menu   Font   Font Size   Italics   Toolbar   Title Bar

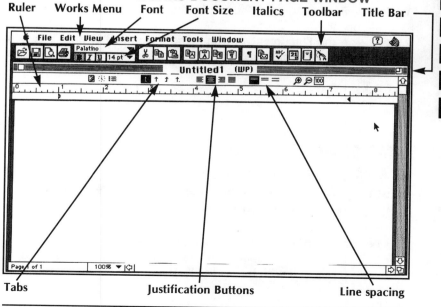

Tabs   Justification Buttons   Line spacing

OPENING YOUR DOCUMENT LATER

1. Follow the steps above to open **Microsoft Works** from the **Application Window.**
2. Choose **Open** from the **File Menu.** An **Open Dialog Box** will appear. **See the Open Dialog Box illustration on page 3-7 in Chapter 3 Basic Macintosh.**
3. Choose the location of your document from the pop-up list. It will be on the **Desktop,** the **Macintosh HD,** or in the **folder** where you saved your document. You may need to click on the pop-up list at the top to see the folders and documents in each location.
4. Use the **scroll bars** to scroll through the files until you locate your document. Click on your document and it will open with its name in the **title bar** and you will be ready to enter text.

MARGINS

The setting for **APA** papers is one inch on top, bottom, and sides which is the default setting for **Microsoft Works.** You can change the margins if required by your instructor, but do not right justify or hyphenate words.

1. Choose **Page Setup** from the **File Menu.** The **Page Setup Dialog Box** will appear.
2. Click on the **Document Button.** The **Document Dialog Box** will appear. Type the modified margins in inches in each of the margins boxes.
3. Click on **OK**.

LINE SPACING

APA papers are double spaced throughout. The default setting for **Microsoft Works** is single spacing. Change the setting before you begin typing.

1. Click anywhere in the first paragraph of your paper.
2. Click on the **2.0 Line Spacing Button** in the **ruler.** It is the third button on the left with the widest spacing.

FONT

Font is the term used to describe the shape of the type used in typing. The **APA** suggests using a standard typeface in 12 point size similar to that found in typewriters. **Courier** and **Times Roman** are good examples. Although **Microsoft Works** enables you to change the font, the size, and a whole range of styles such as bold, condensed, and shadow, select one simple typeface and keep it in the plain text style.

`This is 12 point Courier font.`

1. Click on the **Font Pop-up Menu** in the **Tool Bar**. Drag down to **Courier**.
2. Click on the **Type Size Pop-up Menu** in the **Tool Bar.** Drag down to **12.**

ITALICS AND UNDERLINING

Underlining is used to indicate words which are to be italicized in a printed version. Writers following **APA** style should not use italics unless approved by the instructor. The titles of books, periodicals, volume numbers in reference lists, some test scores, and Latin scientific terms are underlined to indicate italics.

1. Select the text you want to underline or italicize.
2. Click on the *I* or U buttons in the **Tool Bar.**

CENTERING AND JUSTIFYING

Justification describes how words are placed on the page: flush left, flush right, or centered. **Microsoft Word** allows you to spread the words on each line across the page so the right margin is ragged or right justified. Although **APA** papers should not be justified, you will need to center or move some text at times.

1. Select the text you want to center or move.
2. Click on the appropriate **Justification Button** just to the left of the **Line Spacing Buttons** in the **Ruler** to center or move text.

INDENTION

APA papers are indented one half inch. The **Microsoft Works** default setting is one half inch, but you may want to change indents for quotations or other purposes.

1. To change the position of the first line in a paragraph, click on the **First Line Indent Mark** just under the number 1 on the ruler and drag it to the appropriate tick on the ruler. There are two **Indent Marks** on the ruler, the top mark is the **First Line Indent Mark** and the bottom mark is the **Left Indent Mark** which controls the rest of the paragraph. In **Works 4.0,** you must hold down the shift key to move the **Left Indent Mark** to the right without moving the **First Line Indent Mark.**

2. To change the right hand indent of a paragraph, click on the **Right Indent Mark** which is just under the 7.5 inch mark on the ruler and drag it to the appropriate tick on the ruler.

PAGINATION

Beginning with the first page, **APA** papers carry a right justified heading one half inch from the top of the page with the first two or three words of the title of your paper in upper and lower case followed by the page number in arabic numerals. **See the sample pages on pages 9-16 through 9-20.**

Microsoft Works 3.0
1. Open your term paper document at the first page of text.
2. Choose **Show Header** from the **Windows Menu.** The **Header Window** will appear with its own ruler and buttons.
3. Be sure the cursor is at the left margin. If it is not, click on the **Left Justification Button** in the ruler.
4. Type the first two or three words of the title of your paper and move the cursor five spaces to the right by pressing the **Space Bar** five times.
5. Click on the **Page Number Button.** It is just to the right of the **Clock Button.** The number 1 will appear.
6. Select the entire header and click on the **Right Justification Button.** The header will move to the right side of the page and will appear on every page.

Microsoft Works 4.0

1. Open your term paper document at the first page of text. There is a box at the top of the document page which is the **Header Box.**
2. Move the cursor inside the **Header Box** by clicking inside the **Box.** The **Page Number Button** appears in the ruler next to the **Date, Time,** and **Bulleted List Buttons. Special Center** and **Right Tab Stops** also appear in the ruler.
3. Press the **Tab Key** to move the cursor to the **Right Tab Stop.**
4. Type the first two or three words of the title of your paper and move the cursor five spaces to the right by pressing the **Space Bar** five times.
5. Click on the **Page Number Button** in the **Ruler.** The **Page Icon** will appear five spaces to the right of the short title. The actual page numbers will appear when you print your paper or when you select **Print Preview** in the **Print Dialog Box.**

TITLE PAGE

APA papers have a specific format for the title page which contains a **running head,** the **title,** the **author's name,** and **affiliation. See sample title page on page 9-16.**

1. Move the cursor to the top line of the first page.
2. Type at the left margin the words, **Running Head:** in upper and lower case followed by a colon, leave one space and type, all in upper case, an **abbreviated title** of fewer than 50 characters including punctuation and spaces.
3. Center the **full title** in upper and lower case on the page. Double space if two or more lines.
4. Center **your name** in upper and lower case one double space below the title.
5. Center **your school name** in upper and lower case one double space below your name.

ABSTRACT PAGE

Formal **APA** papers include an **abstract page** which summarizes the paper. It is always numbered page 2. **See sample Abstract Page on page 9-17.**

1. Move the cursor to the end of the last word in the **title page.** Press **Enter** to place the cursor on a new blank line.

Microsoft Works 3.0

2. Choose **Insert Page Break** from the **Document Menu.** A **Manual Page Break Marker** of small dashes will appear across the page.

Microsoft Works 4.0

2. Choose **Page Break** from the **Insert Menu.**

3. Center the word, **Abstract**, in upper and lower case on the top line and double space.

4. Type the abstract, a summary of your paper, in a single paragraph without paragraph indention in fewer than 960 characters including punctuation and spacing.

TEXT

APA papers begin text on the third page. **See the sample Text Page on page 9-18.**

1. Move the cursor to the end of the last line of text on the Abstract Page. Press **Enter** to place the cursor on a new blank line.

Microsoft Works 3.0

2. Choose **Insert Page Break** from the **Document Menu.** A **Manual Page Break Marker** of small dashes will appear across the page.

Microsoft Works 4.0

2. Choose **Page Break** from the **Insert Menu.**

3. Center the **title** of your paper in upper and lower case double spaced at the top of the page.

4. Double space and begin typing text.

AUTHOR-DATE CITATION

APA papers use a simple system of citing sources by stating the author's name and date of publication of the work in parentheses. Citations are placed directly in the text. No special keystrokes are necessary. The citations lead readers to the alphabetical list of sources in the **References** list at the end of the paper. Follow the **explanation** and **examples** on **pages 9-2 and 9-3.**

1. Citations are placed directly in the text. No special keystrokes are necessary.

MICROSOFT WORKS
Text Citations

REFERENCES LIST

The **References** list is printed at the end of the paper and presents full bibliographic information for every source cited in the body of your paper. Do not include sources you may have consulted, but did not use. It is a good idea to prepare the **References** list before you actually start writing the paper so you will know how to cite the references in the text. **See sample formats for References entries on pages 9-4 through 9-11 and the sample References Page on page 9-20.**

1. Move the cursor to the end of the last line of text. Press **Enter** to place the cursor on a new blank line.

Microsoft Works 3.0

2. Choose **Insert Page Break** from the **Document Menu.** A **Manual Page Break Marker** of small dashes will appear across the page.

Microsoft Works 4.0

2. Choose **Page Break** from the **Insert Menu.**

3. Center the word, **References,** in upper and lower case on the top line. Double space.
4. Type the entries using the appropriate format for the type of reference you are citing.
5. Indent the first line of each entry one half inch. Double space within and between entries.

TABLES

Tables should be used sparingly. Use them only when data will be better presented in tabular form. Avoid confusing the reader by breaking up text with too many tables. Do not duplicate information in the text which appears in a table. Tables should supplement material in the text, but it should also be understandable alone.

Tables are assigned arabic numerals and brief titles.and are located as close as possible to their mention in the text on a separate page. Every column must have a short

MICROSOFT WORKS
References Tables

heading. The data in the left column usually describes the major independent variable.

Use horizontal rules only and use horizontal spacing to make the table easily readable. Double space within tables. **See the sample Table Page on page 9-19.**

1. Begin each table on a separate page. Move the cursor to the end of the last line of text. Press **Enter** to place the cursor on a new blank line.

Microsoft Works 3.0

2. Choose **Insert Page Break** from the **Document Menu.** A **Manual Page Break Marker** of small dashes will appear across the page.

Microsoft Works 4.0

2. Choose **Page Break** from the **Insert Menu.**
3. Type **Table 1** flush left in upper and lower case without a period on the top line.
4. Double space and type the **title** flush left and underlined. Capitalize only the first letters of major words. Extra lines of title are flush left and double spaced.
5. Double space and type a **solid line** across the page by pressing **Shift** and **Underline Keys.**
6. You must now set up the rows and columns which make up the table. Each column must have a header and these should be spaced evenly across the top of the table. Leave at least three spaces between columns.
7. When you press the **Tab Key**, the cursor moves one half inch to the right and the first character of text will be aligned on the tab stop. This is the **Microsoft Works** default setting. To set up the table you will have to change the **Tab** settings.
8. Find the four upward pointing arrows on the ruler which are the **Tab Stops.** The one on the left is the **Left Align Stop** and has a right pointing tail, the one in the center is the **Center Align Stop** has no tail, the next on the right is the **Right Align Stop** and has a left pointing tail, and the last has no tail but has a decimal point on its right and is the **Decimal Align Stop.** When you tab to the **Right Align Tab Stop**, the last character will be aligned on the stop. When you tab to the **Center Align Tab Stop**, the characters will be centered on either side of the stop. When you tab on the **Decimal Align Stop**, decimal points will be aligned under the stop.

MICROSOFT WORKS
Tables

9. Click on the **Center Tab Stop** in the **Ruler** to select it and click in the ruler to set a tab at the approximate location where the first header should be. Continue the process by clicking in the ruler at the approximate locations where each header should be.
10. Press the **Tab Key** and type the first header. It will be centered at the tab location. Follow the same procedure with the remaining headers. Capitalize the first word of each header
11. Double space and underline by pressing **Shift Hyphen Keys.**
12. Double space and enter data in each column by pressing the **Tab Key** to move the cursor to the next column. Double space. Click on the **Decimal Align Stop** and move it on the ruler to any column containing decimal data.
13. After entering data, double space and underline by pressing **Shift Hyphen Keys.**

SPELL CHECK

1. Place the cursor at the point in the document you want to begin checking.

Microsoft Works 3.0
2. Choose **Spelling** from the **Document Menu.**
Microsoft Works 4.0

2. Choose **Spelling** from the **Tools Menu.**

3. The **Spelling Dialog Box** will appear with any misspelled words on the **Not in Dictionary Line** with the correctly spelled word in the **Change to Box.** Other variations for the word will appear in the **Suggestions Scroll Box.**
4. If the correct word is in the **Change to Box**, click **Change** or **Change All** to correct the word wherever it appears in the paper.
5. If the word you want is in the **Suggestions Scroll List**, click on it and then click **Change**.
6. If the word is correctly spelled as is, and **Word's Spell Check** does not recognize it, click **Ignore.**

PRINTING
See page 3-5 in Chapter 3. Basic Macintosh for instructions.

SAVING
See page 3-6 in Chapter 3. Basic Macintosh for instructions.

MICROSOFT WORKS
Spell Check Printing Saving

ABOUT THE AUTHOR

Alvin Baron taught English and composition for many years in high schools and middle schools. Over two million of his books have been sold featuring the Easy Task Method for Research Papers, Theses, and Reports which makes writing papers so much easier.

He served as principal of the Lawrence Middle School and Lawrence High School in suburban New York and was Superintendent of the Lawrence, Franklin Square, and Port Washington school systems.

Dr. Baron was awarded the Doctor of Philosophy degree from New York University and taught at New York University, City College of New York, Richmond College, and Hofstra University. He now devotes full time to writing and helping students with research projects.

Dr. Baron believes the Internet will surpass the invention of the printing press in its impact on world civilization and he continuously updates his books to include the latest advances in researching on the World Wide Web!

NOTES

NOTES

NOTES

NOTES

NOTES